Albert S. Bradshaw

Wife or Slave?

Albert S. Bradshaw

Wife or Slave?

ISBN/EAN: 9783744796279

Printed in Europe, USA, Canada, Australia, Japan

Cover: Foto ©ninafisch / pixelio.de

More available books at **www.hansebooks.com**

WIFE OR SLAVE ?

BY

Mrs. ALBERT S. BRADSHAW,

AUTHOR OF

"A Crimson Stain," "A Noble Vengeance," "The Queen's Defence,"
"The Young Roman," "Condemned," "Damian's Wife," &c.

LONDON:

HENRY AND COMPANY,

6, BOUVERIE STREET, E.C.

The Author has Dedicated the present work (by kind permission) to

HER GRACE THE DUCHESS OF RUTLAND,

Who, by her efforts, Literary and Philanthropic, has done so much to further the interests and improve the surroundings of those less fortunately circumstanced than their noble benefactress.

INDEX.

Chapter		Page
I.	At the Village School	1
II.	The St. Kestor Inheritance	14
III.	Do you Believe in Destiny...	19
IV	Narrative by Hugh Penwood	28
V	Conjugal Felicity	43
VI.	Hugh Penwood's Narrative Continued	48
VII.	Sir Peter Fairbairn, Knight	64
VIII.	The Apple of Discord	72
IX.	A Dangerous Guest...	81
X.	A Simple Funeral	88
XI.	Hugh Penwood makes his First Experiment in Thought Reading	95
XII.	Driven into Exile	106
XIII.	A Mother Steals her Own Child	121
XIV	Cruelty and Treachery	127
XV	A Terrible Discovery	137
XVI.	Further Conspiracies	145
XVII.	Lady St. Kestor Discovers Sir Peter's Family Skeleton	150
XVIII.	Sir Hardress is Brutally Candid	162
XIX.	Let me be Your Friend	173

Chapter.		Page.
XX.	Mathilde Offers Her Suggestion	180
XXI.	I Don't Want Your Love	186
XXII.	Hester Barnforth Plays Her Part	200
XXIII.	Mary Haldane's Make-up	215
XXIV	Hester Barnforth Overhears a Conversation	234
XXV	A Threatened Storm	240
XXVI.	The Storm Bursts	250
XXVII.	Hugh Penwood's Second Experiment	255
XXVIII.	Master Dick	265
XXIX.	Mons. Pierre's Romance	279
XXX.	Ashley Dallas Pleads His Suit	294
XXXI.	Sir Peter's Family Skeleton	300
XXXII.	Hugh Penwood's Narrative Concluded	309
XXXIII.	So Soon	315
XXXIV	Wedding Bells	319
XXXV	Nil Desperandum	325

Mrs. Albert S. Bradshaw's Press Notices

"A CRIMSON STAIN."

A vigorous tale of Spain in olden times.—*Daily Chronicle*.

Readers who desire exciting literature with plenty of mystery, will find that this story more than fulfils their expectations.—*Public Opinion*.

The tale is graphically told!—*Bookseller*.

An extremely well-written story of a type likely to find favour with the public. It will certainly please the great bulk of readers.—*The Scotsman*.

A striking novel. The plot is a very peculiar one; perhaps it is this which gives a certain air of unreality. We are carried on by the mystery which is indicated from the beginning, but not revealed until the interest is at its height; then we acquire a double interest in finding out how the destiny which is involved in the mystery is avoided. The story is well written. Mrs. Bradshaw's style is clear, nervous, and forceful; she has the art of carefully concealing mystery until the time comes for revelation.—*The Glasgow Herald*.

To a story of Spain, in the reign of Ferdinand VII., and is a thrilling narrative.—*Manchester Courier*.

There are many travellers who will welcome such [a novel] as a companion for their journeys. The plot is not too complicated, but is sufficiently uncommon to be read without the unwelcome conviction that one knows exactly what is coming.—*Yorkshire Post*.

If it is an attraction, as we believe it is, to sustain no ordinary thrill of interest from the first to the last clause in a book, this production has a claim upon the novel reader. The reviewer, out of sheer curiosity, has read it through carefully, and can give it an unqualified word of praise. It is a remarkable story.—*Sheffield Daily Telegraph*.

An interesting and original novel.—*Sheffield Post*.

A narrative of Spanish revenge. The incidents have been wrought into a clever story.—*Bristol Western Daily News*.

The story is thrillingly sensational, but it is remarkably well written, and it would require a singularly unemotional reader to lay down the book now before us, without having read it to the end. It is a most remarkable romance. We shall watch the future work of the writer with more than ordinary interest.—*Bristol Mercury*.

The opening of this remarkable story reveals to the reader one of the loveliest regions in the South of Spain. The beautiful Maria Bolurski's love for Felipe forms a fine feature in this beautiful story.—*Western Morning News*.

A work of thrilling interest. The plot is both powerfully conceived, cleverly written, and the interest fully sustained from beginning to end.—*Leicester Journal*.

The story is worth reading, giving a truthful description of the national prejudices, on which the plot hinges. "The sins of the father shall be visited on the children" sums up the exciting story.—*New York Literary News*.

POEMS, &c.

Mrs. Albert S. Bradshaw also recited with feeling a dramatic poem of her own, "Condemned; or, Told to the Chaplain," cast in the familiar mould of the Dagonet Ballads.—*Stage*.

Mrs. Albert S. Bradshaw recited a poem of her own, entitled, "Condemned," with good facial expression and appropriate gestures.—*Society*.

Mrs. Albert S. Bradshaw recited "Condemned," a powerful story of retributive justice, of which she is the authoress.—*Islington Gazette*.

Amongst the conspicuous items of the programme was the recital by Mrs. Albert S. Bradshaw of her own poem, "Condemned.—*London*.

The capabilities of Mrs. Albert S. Bradshaw as an able writer and an extremely-gifted elocutionist were fully displayed in her rendering of the pieces "Condemned" and "Idalia," which are her own composition. Mrs. Bradshaw's forcible and skilful pourtrayal of the alternating feelings of sorrow, pain, and vengeful declamation expressed in the two selections, with the interesting nature of the narratives themselves, combined to excite and sustain the attention of the audience throughout from beginning to end; and the lady's efforts were thoroughly recognised as among the most pleasurable items of the programme and were heartily applauded.—*Middlesex County Times*.

Mrs. Albert S. Bradshaw recited "Condemned; or, Told to the Chaplain," in most effective style.—*Nottingham Daily Express*.

Mrs. Albert S. Bradshaw recited a poem of her own, much after the style of Mr. Geo. R. Sims, entitled, "Condemned." Mrs. Bradshaw was sympathetically received, and both the pathos and passion of the poem, and the method of its presentation, were thoroughly appreciated.—*Nottingham Daily Guardian*.

Mrs. Albert S. Bradshaw made her second appearance at Long Eaton. She recited two pieces of her own composition, entitled, "The Young Roman" and "Condemned," and the hearty re-call she received must have assured her the audience highly appreciated her elocutionary ability. "Condemned" has plenty of room for dramatic delineation, and it is little enough to say that Mrs. Bradshaw's intellectual interpretation of it was quite natural and evidently enjoyed, her hearers being spell-bound to the last.—*Long Eaton Advertiser*.

Of a totally different character was the strong poem "Condemned," the fruit of her own pen, in which Mrs Bradshaw delineated a striking hero of seventeen, and held the sympathetic attention of all The burst of applause which greeted the conclusion of this long dramatic effort must have assured the talented lady that her work, literary and dramatic, has merit.—*Alfreton Journal*.

"Idalia" is full of pathetic and tragic interest, and Mrs. Albert S. Bradshaw, who, besides being an authoress, is a trained and polished elocutionist, was loudly and deservedly applauded for the taste and intellect she brought to bear in its interpretation.—*Dramatic Review*.

Among the principal items was the recital by Mrs. Albert S. Bradshaw of her own poem, "Idalia." The piece is full of pathetic and tragic interest, to which Mrs. Bradshaw did full justice.—*The Star*.

Mrs. Albert S. Bradshaw is a novelist and a lady of unusual

accomplishments, both as a writer and an elocutionist. Delighted the audience with "Idalia."—*Newark Advertiser.*

Mrs. Albert S. Bradshaw recited "Dick," a touching narrative of the evil effects of drink, with much pathos, which elicited loud applause.—*The People.*

Mrs. Albert S. Bradshaw appeared in her monologue, entitled, "Cousin Tom," which was amusing, and, in the course of it, she sang "Annie Laurie," in a sweet and sympathetic voice, fully deserving the basket of flowers which was handed to her.—*Nottingham Guardian.*

Mrs. Albert S. Bradshaw appeared in a monologue sketch as a petulant school-girl, with a hatred for her governess, whom she dubbed "the cat," a dislike for her books, and a decided preference for her "Cousin Tom," with whom she was desirous of eloping.—*The Stage.*

WIFE OR SLAVE?

CHAPTER I.

AT THE VILLAGE SCHOOL.

IT was the month of August in the year 18— The heat had been more than usually intense, and the long Devonshire lanes seemed at one and the same time to scorch the feet of the pedestrian, and almost to blind him with their dazzling whiteness. But the occupants of a handsome barouche, which came bowling along between the hedges abounding with great clusters of large tempting blackberries, failed to discover such little discomforts, as they lounged luxuriously back upon the cushions beneath shady umbrellas and fanciful sunshades. To them the drowsy hum of insect life was but a fitting accompaniment to their own pleasurable idleness. The sky overhead was one broad expanse of unsullied blue. Not a leaf stirred, and not even a bird could be seen on the wing. All nature seemed to be under the spell of some soporific influence.

A sudden turn in the lane revealed the upper portion of the village of St. Kestor, which consisted of about half-a-dozen low-roofed thatched cottages, almost buried amongst the luxuriant fuchsia trees, which in most cases overtopped the houses. Before each cottage was the proverbial little square of cottage garden, in which mingled indiscriminately the useful with the ornamental. There were rows of peas, and scarlet-runners interspersed with straggling sunflowers, lupins, and foxgloves. There were flourishing beds of mint and herbs to delight the hearts of housekeepers, and side by side were golden marigolds and purple heartsease in company with bright-eyed daises and modest lilies of the valley. A little further on, and the old weather-beaten church came into view, or as much of it as could be seen from amongst the forest of trees which surrounded it. It had stood for upwards of a century, and presented various signs of decay, the result of funds not being forthcoming at such times as it had suffered from the violence of the weather. There were crevices in the exterior that had been filled up with the parish mortar, which should have been town cement, and there were crevices in the interior, through which the damp had made its way, and left its mark in varied streaks and discolorations. One by one the pinnacles had been blown from their proud positions on the square grey-stone tower, until it was left desolate of ornament; and now the tower itself had given several warnings that it also sought to rejoin its severed members in the crumbling dust, for it had been pillared and bolstered up on its several sides during the last few years, and now stood maimed, patched, and frowning upon the rustic worshippers as though longer begrudging them its shelter.

A long gravel path led up to the west door, which was the principal entrance, though there was another door at the north end, which was rarely used. The ground, or rather the churchyard, was somewhat extensive, and pretty well covered with tombstones of various sorts and sizes. At the back of the church the ground rose to a considerable height, and gradually sloped downwards until the extreme front portion reached the level of the road. A low wall enclosed it from the high road without shutting any part of it from view.

On the opposite side, and standing back some distance from the road, nestled the parsonage house, which was also built of gray-stone, with gabled roof and dull red tiles. A broad, smoothly cut lawn extended the full length of the house in the front, and was only separated from the road by low iron railings. A small iron gate led to a side path to the front entrance, and on the left side a thick shrubbery formed a boundary between the rector's garden, and the St. Kestor plantation, which just skirted the park in which was situated the residence of Sir Hardress St. Kestor.

At a second turn in the lane, about a hundred yards beyond the rector's kitchen garden, was the lodge belonging to the Hall, but the house itself was not visible until you came close upon it, so winding was the path, so thickly grew the trees, and so interminably long seemed the carriage drive by which it was approached. A short cut on the other side of the park was the one more generally used, as it led straight into the village. The first house in the village street was occupied by the doctor. It was built of red brick, and came right up to the road. Beyond the doctor's house were the post-office and general drapery stores, the grocer's and the blacksmith's shop and forge, and a few more cottages rather more pretentions than those on the outskirts; and the end of the street was marked by the village school and school-house. The door of the shoolhouse stood open, and the window panes were swung back to the fullest extent. From the open windows on the one side, which was the girls' portion of the house, the voices of the children were borne on the sultry summer air as they chanted a verse of poetry in the way peculiar to that form of village education; while from the other half, which was the portion set apart for the boys, the droning voices of the youthful rustics rose and fell as they mechanically repeated in sing-song cadence the orthodox multiplication table.

The barouche came to a sudden halt at the schoolhouse, and the smart footman jumped from his seat on the box, let down the steps, and held open the door for the occupants to alight. The first to descend was a tall, finely-built young Hercules, clad in a light tweed suit, who offered his hand to assist a lady who had risen to follow him. As she stood beside him, she leaned over to speak to some one in

the carriage, but the someone was so buried beneath
a large umbrella that it was impossible to obtain a
view of him, and it was with difficulty the querulous
tones could be understood. A swift expression of
sadness crept over the lady's face as she turned and
took the proffered arm which her companion held
out for her, and in silence they proceeded up the
half-dozen steps and entered the school-house.
Turning into the room on the right, which was the
one occupied by the girls, the lady advanced towards
the upper end and met the mistress, who had
vacated her post immediately upon their entrance.
The gentleman soon ingratiated himself among the
white pinafored, rosy-cheeked youngsters, by an in-
discriminate distribution of pence, which he varied
by mischievous pulls at some tempting lock of hair,
or by pinching some plump little cheek between his
aristocratic fingers, accompanying the action with a
comic grimace of simulated terror of the mistress
discovering his pranks. Of course he soon brought
the whole school into a state of anarchy and confusion. The multiplication table thereupon suddenly
ceased in the next room. Wonder and curiosity
were evoked by the strange sounds, in the breasts of
both pupils and master, and they, too, left their
benches and rushed to the door to stare open-
mouthed at the vision of the great lady from St.
Kestor, who stood in deep converse with the teacher
of St. Kestor's day-school. Then a burst of merriment issued from the lips of the group of urchins
assembled at the door, as they, too, caught sight of

the droll antics of the young gentleman. But they were sharply pulled up in their merriment by the master's voice.

"Now then, boys, back into your places instantly"

He had forgotten himself momentarily when he allowed his curiosity to draw him from his duties, and even as he returned to his vacated desk, he had not thoroughly regained his wonted command over the youngsters committed to his charge. With an effort he resumed the lesson. He turned his back upon the rows of children seated before him, and chalked some figures upon the blackboard, but with each figure he felt as if he were tracing the lineaments of the stranger's face, and wondered what was the business which had brought Lady St. Kestor to take counsel with the schoolmistress. As he turned to harangue his pupils, his eyes again fell upon the stranger who stood just within the doorway. Curiosity had brought him this time to the boy's schoolroom. A curiosity to again look upon the schoolmaster's face, of which he had caught a glimpse as he towered above the heads of his pupils, and which had been sufficient to arouse a vague sort of interest which he did not attempt to define even in his own mind.

The tutor was above the usual height, even for a man, and correspondingly thin. His head was massive, with a projecting forehead, and large dark eyes, deeply set. The nose was purely aquiline, and the chin oval and smooth as a woman's. From his high, broad forehead his thick black hair was swept back in a luxuriant mass, revealing the contrast of his fair, delicate skin. His hands were small and white, with the blue veins plainly visible. He had a nervous habit of constantly keeping his hands employed. He would either fidget restlessly with a steel watch-chain which depended from his waistcoat, or he would toy with a penknife, as though he found relief in some way by constantly opening and shutting first one blade and then the other. His clothes, too, had a habit of hanging loosely upon him, which tended to give him a somewhat slovenly appearance. Though really possessing all the attributes of a gentleman and a scholar, both in form and feature, there was a peculiar shrinking in his manner, a nervous diffidence in his expression, which was apt to give to strangers the erroneous impression of sullenness. Despite his fragile build there was a certain rugged grandeur about Hugh Penwood which invariably commanded respect and even obedience, and there was also a winning gentleness, which won for him the love and confidence of the little ones with whom he was brought into contact.

A greater contrast could scarcely have been imagined than that presented by the two men, the one shy and sensitive almost to an absurd degree, the other characterised by a straightforward bluntness of manner which, had it not been blended with an equal amount of soft-heartedness and ingenuous simplicity, would have frequently rendered him somewhat obnoxious. He was a good-looking fellow, which, as far as the ladies were concerned, was very much in his favour. They admired the fine proportions of his stalwart figure, and raved over his tawny hair and waxed moustache, suiting to perfection the warm-coloured tint of his skin, which exposure to the sun had slightly bronzed. And as for eyes—in which shone the depths of heaven's own blue, and were capable of looking things unutterable—well, there were those in plenty who were of an envious or disagreeable turn of mind who were ready to take every opportunity of testifying to the amount of havoc they had worked in various blighted hearts; and there were many more by far who sang his praises, enjoyed his society, laughed at his drollery, and were content to be put off and overlooked whenever his royal fancy led him elsewhere.

The tutor administered a second rebuke to his refractory pupils, laid his chalk inside his desk, and went down the room to speak to the stranger who was the cause of all the mischief. As he advanced he fidgetted uneasily with his chain, and a nervous flush rose to his face.

"The boys are so unaccustomed to strangers, sir," he said, in low, hurried tones, "that you must excuse their ——," and he glanced across at them as though unable to finish the sentence.

"Oh, pray don't offer any excuse for the youngsters, Mr. ——."

"Penwood," supplemented the schoolmaster, with a slight bow.

"Mr. Penwood," he continued, "It is I who should apologise for disturbing you. What a mischievous set of young urchins they look to be sure. By Jove! Mr. Penwood, if I were in your place, I should always be up to some pranks or other with them. I should want to teach them fencing and boxing, set them scrambling for pence or fighting over candy."

The schoolmaster ventured to cast an admiring look at the young man who was invested with so much light-heartedness and good humour, but the admiration was mixed with a good deal of wonder and surmise, and he answered with a slow shake of the head and a half-amused smile—

"Ah, sir, if you had been pegging away at it as many years as I have, you would have become used to the monotony and the drudgery, and forgotten the frolicsomeness of youth."

"Why you talk as if you were an old man rather than a young one who has scarcely reached the prime of life," exclaimed the stranger in astonishment, looking at the schoolmaster from head to foot, who coloured, and shifted his eyes uneasily under the scrutiny. "I see what it is," he continued, "you are mewed up in these stuffy rooms all day, and one has only to look at you to see that you are one of those fellows who is for ever studying and taxing his brain to the utmost stretch, never thinking of recreation or relaxation of any kind. Now, what do you say to a day's fishing, just to clear the cobwebs from your brain? It's Saturday to-morrow, so I'll call for you or meet you anywhere. We'll say at ten o'clock, and have a good long day of it. You'll come, there's a good fellow! I knew you would. Oh, here comes her ladyship so I must be on duty again ; and here's my card," he said, thrusting it into the schoolmaster's hand, as he rushed off to join Lady St. Kestor, who was waiting for him in the porch.

"Shall we walk on and meet the carriage?" he asked her as they left the school-house.

Lady St. Kestor nodded assent, and they pursued the direction which the carriage had taken. "You seem to have found a friend, Ashley," she said, "while I was transacting my little bit of business."

"Yes, cousin Laura," he replied, "Penwood seems a very decent sort of fellow. I have invited him to have a day's fishing with me to-morrow. He looks as if he didn't get half enough fresh air."

Lady St. Kestor gravely shook her head, "You are so impulsive, Ashley. I don't know what Hardress will say to your striking up a friendship with Mr. Penwood, of whom you cannot possibly know anything; I am afraid he will not approve of it."

"Oh, you think your august husband won't approve of my friendship for Mr. Penwood, do you?" said Ashley, suddenly halting and looking down upon his companion from his own lofty height, as they both came to a standstill in the middle of the path. "Well, then, my dear, all that I can say is, that if he don't like it, I'm very much afraid he'll have to lu-ump it! Oh, now, cousin, I have offended you. I know I have; but really, how else can a fellow express himself under such circumstances? Here, have a piece of toffy?" and he fumbled in his pockets until he drew forth a quaintly-carved wooden box containing little strips of barley-sugar, a comestible with which he was in the habit of regaling himself, and which he looked upon as the panacea for all ills. How anyone could possibly refuse so tempting a luxury he was utterly at a loss to imagine! it was his friend and consoler at all times and seasons; it served him now in the hour of his need. With the open box held towards his cousin he importuned her forgiveness, and acceptance of his peace-offering in one and the same breath.

With her dainty fingers Lady St. Kestor abstracted one of the yellow golden bars, and conveyed it to her mouth, with a half-laughing protest on her lips.

"I must keep you company to be gallant," he said, with one of his comical grimaces; "sweets to the sweet, my dear cousin," and he popped a piece of his favourite barley-sugar into his somewhat capacious mouth, and Richard was himself again.

A little speck became visible in the distance, followed immediately by a cloud of dust. It was the carriage returning. As Lady St. Kestor noted its approach she laid a hurried, trembling hand upon Ashley's arm, and there was a suddeen tremor in her voice when she addressed him.

"Ashley, what will you think of me if I tell you that, perhaps more for my own sake than even that of my husband, I don't wish you to cultivate an intimacy with Mr. Penwood? No, don't misunderstand me," she continued, her tone growing momentarily more agitated, "it is no class distinction that moves me to speak thus, for who was I but the daughter of a country clergyman, whose ambition never soared beyond the spire of his own church, or led him beyond his parsonage grounds? No, it is not on that score that I object to Mr. Penwood; but there is a subtle instinct, a vague something which warns me to shun him. In vain do I try to crush it, to stifle it, but it is stronger than I am. It may be that fate will be even stronger still, and that in the future—my future—Hugh Penwood will yet play the part to which I feel he is destined, but which is yet a mystery. I know nothing of him, have not exchanged a dozen words with him in my life. I know not whether he be false as base metal or true as steel. But I know this, that there is a strange inexplicable something between him and me, which at one moment rises like a wall of snow or ice between us, and the next moment melts away before the fires of a dangerous fascination, which, like a vibrating chord or an electric thrill flashes, wordless and untongued, from one soul to another—from his to mine!"

"By Jove, Laura, you put it hot and strong, there's no mistake!" said Ashley, swinging his cane nervously backwards and forwards as he spoke; but there was far more gravity expressed on his face than he allowed to be manifest in his reply. "You have been out of sorts lately Laura, and your nerves are unstrung. How on earth could a fellow like Hugh Penwood, holding, too, such a different position in life from you, ever be associated with you in any way whatever? Why, the greatest luck that is ever likely to befall him would be that which would offer him a better appointment, a higher salary, and remove him at the same time miles away from sleepy St. Kestor and yourself."

"I may be out of sorts and unstrung, but these are no vagaries of which I speak. I have trusted you, Ashley, will you help me by keeping him away from me? and—if you can get him away from St. Kestor, why, then, you will help me still more."

At her last words, Ashley could not refrain from looking round upon her with a little start of surprise. How very firmly must the idea have gained a hold upon her to cause her to treat it so seriously, and an uneasy suspicion began to enter his mind as to whether the many troubles and worries which he guessed were her portion, had at last conspired to turn her brain. He had only time to whisper to her under his breath, "you can trust me cousin Laura," as the carriage drew up to the high road for them to again take their places.

"Excuse me, I shall take a stroll across the fields before dinner," he said, and closed the door of the carriage. He wanted to think over the very strange communication which his cousin had made to him. "I never could see more than half-a-dozen yards ahead," he muttered to himself, as he left the road, and vaulted over a style into a field, "and, confound me, if I can make head or tail either out of this business."

CHAPTER II.

THE ST. KESTOR INHERITANCE.

AS Laura, Lady St. Kestor, had stated she was before her marriage but the daughter of the village clergyman, who, with her younger and only sister still inhabited the gray stone parsonage house, the grounds of which were only separated from those of the Hall by a thick shrubbery.

But it was not to become mistress of the Hall that she left the parsonage. When she solemnised her marriage vow with Hardress Carew the probability that he would ever inherit the St. Kestor title and estates was one of those vague contingencies, which do sometimes, but very rarely, occur. In this case it had occurred. Five years before, Hardress Carew had been on a visit to his uncle, then baronet, who was at that time the owner of St. Kestor, Hardress himself holding a captaincy in an Irish regiment and possessing only a moderate income of five hundred a year, beside his pay.

The baronet had two sons, both of whom preceded their cousin as to right of inheritance, so that setting aside his uncle altogether two distinct lives still separated Hardress from succession. And, to render the chance still more remote, should either of his cousins leave sons they in their turn would become the rightful heirs, to his exclusion.

At that time, however, the baronet was hale and strong, and was, indeed, only just bordering on his sixtieth year, and the elder cousin had about the same time attained his majority. Between him and the younger brother there was a disparity of four years, a little daughter having been born in the interim, but who had passed away in infancy. There was every reason for supposing that his uncle would live many years to maintain his own, and there was still more reason to suppose that one, if not both of his cousins would in their turn seek a wife, and, as a natural consequence, bequeath a direct line of descendants to the title and estate.

Such was the relation in which Hardress Carew stood with regard to his future inheritance when he wooed and won Laura Haldane for his wife; when he led her to believe in his honour as a gentleman, in his noble ambition, which was but paltry pride, and in his self-sacrificing efforts for the world at large, which he made a stepping-stone towards raising the pedestal for his own glorification.

It is only charitable to give him the benefit of supposing that he believed in some degree in himself, and that he was really not aware of the full extent of his own hypocrisy. Though he would accompany his *fiancée* to her father's church on Sunday, kneel reverently by her side and devoutly murmur the responses, liberally and out of the fulness of his heart drop a golden piece on to the offertory plate as it was passed from pew to pew, as with the rest of the congregation he repeated "Lay not up for yourselves treasures upon the earth, where the rust and moth doth corrupt, and where thieves break through and steal," yet it never occurred to him that he had but been acting a part; even when, freed from the restraint which had surrounded him, he would hasten to shake off the cloak which he had been wearing and give vent to his hitherto only suppressed irritability in a tirade against the "cursed old parson," as was his customary mode of designation. Could the gentle, silver-haired old man have seen him in one of his tyrannical moods, or the outbursts of almost ungovernable fury which sometimes possessed him, he would have trembled at the prospect of his treasure ever being placed in such keeping.

But, so far, Hardress had been quite sincere concerning his attachment for Laura Haldane. He admired her truly, and not merely for her personal appearance, though that had first claimed his attention, for she was very fair and sweet to look upon. Though neither tall, nor particularly slender, she had a certain grace of movement and repose of manner which never failed to please. Her complexion had that healthy fairness induced by simple living and the baths of early morning dew which the Gods prescribe. Her eyes were of a deep unchanging blue, a frank trustfulness seemingly reflected in their depths; they were indeed the true index to her nature, and in their mute language spoke volumes to those who had sufficient perception to grasp their testimony.

Hardress Carew soon observed that she possessed all those finer qualities which are supposed to be the necessary adjuncts for the making of a true lady, while at the same time she was in a certain measure ignorant of the usages and rules of city society, inasmuch as she had never been thrown amongst it, having lived an almost secluded life with her father ever since the death of her mother, which had occurred while she was still in the schoolroom.

"I will go in and win," Hardress had mentally reflected, after renewing his acquaintance with her while on a visit to his uncle, the baronet.

"She is a little Puritan, but so much the better. I can mould her the more easily to my own liking, and make of her what I will."

His keen intelligence had not enabled him to grasp the entire depths of the nature of the woman whom he thought he had so easily fathomed.

So tenderly did he plead his suit, and with such *finesse* and old world chivalry did he conduct his wooing, that a heart less guileless by far than Laura's might have fallen even a readier prey to the honeyed machinations of so ardent a lover.

Upon the announcement of his engagement, followed by his speedy marriage, relatives and acquaintances were all unanimous in declaring it to be the first time that he had ever allowed his heart to get the better of his head, for everyone supposed that so ambitious and so calculating a man as he was always considered to be, would have sought, if not a wealthy bride, at least a titled one. That Hardress Carew could have married for love, purely and solely, was beyond the comprehension of any of those who were in any degree intimate with him.

Perhaps after all he was not so sanguine himself as to his chances of securing a wife possessing the attributes which his friends deemed he would require in making a selection. Could he have foreseen the events which were destined to take place during the next two years, the probability is that he would have waited a while ere fettering himself with matrimonial chains. Just two years afterwards, to his utter amazement he received a letter from his uncle's lawyer requesting his immediate presence in England at St. Kestor, and informing him that his uncle and two cousins had been accidentally killed by the fall of a cliff.

Great as was the shock caused by the hearing of the news, he could not wholly stifle the elation which he experienced at the sudden change in his own prospects, though by the time he arrived at St. Kestor he had trained his voice to the exact pitch of gravity and sympathy which he thought to be consistent with the circumstances.

It was now three years since Laura Carew had returned to her native village to take her place as Lady St. Kestor and mistress of the Hall.

CHAPTER III.

DO YOU BELIEVE IN DESTINY?

THE dining room at the Hall was a long room, with three French windows, opening on to a lawn. The ceiling was low and old-fashioned, with wainscots and doors of oak. The walls were hung with family portraits, most of them darkened and mellowed by great age. Around the walls were placed huge silver branches for wax candles, which when lighted gave a singularly cheerful aspect to the otherwise sombre appearance of the apartment.

It wanted just five minutes to the dinner hour as Ashley Dallas entered by one of the open French windows.

The old butler was placing a handsome silver candelabrum at each end of the table, for though the daylight had not faded, still it was the master's whim always to dine by artificial light; so the Venetian shutters, which were then quite a modern innovation, were always carefully closed, in order to exclude the golden glory of the beautiful summer evening. The table, covered with its spotless damask linen napery, was laden with temptingly luscious fruits, held in massive gold and silver bowls. The richly cut glass of crystal and ruby shone amongst the elegant silver appurtenances of the table. There were rare orchids, ferns, and exotics, grouped in careless profusion in vases of almost priceless china. The table might have been spread for a banquet, and yet there were covers laid only for five. It was another of the master's whims that the same state should be observed whether they were entertaining fifty, or whether, as on the present occasion, they were simply dining *en famille*. The only difference ever observed in the matter was, that on state occasions Sir Hardress reserved his ebullitions of discontent at everything provided, to be poured into his wife's ears as soon as the guests should have taken their departure, while on ordinary occasions, such as the present one, the vials of his wrath were plentifully distributed with each separate course as it made its appearance.

By this time, too, the effect of his father-in-law's presence had ceased to be sufficient to put any restraint upon his ill-humour, and Lady Laura with a sinking heart watched the angry frown settle upon his brow, as he allowed the butler to remove his dish of soup almost untouched. As the tureen was at last removed, she heaved a sigh of relief that at least he had allowed it to pass without comment. But again she nervously watched him as he toyed with the delicate flaky white morsels of fish lying upon the plate in front of him. A second or two later he pushed the plate away, and threw himself back into his chair with a motion of disgust.

"Since when have you condemned us to prison diet, Laura?" he said, half savagely, half satirically; "three times within the last ten days have you treated us to this especial member of the finny tribe. I don't doubt your good taste for a moment, but you should remember one likes a change sometimes."

And so the dinner progressed. From that day the butcher who had served the family for over twenty years, must be given up; he was simply trading on his long connection by serving them with meat that was badly fed. The poultry was tough, and the ducks were far too disgusting in their mode of living to be suitable food for decent people to eat.

The discontent of the host, and the apparent distress of the hostess, which she so vainly endeavoured to conceal, caused a corresponding restraint and depression to be felt by the guests. Each one tried to be cheerful, or at any rate to appear at ease, but felt it to be a failure, and the signal for withdrawal was alike welcome to all.

They had just risen from their seats when Grames, the butler, entered. "Mr. Penwood has called and left this note for you, sir," he said, handing it to Ashley as he spoke.

It contained only a few lines, and Ashley passed it over to Sir Hardress as soon as he had read them. "I saw Penwood this afternoon and asked him to have a day's fishing with me to-morrow, but it seems there's a treat or something of the sort on with the youngsters which he had forgotten, so he writes to tell me he can't go."

Lady Laura heard so much as she left the dining room, followed by her younger sister Mary, but she was not able to draw any inference as to how her husband would take it from the expression of his face as he read the letter.

When they reached the drawing room Mary Haldane sank into a low rocking-chair, and leaned back with her hands clasped at the back of her head, fixing her eyes upon her sister, who had walked across the room and stood looking from one of the open windows upon the sun, as it was sinking to rest behind a silver tipped cloud.

Mary was neither so tall nor so finely modelled as Lady St. Kestor. Her figure was round and plump, and yet graceful. On seeing her face for the first time a stranger was almost invariably disappointed, for she could not boast of the possession of one perfect feature. The mouth was wide and the chin square and heavy for a woman, and the teeth though faultlessly white and even, were still too large to be pretty. The nose could neither be termed Roman nor aquiline, but it was very determined, and much too prominent a feature to be overlooked. Had it not been for the two soft brown eyes which fully equalled those of her sister in gentleness and tenderness, and yet so often flashed with mirth and roguery, there would have been no point of resemblance between them. Her rich wavy brown hair was brushed back, revealing a low square forehead. Her skin was dark, but clear almost to transparency, and it was rarely that ever a tinge of colour was visible.

She wore a dress composed of a very thin fabric of a peculiar pinky shade, very simply made and trimmed with old-fashioned yellow lace. It was pretty and tasteful, though it would not bear comparison either in richness or style with the elaborate Parisian toilette worn by her sister, Lady St. Kestor.

"However you bear your husband's ill-humour and disagreeable speeches so calmly I cannot imagine. You must be a saint, Laura, and I am not sure but that it is a mistaken saintliness after all. It might be better if you were to assert your independence a little more; you give in to him a great deal too much, and allow yourself to fear him without any adequate reason for it."

Lady St. Kestor did not move from her position at the window, and it was fully the space of a minute ere she replied to what her sister had said.

"It is too late now for me to assert myself. I do fear him, and he knows it. As soon as he speaks to me in that cold, cruel way I tremble so that I can scarcely stand, and the tears will come in spite of all my endeavours to repress them. I know he hates me for my very weakness and takes advantage of it. I never had your courage and spirit, Mary," and she looked admiringly at her sister, who had risen from her chair, and was pacing up and down the room as she listened to Lady St. Kestor.

"No! more's the pity that you hadn't, Laura. He should have had a woman like me, who would neither shrink from his sneers, nor fear his tyranny; and if you would only let me, I would take up the cudgels on your behalf even now. I should not hesitate to tell him a few plain truths without stopping to garnish them either."

"No, no, Mary! You must do nothing of the kind," exclaimed Lady St. Kestor, in excited, hurried tones; "you would only make it still worse for me, and at the same time alienate yourself from him, and I really believe that you are a favorite of his so far."

Mary Haldane shrugged her shoulders, as though to possess his favour might be a somewhat doubtful cempliment. "Well, dear," she said, "I hold my tongue because I think I may, perhaps, be better able to befriend you by doing so; but there are times when—well, perhaps, I had better not finish what I was about to say. But I do believe, Laura," and she lowered her voice as she spoke, "that papa is beginning to suspect that Hardress is not the good man that he led him to suppose he was."

"Poor papa! if he only knew—if he only knew," sobbed Lady Laura; "but the truth must be kept from him at any cost; it would kill him."

"You may be sure he will never know from me," said Mary; "but I smell the scent of a cigar in the hall. Be on your guard, my dear, or those sharp eyes of your husband will be upon us, and woe be to both of us should he guess that he has been under discussion."

The sound of voices now became nearer, and the

next moment the door was opened from without to admit the gentlemen. Sir Hardress entered first, and accompanying him was Mr. Penwood. Behind them came Mr. Haldane and Ashley Dallas, who cast a nervous uncomfortable look at Lady St. Kestor.

"Laura, I wish to introduce you to Mr. Penwood," said her husband.

She advanced and met them half-way across the room. As she bowed her head in response to the introduction, a shiver ran through her from head to foot, and she found it almost impossible to meet Penwood's eyes. But as she raised her head again, she could not resist casting a swift keen look at Ashley, which he saw and understood, and he too shivered as with a chill presentiment.

"Miss Haldane and I have met before," Hugh Penwood said, as he cordially shook hands with Mary. "Have you seen poor old Mrs. Groves lately? The last time I was there, she told me you had been writing to her sailor son for her."

"Yes, I have written to Jack ever since he started on his first voyage, three years ago. Poor creature, it almost broke her heart when he left home, and I believe those letters are now the greatest joy of her life. And she tells me of your goodness to her," Mary Haldane contidued, fixing her large brown eyes upon his face. "Nay, don't attempt to deny it," she said as he became confused and stammered out something about it being a mistake, "don't spoil your good deeds by afterwards being ashamed of them."

But Hugh Penwood had scarcely paid any heed to her words, his attention was fixed upon Lady St. Kestor who sat on the opposite side of the room engaged in conversation with her father. Mary guessed that his thoughts were straying from her, and the subject in question, and followed the direction of his gaze.

Mary Haldane was a shrewd woman. She saw the almost rapt intent expression in Hugh's eyes, as he kept them fixed upon Lady St. Kestor.

"You admire my sister, Mr. Penwood?"

She had changed her tones entirely; there was a ring of contempt, and a certain meaning in her words, which might be taken either as a query or an assertion. They were sufficient to cause him to abruptly withdraw his eyes, and to crimson with vexation.

"Yes, Miss Haldane, I admire your sister—who could help doing so?" he answered.

During the remainder of the evening, Sir Hardress was the pink of courtesy, his ready smile and spontaneous wit enlivening the whole party. When he chose to exercise his powers of fascination he was sure to succeed, and in that dangerous gift which had been bestowed upon him to an almost unlimited extent, lay the secret of his popularity.

As they separated for the night, Lady St. Kestor put a question to Mr. Dallas, "Ashley, do you believe in destiny?"

"No, Cousin Laura, I do not," was his somewhat curt response.

But there was a strange look of perplexity on his

face which belied his words, as he restlessly paced the floor of his room a few minutes later. "Of course I wasn't likely to tell her that I believed in destiny—what has destiny to do with our lives? But after all, it's the queerest go that ever I heard of. Here Laura makes me promise to get Penwood away, and just five minutes before, I had done the very thing which leads him to come to the house, and into her very presence. In fact I've actually brought them nearer than they have ever been before—broken down the barrier of social etiquette which hitherto divided them—by introducing them to each other. It's odd, to say the least of it. How can I stand a chance for one moment of getting him away when her husband is at the very same time making him a handsome offer to stay? No, Laura, I am afraid it is your *destiny* that Hugh Penwood shall stay, if that is the name you choose to use for it.

CHAPTER IV

NARRATIVE BY HUGH PENWOOD.

AUGUST 25th, 18—. Have just returned from St. Kestor. It is now close upon twelve o'clock, and I have had the honour of spending fully two hours in the company of the great folks at the Hall, as the rustics are in the habit of describing them. How mean and insignificant appears my humble abode after the spacious rooms and magnificence of St. Kestor, and yet there is a depressing influence about the place which seems to fall mantle-like upon you as soon as ever you set foot within its precincts. It may be that I am preternaturally and unfortunately sensitive to outward influences, or that I am inclined to be morbid, for I have frequently been subject to such impressions when others have been unable to perceive them.

As I waited for Mr. Dallas to send me a message in reply to my note, I felt instinctively that the household was regulated on a sort of clockwork system; that rule and ceremony were the standing order, for the very atmosphere seemed weighted with precision.

I had not waited long, when, to my surprise, Mr. Dallas entered, accompanied by Sir Hardress himself, whose greeting was unusually cordial. After shaking hands with me, and referring jocularly to the duties which had interfered with the promised day's sport, he invited me to return with them to the dining room for a glass of wine and a smoke. Informing him that as I neither indulged in the one nor the other, I should only prove an unsociable companion, I declined, at the same time thanking him for his proffered hospitality.

"At any rate, you won't refuse to stay for an hour's chat," he said. "Mr. Haldane is in the dining room, and both he and myself had arranged to come and have a talk with you, but it will be the best to take this opportunity—that is, of course, if you can spare us your time."

To this second proposition I could not but assent, and together we adjourned to the dining room, which was a perfect blaze of light. As we entered, my first idea was to suddenly withdraw, for I thought they must have been entertaining a large party, so gorgeous were the table decorations and so sumptuous appeared the repast, the remains of which were in course of removal.

"Glad to see you, Mr. Penwood," said the old clergyman, as we shook hands, "I had intended calling upon you for several days past, but waited for Sir Hardress, who seems to be always engaged over something."

"Yes! so I thought I would secure Mr. Penwood

while I had the chance," said Sir Hardress, speaking between the puffs of his cigar which he was in the act of lighting, "and as Mr. Penwood informs me that he neither smokes nor drinks, it is useless my inviting him to partake of either, so suppose we get our bit of business over and then join the ladies."

"I think before you came to St. Kestor a year ago you had been fulfilling the position of a curate, if my memory serves me rightly," said Sir Hardress, as he pushed a chair towards me opposite to his own.

"That is correct, sir," I replied, fumbling nervously at my chain as I spoke, for reasons known only to myself. I did not care for a raking up of the past."

"Well, we have a proposition to make to you," Sir Hardress went on, looking at me very kindly. "Mr. Haldane has, I regret to say, been in a somewhat enfeebled state of health during the last few months, and finds the work of the parish to be beyond his strength, to say nothing of the three services every Sunday and two during the week. So I have resolved that he shall have assistance, and his choice has fallen upon you, if we can persuade you to look favourably upon the proposal. It might be managed in this way—you could still retain your post as master of the school, but engage somebody to undertake the management during your absence, and be a sort of general factotum. You would take up your abode at the Rectory, and hand over to your substitute the house at the school with a yearly salary of fifty pounds. I daresay there are plenty of young fellows just starting in life to whom it would appear as a God-send, if only as a stepping-stone to something more lucrative."

A house and fifty pounds a year beside! Why to me, not so very long ago, that would have been as the luxury of untold wealth. It is only those who have known the want of a roof to shelter them, of a bed upon which to rest their wearied limbs, or of a pillow upon which to lay an aching head, who can realise what it means to become possessed of what are looked upon as such ordinary every-day comforts, and perhaps to them only is granted the ability of appreciating fully and keenly the luxury of such advantages—or so reasons the law of averages. But I must not permit myself to moralise or stray into the region of ethics; my purpose is simply to relate events as they occur. So to continue :—

After Sir Hardress had acquainted me with his proposition, I was bound to make some reply, though for the life of me I could not frame a suitable one. The offer was a tempting one in every sense of the word. My salary would be doubled, I should be relegated to comfortable quarters at the Rectory, and my social position would at the same time be considerably improved. And yet I hesitated at accepting it. I, who a twelvemonth back was a wanderer and outcast, little less than a vagrant. Here was comfort, money, and position within my grasp, and yet I was mad enough to feel a doubt about accepting it.

"You are kind, very kind," I stammered nervously, addressing Sir Hardress, "and you, sir, do me too much honour," I continued, looking at Mr. Haldane. " Why your choice should have fallen on me, sir, I am at a loss to suppose; there must be so many others who would be more fitted in every way to fulfill the position than I could ever expect or hope to be. I must confess that I am surprised and startled at this very unexpected news."

"Nay, nay, Mr. Penwood," put in the rector. "I am sure you would be capable of fulfilling whatever you undertook, and besides having both esteem and liking for you myself, I am sure that the parishioners would take more kindly to you than to a stranger. Indeed, I think they are already fairly accustomed to your visits among them, and I know that you have won your way into many of their hearts. But we will say no more about it to-night, Hardress. Mr. Penwood is sure to want a little time to consider the matter."

"Oh, certainly," said Sir Hardress. " There need be no hurry over it "

Again I thanked them, and rose from my chair preparatory to taking my departure, but Sir Hardress would not hear of it, and insisted upon my adjourning to the drawing room with them.

"Well, have you settled your business?" yawned Mr. Dallas, stretching himself, as he lazily rose from the depths of an easy chair where he had ensconsed himself, indulging in forty winks, from which we had rudely aroused him on rising from our seats. "Here, Mr. Penwood, you must want a reviver after talking business at this hour of the night," and he held towards me a quaintly-carved oak box filled with barley sugar.

"You'll never repent it," he said, with a comical grimace and a shrug of the shoulders, as I declined; "but you may live to regret it. Joy of my life, comfort in my hour of need, I eulogise thee," and he departed with the succulent morsel between his teeth, Sir Hardress and Mr. Haldane following, with an amused smile on each of their faces at his humour.

Upon our arrival in the drawing-room Sir Hardress introduced me to Lady St. Kestor. I almost fancied that she responded to the introduction with reluctance, and that if she could have avoided it she would have done so. At any rate, I felt rather than saw her shiver, as she bowed somewhat coldly to me. Is this, too, one of my morbid fancies? No, honestly I think not. Her sister, Miss Haldane, was there, too. She must have noticed my unusual interest in her sister, for she positively pulled me up quite sharply once when I had been watching her. If it had been any other woman I might have attributed her motive to jealousy, or to pique, as detracting from herself; but neither jealousy nor vanity form any part of Miss Haldane's nature. Perhaps I was really rude and deserved it. What can there be about Lady St. Kestor to interest me so strangely? There is nothing striking in her appearance; perhaps the most noticeable feature is a sad wistfulness in her eyes which at once demands attention. Her deportment is dignified, and her manner somewhat reserved, but not from any stand-offishness or pride. When she converses she has a sweet smile which thaws all former reserve and sets you at ease at once.

A few minutes after our entrance, a lovely child, about six years of age, came in to say good-night before going to bed. For a short time Sir Hardress kept her beside him, twining her long golden curls around his fingers, or pinching the plump little cheeks to provoke her into expostulating against such treatment.

As I watched the father and child I said to myself, "He is a good man; his heart is tender enough to admit the love of his little daughter." The next instant he pushed the little one roughly away from him while a frown black as night gathered on his face.

She had interrupted him as he spoke, and for that trivial offence he allowed her to depart with her blue eyes brimming over with great glistening tears which fell like crystal drops upon the lily-like fairness of her transparent skin.

"Please to see that the child goes to bed at the proper hour for the future, Laura," he said, in a hard metallic voice, as his wife, holding the child's hand, led her from the room.

A hot flush had risen on her own face, and her eyes were lowered, it might be to hide her own tears.

"The man is a brute," I said to myself, and at that moment I decided not to accept the position which he had offered to me.

Ten minutes later Lady St. Kestor returned

"Well, my dear, have you got rid of chatterbox?" he asked her with his usual good humour. I looked up, curious to observe her manner as she replied. But she evinced no surprise and was evidently accustomed to the variable moods of her lord and master. Then somebody suggested music. But Lady Laura begged to be excused when Mr. Dallas asked her to sing, and Miss Haldane, after casting an uneasy glance at her sister, turned to Sir Hardress and requested him to start the programme.

Laying aside his half-finished cigar, he went over to the piano without a word, and after seating himself commenced to play from memory one of those delightful sonatas of Beethoven's. He was a skilled musician so far as a perfect rendering as to time and manipulation go, but yet it sounded as though he had not possessed himself of the embodiment of the great master's idea which the music had intended to convey. He failed to reach the mellowness of the harmony, which should breathe in every strain; it rather seemed as if a swift cold current of air was born beneath his fingers, and permeated like a running stream to quench the melody ere it came to life. It was automatic and hard.

Again I formed an unpleasant comment in my mind. As he concluded his performance, I said to myself, "Sir Hardress, you are a cynic," and again I congratulated myself that I had come to a right decision.

"Thanks, old fellow," said Mr. Dallas; "now I suppose I must go in and do my bit," and I was not surprised to hear him dash into a waltz of Mozart's. The bright sparkling character of the music seemed a part and parcel of his own identity. His fingers seemed to fly along the keys, and each note to be giving utterance to the thoughts and expressions of his gentle nature. From Mozart, he went to Liszt, and from Liszt to Schumann, swaying us backwards and forwards to the spirit of his fancy or emotions.

When at last he stopped, I drew a long, deep breath, and my looks must have conveyed the thanks I could not utter, for he turned to me with a smile, "You enjoy music, I see, Mr. Penwood."

I told him that "my liking for it amounted almost to a passion, and with an instrument like that too," I said nodding my head in the direction of the piano.

"Perhaps Mr. Penwood will play for us," said the sweet voice of Lady Laura, who with her sister, was coming from the conservatory, which adjoined the drawing-room, and had just been in time to hear my remark.

"Certainly," responded Sir Hardress. "How very stupid of us not to think of asking him sooner, but if Mr. Penwood will oblige us we shall be delighted."

"Yes, do please, Mr. Penwood," chimed in Mr. Dallas and Miss Haldane together.

Any other time I should have been overwhelmed with nervousness, but Lady Laura had asked me; Lady Laura's eyes were upon me, and acting under her impulse, I obeyed without even the wish to do otherwise. Involuntarily, I strayed into the sweet subtlety of one of Mendelsshon's "Leiders," and had soon lost myself among the mazes of the enchanted visions which I had conjured around me. The keys felt like so many human throbbing chords, wakened into life beneath my touch. A strange sensation was stealing over me, steeping my physical senses in a sort of coma. The room and all external objects faded from my vision, and yet I played on and on, unceasingly, impelled by a power, the like of which I had never known before.

On the right hand of the piano, and in a direct line with it, was one of the long windows leading on to the lawn. It had been left uncurtained, and the pale shimmering light from the moon, which had just risen, fell full upon it. Again impelled by that strange power, I turned my face towards the window, set my teeth firmly together, and braced my quivering nerves to meet the sight I knew my eyes would rest upon.

There stood a white-clad figure bearing the face and form of Lady St. Kestor, but oh! with such an expression of utter misery upon her features as I shall never be able to banish from my memory! I dashed into a *crescendo*, and, as with the movement, I saw the figure of a man glide towards her—a man, tall and slender, with a thin white face shaded by a soft felt hat. The figure of the woman stretched forth her hand towards the second figure. The man held out his hand towards the woman. The instant that their hands clasped each other's, I recognised in the figure of the man—myself!

The music ceased abruptly, the vision had disappeared.

"Wonderful! Wonderful!" ejaculated Miss Haldane as I paused.

"Why, you are a born musician, Penwood!" said Mr. Dallas, shaking me by the hand in his enthusiasm. "You must often come up here and give us s treat—by Jove you must!"

But I looked up at Lady Laura, who was standing beside the piano, a new strange light in her gentle eyes. There was a question in her glance as it rested upon me. Perhaps she was mystified at the strange attraction of my music.

The spell was broken by the highly polished tones of Sir Hardress as he questioned me. "Where did you pick up your musical knowledge, Mr. Penwood?"

Again I felt the foolish colour suffuse my face at the simple question which required an answer. How could I tell him that my proficiency, if not my knowledge, had been gained by incessant playing neariy every night of my life for years, to a half savage crew, in a low public-house in one of the least civilised parts of Scotland; that I had been accustomed to sit until the early hours of the morning, grinding away at a wretched instrument dance tunes by the yard, until my brain had become confused and my eyes had grown almost blind to the flying steps of the ribald crowd arouud me, and by instinct alone had my fingers performed their ceaseless task? One night—ah! I can never forget that night—when worn out with fatigue, and faint from hunger, I had the greatest difficulty to remain at my post, I was horrified at hearing strange sweet sounds stealing in horrible contrast right into the midst of the Scotch jig which I was playing. Without being aware of it, I had glided into a sweet sacred air learnt in my childhood, and cherished as a favourite of my mother's. I must have been playing mechanically, with my thoughts far away, and involuntarily introduced the memory of those associations into my playing.

In an instant all was confusion and uproar; the Babel of sounds was simply barbaric, and had it not been for the interposition of the host I should have been subjected to treatment almost as rough. For weeks afterwards my appearance was greeted with jeers and coarse jests, and I was looked upon as little less than a lunatic; but as I bore it all with good nature, and took care not to so offend again, in time it was forgotten and I was allowed to pursue my duties without interruption.

All the circumstances that I have related, seemed to rise before me and force themselves into recollection as I replied to my host, and my voice sounded tremulous to my overstrained fancy as I said, "It is a gift which I inherit from my mother's family; she herself was a skilled musician, and it was from her that I received my earliest instruction."

Sir Hardress made no further comment, but bowed slightly as I finished speaking, a mannerism in which I found he frequently indulged in when he considered words unnecessary.

Thinking that it must be growing late I drew out my watch, but Lady Laura, as though divining my thoughts, "begged me not to think of breaking the party up so soon," in a voice which had certainly more than a touch of pleading in it.

Again I noticed that Sir Hardress echoed his wife's words, and there was even more than ordinary cordiality in his manner towards me as he invited me to "take a cup of coffee," which the butler had just carried into the room. "A game at nap to finish up with, eh, Ashley?" he said, a gleam of real mirth in his eyes as he turned them upon Mr. Dallas. "Fetch the cards, my boy, and let's have a round!"

"Perhaps Mr. Penwood does not play 'nap,' or care for cards," he replied, looking at me.

"Nonsense," interrupted Sir Hardress, "of course he cares for cards, and if he doesn't play 'nap' we'll soon teach him!"

As I took my place at the card table, saying that I had frequently played the game a few years previously, he laughed and fixed me with a curious look. "Yes, of course you have," he said; "you've seen more than our friend here gives you credit for," and he nudged Mr. Dallas with his elbow as he spoke.

I asked myself at the time what Sir Hardress meant by that remark.

I ask myself again now!

As the game progressed, another phase of his character developed itself. What was at first hilarity of spirit, by degrees swelled into boisterous mirth which evoked an appearance of childish exuberance in so apparently grave and dignified a man. During the few hours which I had passed in his presence, I found him by turns to be courteous and cold, genial and cynical, affable and brutal, playful and humorous.

What a conglomeration of virtues and vices. But I also discovered that he possessed all the cruelty of a tyrant and a despot.

When we at last rose from the card-table, I was again hesitating whether I might not after all accept the offer made to me.

As we parted at the Rectory gate, and I felt the firm clasp of Mary Haldane's hand as we bade each other adieu, I knew that I should find a true friend in her, and that she, too, might perhaps be grateful some time to have a friend at hand in whom she might trust and feel reliance.

Now for a final settlement! I must, of course, be prepared to resign my situation at the school if I decline the curacy, as Sir Hardress evidently wishes to combine the two offices. Well, chance in the shape of the elements shall decide it. The clouds are shifting uneasily along a somewhat angry sky, and at the present moment the moon is obscured behind a purple black mountain. If she emerges and reaches a certain point, which I have fixed, within the next three minutes—I stay. If she does not reach the point or passes beyond it—I go!

Now for it. With the curtain held in my right hand back from the window, and my watch in the palm of my left hand, I gaze alternately from the one to the other, at first with an interest in the race, for which I hold the stake, but as the seconds and moments pass each other along, I grow fascinated and excited, almost breathless as my fate hangs in the balance.

She is sailing along proudly now, the dark cloud is left behind, and the golden light comes streaming through the uncurtained window and falls upon the register in my hand as though in playful banter. It is growing nearer and nearer to the fatal point which I have fixed as the boundary line, and yet the recorder ticks on with slow and even beat, and never hurries, even though my own heart beats faster and faster as the last moment approaches. She is nearly there. At the rate she is travelling now she must beat time—and I—and I must be again a homeless wanderer. What! she pauses' Could I but see the obstacle which impedes her course. It is passed, and there is a second gained. Now, now, it becomes an even race. It is over; I have won.

Chance has decreed that I shall be curate of St. Kestor, and—shall I write it—

" No! Discretion says—' Better not!' "

CHAPTER V

CONJUGAL FELICITY.

HALF an hour later, after the departure of the guests, Sir Hardress entered his wife's dressing room. There was no trace left of the genial host. His brow was puckered in an angry frown, and the gleam of merriment, playing in his eyes so shortly before, had given place to one of almost fierce hatred.

Lady St. Kestor was seated in a low chair by the window, looking down into the garden below, seemingly absorbed in the beauty of the night.

"I thought I should find you mooning there," he exclaimed, in a burst of impetuous wrath. "I want you to explain the meaning of your extraordinary conduct this evening. As you seem to have forgotten your position as Lady St. Kestor, it becomes my duty as your husband to remind you of it."

"Oh, Hardress, what do you mean?" Lady Laura said, her voice trembling and agitated, a startled frightened look in her gentle blue eyes. "I have fulfilled my duties as hostess to the best of my abilities; if I have failed to please you I am sorry."

"Stop that school-girl clap-trap," interrupted Sir Hardress. "You are always ready with a lot of puling sentiment, and I am sick of it. You know very well what I refer to, and let me warn you that if I see any more of it I shall not hesitate to speak to the young fellow next time, and let him know that I am not the man to be trifled with."

"Hardress!"

Contempt and indignation were both expressed in voice and gesture as she left the window and crossed over to where her husband stood. Though the tears still glistened in her eyes they had ceased to fall, and as she confronted him there was in her attitude a fearless dignity which was entirely new to her.

"When you address such words as those to me you do not disgrace *me*, but yourself. As for the threat which you have mentioned, the mere carrying of it out would stamp you as a coward who seeks to destroy his wife's fair name and honour rather than fight for it and protect it, even should his own be the sacrifice that he must pay. Why do you have Ashley here if you hold his character and honesty so lightly? Is he your guest or mine?"

"Ashley, indeed!" and Sir Hardress gave way to an ill-timed burst of laughter, though it was a laugh which had no true ring in it. "No, no! I don't refer to 'lollipops.' I am not afraid of his encroaching upon my preserves; he doesn't possess heart enough to run the risk—he prefers barley sugar."

Lady Laura winced under his vulgar sarcasm, and an expression of disgust swept across her face.

"Ah, my lady, I see a little deeper than you thought I did, do I?" he continued, as he caught the transient look which his words had caused, but upon which he had placed a different interpretation. "No, I don't refer to Ashley, but I do refer to Mr. Penwood."

There was a malicious brutality in his words as he dropped them slowly one by one, and of triumph in his gaze as he noted their effect. The crimson flush which had mounted to her ladyship's cheeks, paled visibly to corpse-like whiteness, and back again to vivid red; the hunted, frightened look crept back into her eyes as she fixed them on her husband's face. But her reply betrayed none of her emotion.

"Hardress, you are aware that I have been entirely unacquainted with Mr. Penwood until this evening. That is the only answer I have to give you."

Before he had time to reply, or scarcely be aware of it, she had locked herself in the bed room adjoining, and left him standing alone.

"Laura, I insist upon your unlocking the door immediately," he demanded with an oath, at the sound of which his wife shivered, as with trembling fingers she proceeded to obey his commands.

"I suppose you thought it was time to go when you had forced me to speak so plainly to you," he said, when she appeared on the threshold; "but I have not quite finished with you yet. I have some pleasant news to impart to you now. This morning I received a letter from Peter Fairbairn, stating that if convenient to me, he would like to come and spend a week or two with us, and bring his niece, who has only just returned from Paris. Now I want you to have rooms prepared to-morrow for their reception, and, mind you, you are to treat them not only civilly, but cordially, as honoured guests. Do you quite understand?"

"No, I don't understand at all, Hardress," and now there was something like horror in her tones and in her eyes, as she listened to his "good news."

"Then, by Heaven, I must make you understand, Lady Laura," he stormed. "They are coming at my invitation, and I choose that you shall shew them that they are welcome."

"But I thought you disliked this man so much. I have heard you speak of him as a vulgar parvenu."

"And if I have, what has that to do with you? Such airs as you assume are exceedingly bad taste on your part. At any rate, he is better than a beggarly parson!"

"I am becoming almost used to your insults by this time," she replied to him. "So long as they are addressed to me I can bear them, but when you hurl them at my father as you have done lately, they sting and rankle more than I can express to you."

"Well, I'm off to smoke a cigarette before turning in. I think I've said all I wished to say, so there's no use prolonging a not particularly pleasant interview."

Lady Laura watched him until he reached the door of the dressing room. "Hardress, won't you say good-night to me?"

The wistful pleading in her eyes and the pallor of her delicate face would have been sufficient to soften even the hardest heart, but Sir Hardress only cast a glance at her, and with a sneering laugh upon his lips, hurriedly passed out of the room.

With a despairing gesture, Lady Laura flung herself upon her bed and at last gave way to the hysterical sobs which she had so long been striving to stifle.

"What was it that Hardress saw?" she asked herself. "Is the vague something for which I have no name, so near at hand that the first step upon the path has been trodden to-night? Why is fate forcing Hugh Penwood into my presence—into my life, even as I have taken the first step towards shutting him out of it?"

CHAPTER VI.

HUGH PENWOOD'S NARRATIVE CONTINUED.

SEPTEMBER 15th. It is three weeks ago to-day since I left chance to decide for me the momentous question which I dared not settle for myself. And the result of it is that I am now a resident under the rector's roof, looked upon and treated as "one of the family," not in the sense of the much abused advertisement inducements, which one so frequently sees held out to entrap an unwary girl for the post of governess, when she, highly cultured, and probably also, unfortunately, highly sensitive, finds that being treated "as one of the family," means on all social points to be entirely ignored.

The respect which I have always experienced for Mr. Haldane increases day by day under the opportunities which I have had of observing more closely his daily life and habits, and a more charitable, genial temperament I have never before met with. From the first moment I entered the house I felt that I had found a home. Miss Haldane is kindness itself, though not resembling her father in disposition in the slightest degree. She is bright and brisk, inclined to be somewhat hasty, but just and practical. She is the old man's right hand, and the link which binds them together is even a stronger one than that usually existing between parent and child.

Last Sunday I read the prayers in church for the first time. How was it I could not rid myself of the consciousness of the fact that Lady St. Kestor knelt just below me! Why should her presence affect me more than that of any other person who formed a part of the congregation? I only know that I cursed my own folly more than once that I had not taken my departure from St. Kestor while I had been free to do so.

And yet I have not paid another visit to St. Kestor since the one recorded here three weeks ago, though Sir Hardress has invited me on two occasions. But on both I have excused myself from accepting, on the plea of duties to be performed. I have heard that there are visitors staying in the house, and from various remarks let fall by Miss Haldane, I infer that they are anything but pleasant ones.

This morning as we sat at breakfast a groom came over with a note for Miss Haldane from her sister. A troubled look overspread her face as she received it from the maid servant, and apologised to me for opening it immediately. As she read the contents, she bit her lip nervously, and then cast an uneasy glance across the table at her father, but he was immersed in the perusal of a paper which had come by the morning's post, and had not even noticed the

E

arrival of the letter; so, satisfied on that point, she resumed her reading. With a quick decisive movement, she replaced the letter in the envelope as soon as she had reached the end, and made an effort to pursue the conversation. But all the time I could see that her thoughts were elsewhere, and during the rest of the meal she remained thoughtful and pre-occupied.

When we again met for dinner, I was not surprised to learn from her father that she had gone to St. Kestor, at Lady Laura's request.

She was back again, however, to preside at our six o'clock tea, which always appeared at precisely that hour to enable me to reach the church in time for evensong, which now regularly develoved upon me. She did not allude in any way to her absence or to her visit, but of course the rector might have questioned her immediately upon her return when I was not present. Though I felt an indescribable amount of curiosity and anxiety to know whether Lady Laura had been in serious need of Miss Haldane's assistance, I instinctively knew that I must be silent before the rector, and that it was also probable that in any case Miss Haldane might resent my questioning her upon the subject of her sister.

Half-an-hour later, as I came downstairs preparatory to setting off for church, the door of a small apartment just opposite to the study was slowly opened. It was Miss Haldane's private room, and as yet I had not been privileged to enter it. But now she beckoned to me to follow her inside, and, with her finger upon her lip to enjoin silence, nodded her head towards the study, by which sign I understood that her father was within, and she did not wish him to be disturbed.

I had expected to see the room fitted up after the usual prescribed form of ladies' boudoirs, a sort of fancy work repository, or shrine for those various elegant trifles in which the fair sex find delight. But no such objects met my eye as I glanced around the room; on the contrary, a uniform plainness was manifested in every detail. The centre of the floor was occupied by a solid mahogany leather-topped knee-hole desk, on which were placed the various requisites for writing. Fixed to the wall, behind the door, and opposite to the window, was a large cupboard fitted with pigeon holes, and containing little bundles of papers neatly tied with pink tape. There were also memoranda and account books. Everything was arranged with a perfect nicety and precision, the only sign of feminine occupancy being a heap of flannel and calico garments which were in course of progression, piled upon the round table in front of the window. Beside them stood an open work basket, and on the floor lay a reel of cotton and a pair of scissors which had fallen unnoticed. So soon as I closed the door Miss Haldane walked over to the table by the window and stooped to pick up the reel of cotton and the scissors keeping her back to me as she did so.

Nervousness or hesitancy was so foreign to her nature that I felt she must have something of a serious nature to communicate, or something, at any rate, unpleasant. When she had replaced the cotton and scissors in her work basket, although she had braced herself to perform the task for which she had summoned me a minute previously, there were traces of agitation still apparent both in voice and manner. Again she glanced nervously at the little timepiece standing on the mantle-shelf as though half inclined to put me off even then.

"I am afraid I ought not to keep you now," she said; "you will think I have chosen an inopportune moment for speaking to you."

"Oh no! I have still several minutes to spare" I replied "if there is anything I can do for you, Miss Haldane, I am at your service, and shall look upon it as a favour conferred upon myself."

My words seemed to sat her at ease; her face brightened, and the constraint which sat so ill upon her vanished as if by magic.

"You are very good, Mr. Penwood, to make so generous an offer when you have no idea of the services which I may ask you to render me; and first of all let me thank you for your silence just now concerning my absence during the day. You must have guessed that I did not care to be questioned before my father, and I appreciate your delicacy and keenness in divining it, and still more for respecting it. Since you have become an inmate under our roof, it would be impossible for you not to discover that there is the proverbial skeleton behind our door. That skeleton, Mr. Penwood, is my sister's husband, Sir Hardress St. Kestor."

"You are astonished I see," she commented, as I gave an involuntary start, and leaned my hand more heavily upon the table. "I cannot stay to explain details now, but it is absolutely necessary that my sister should be prevented from carrying out a plan on which we agreed this afternoon, but which circumstances now render impossible. If I were to be absent again this evening my father might be uneasy, and even suspicious, and in this extremity I have dared to appeal to you; something tells me that you are to be trusted!"

"Try me, Miss Haldane," I replied. "And now what must I do?"

"Mary!"

It was the rector's voice, calling her by name.

"Yes, papa, I will come," she answered him. "I must go—I cannot keep him waiting. Come in here on your return from church, and in that work-basket I will leave a note giving you instructions how to act."

In an instant she had vanished. The next I was on my way to the church, my mind occupied with the mystery and trouble in which it seemed I was destined to share.

September 16th. Before me lies the note to which Miss Haldane referred last night. I will copy it into my diary, and then destroy the original.

"Dear Mr. Penwood,—When I left my sister this afternoon it was arranged that she should come to the rectory during the early part of the evening, bringing with her the two children. But owing to a letter which

I have since received from Sir Hardress, I wish you to give her to understand that the plan is no longer feasible, inasmuch as her husband overheard our conversation, and threatens to deprive her of her children if she persists in carrying it out. Whether this is a mere threat, or whether it is true he really has the power so to act, I am at present unaware, but, that, I will ascertain by some means; until that time, she must at any cost remain where she is. Be on the terrace a few minutes after eight o'clock, and you may be able to intercept her flight. I will take the night to consider whether it will be advisable to shew you Sir Hardress's letter. In the meantime let me thank you for thus constituting yourself our friend. Trusting that you may never have cause to repent having done so,—I remain, yours faithfully, Mary Haldane."

There! I have destroyed the original by burning it in the flame of my candle, all that is now left of it being a little heap of charred fragments which tell no tales. I always make it a strong point to destroy whatever evidences might prove dangerous or in any degree unpleasant should they happen to fall into other hands than those for whom they were intended, and one never knows what even an hour may bring forth. I have even taken the precaution of pasting a label on the cover of this diary on which I have written, " Should this book, in the event of my death, fall into the hands of a generous and honest person, I beg that he or she will destroy it without perusal."

Holding these opinions it would probably strike an outsider as somewhat of an anomaly that I should persist in keeping such a record. There are times when I acknowledge it myself. And yet I should find it very hard to discontinue it altogether, for it has been a solace to me in so many of my lonely hours, my sole confidant in so much trouble and perplexity that I have come to regard it in the light of an old friend. Other youths and men have their companions and their women friends, maybe their sisters or a mother. Hitherto my one companion has been my book. Now all this is to be changed, and I, Hugh Penwood, am no longer the solitary being, denied the boon of home, but one who helps to form a family circle; whose advice is solicited in the name of friendship, by the two women for whom he would go to the ends of the world, if by so doing he might serve them!

No sooner had I mastered the contents of Miss Haldane's letter than I was even more eager than she could have been, to accomplish the service which she had requested of me; for, alas! I knew the importance of it, while she had only surmised it. Strange if I did not know, as it was owing to that same accursed law that I became an outcast, bereft of a mother's love and care, my life embittered by the knowledge that its power had also driven that mother to desperation and death.

Oh, man, who art thou, that thou shouldst in thy arrogance and conceit take upon thyself to repeal even Nature's laws?

Why should God have not only endowed woman with the power of maternity, but also implanted in her bosom that strongest of all affection's ties—the natural love of a mother for her offspring—if it was not intended that she should be its natural guardian?

And yet men have dared to cavil at the great Creator's plan; and in their egotism and selfishness have framed the law which is the blot on the fair page of England's justice; the law which vests in the father solely the custody and guardianship of the children—the control over their persons, education, and condition, to the entire exclusion of the mother. Surely the day will dawn ere long, which will mark the shattering of such an engine of tyranny!

Fearing that Lady Laura might have already left the house, I rushed headlong through the private cut from the rectory, and in my haste stumbled right upon Mr. Dallas, who was making his way from the opposite direction.

"Holloo, old fellow; are you going up to the Hall?"

Dismayed and confused, I knew not how to answer him. I had tumbled into my first difficulty, and not knowing how to get out of it, I finally stammered something about my visit not being to the Hall.

"Well, you looked as if you were in an uncommon hurry to get there a minute since, for I'm not aware that the path leads in any other direction," and there was a tone in his voice which decided me that it would be best to make a clean breast of my errand and trust to his good-nature not to betray me.

The result proved that I had acted wisely. After I had explained my object he remained thoughtful for a few seconds, and then fixed his eyes upon me with a somewhat curious look. "Well, I suppose what is to be will be," he said, turning upon his heel and switching the grass and fallen boughs which lay in his path with his cane, as he spoke, then I saw him take from his pocket the box containing his succulent solace. Once more I hastened my steps, I knew he would not appear in sight of the house until he had disposed of his comfort.

As I reached the steps in front of the terrace my heart began to throb so violently, and each pulse to quicken its beating, that I covered my eyes for a moment ere I dare ascertain whether Lady St. Kestor was there or not.

And then, as my eyes fell upon the form which I had come to seek, a cold shudder seized me from head to foot as mechanically I advanced with the note outstretched between my fingers. It was the actual realisation of the vision which occurred to me upon my first and only visit to St. Kestor, and which I described in these pages when writing on August the 25th. Advancing towards me was the white-robed figure, with a face white with misery and despair, while I represented the second figure as I glided to meet her my face shrouded with the soft felt hat which formed a part of my clerical garb, stretched forth her hand to receive the note which I still held. As soon as I placed if there, she turned and vanished in the fading light without uttering a word.

I was alone! Once again I rushed over the ground which I had so recently trodden, and upon reaching the rectory, made my way to my own apartment without seeing or speaking to anyone.

With the exception of having come across Mr Dallas my mission had been successful, and though the incident may have aroused his curiosity, the secret is safe in his keeping. I will just refer to Miss Haldane's letter, which I copied before destroying. "Yes," she says, "I will take the night to consider whether it will be advisable to shew you Sir Hardress's letter!"

Well, the day has passed, and she has not yet shewn it to me, but I am under the impression that she will do so sooner or later.

September 17th. This morning I was again summoned to Miss Haldane's morning room, but this time it was the cook who brought me the message. When I entered, Miss Haldane was seated by the table near the window, busily engaged upon one of the garments which helped to constitute the pile which I had noticed before. She was wearing a simple morning print dress of a delicate lilac shade, and which fitted her neat plump figure with the accuracy of the proverbial glove. The sun shone full upon her wealth of hair, and tipped its natural waves with the sheen of his golden glory. I thought I had never seen her look more sweet and womanly than she did then, engaged upon her feminine occupation; the stern lines about her mouth seemed to have relaxed and softened, and the grave brown eyes to beam with a tenderer light.

"I have not yet had an opportunity of thanking you for being the bearer of my note, and my sister tells me that in her excitement she quite omitted doing so, but begs that I will apologise for her."

"My dear Miss Haldane," I interrupted, "neither thanks nor apologies are at all necessary. Lady St. Kestor was naturally agitated, and did not expect to see me; even I felt more than a slight degree of embarrassment."

A slight frown puckered her brow, and she tapped her foot nervously upon the floor, ere she next spoke. "When I asked you to come to me this morning it was not only to apologise to you, but to show you a letter which I have received this morning from my sister. After what occured the other evening, I am afraid you will think that I made a mountain out of what was in reality but a mole hill, for that is what the affair has now resolved itself into."

She passed the letter over to me, and subjoined are the contents as nearly as I can remember, for of course I had no excuse for detaining it.

"My dear Mary,—Please forget our conversation of the other day. It was foolish and wicked of me to say what I did about Hardress, and I repented my cruel words almost as soon as they were uttered. But I spoke in a fit of insane and uncalled-for jealousy. Hardress told me afterwards that he overheard part of what was said, but in order to show that he fully forgives us both (though, of course, I told him you couldn't help listening to me) he wishes me to ask you, dear Mary, also Papa and Mr. Penwood, to come and dine with us this evening. With fondest love, from your affectionate sister,
                                    "LAURA."

"P.S.—Please remind Mr. Penwood that he promised to bring his book of sonatas the next time he came, also his own prelude in E minor! Adieu."

As I refolded it and laid it upon the table, Miss Haldane rose from her chair, selected a bunch of keys from the key basket, which stood on the leather-topped writing-desk in the centre of the room, and unlocking one of the drawers took from it another letter.

"I hesitated about shewing you Sir Hardress's letter before—now I do so no longer. You have seen my sister's—it is only fair to me that you should also see her husband's."

A shadow fell across the window, and footsteps were to be heard approaching. I glanced at Miss Haldane, and still held the letter in my hand.

"Yes, you may take it away with you, and return it whenever the opportunity occurs."

As I passed out of the room I heard the rector speaking to her, and a short time afterwards saw them walking together towards the village bent on some errand of mercy, I do not doubt.

And now for the letter. My impression has proved correct, but sooner even than I had anticipated. Another confidence for my diary :—

"My dear Mary,—I feel it incumbent to address to you a few words of warning, which I hope you will be inclined to accept in the same kindly spirit as that in which they are offered.

"Unintentionally, but fortunately, I was in my dressing room this afternoon, and so overheard the conversation between you and my wife. I must confess that I was considerably astonished at hearing such a discussion of my peccadilloes, though for some time past I have had reason to believe that Laura had contracted the very unwise habit of airing her domestic grievances in society, or rather her supposed grievances; but I was still more astonished that you, whom we are all apt to credit with more than the ordinary amount of practical good sense, should not only listen to such tirades, but positively encourage your sister to open rebellion. I am not only surprised but grieved at this very painful discovery, and I beg of you to consider well the dangerous step which you have taken in coming between husband and wife.

"Laura has taken an absurd and childish idea into her head, without the slightest reason or foundation for it. If there is one thing on this earth that I detest more than another—it is a jealous woman, and it seems to me that Laura is developing that fatal passion very rapidly. If you wish to befriend either one or both of us, you will use your influence in persuading Laura to dismiss such foolish and wicked thoughts from her mind. If, on the other hand, she, aided and abetted by you, insists upon pursuing the ruinous course at present entertained, namely, that of voluntarily leaving the home which I have provided for her, even to seek protection under her father's roof, I shall feel it my duty to exercise the privilege which the law of England gives to me, and insist upon the children remaining here. I can only suppose you to be unaware that a wife who absents herself from her husband and her home has neither the right nor the power to take away the children. I give you this warning in order that you may be prepared for the contingency which will most surely follow. I think I have now said all that is necessary.—I still remain, yours sincerely,

"HARDRESS."

I hear voices below in the garden; Miss Haldane and her father must have returned. I am pleased to have been able to finish copying the letter, as I shall now take an early opportunity of returning it.

As I guessed, the rector has gone into his study,

and shut himself in. Now is my chance for seeking Miss Haldane.

Miss Haldane was standing by the hall door as I passed down the stairs. She turned her head in my direction, but still remained standing until I joined her. I restored the letter without offering any comment, and followed Miss Haldane to the lawn, where we paced to and fro for a couple of minutes in absolute silence.

"Well! Have you nothing to say?" she broke in at last. "You have read the two letters; have you no opinion to express concerning them?"

"It is somewhat difficult to state an opinion under the circumstances," I answered. "Sir Hardress's letter, taken by itself, reads fairly, though I can trace an undercurrent of hardness beneath the smooth and carefully-chosen words. But, placing it beside the one written by Lady St. Kestor, it assumes quite a different complexion, and I should say that it was to serve a purpose of his own that he addressed the letter to you, keeping his wife in ignorance of it, and that the one sent by Lady Laura, was also written at his dictation, and sent under the same coercion. Of course, I only base my judgment on what you have told me as to the previous relations existing between them from your own personal observation. It is not likely that Lady Laura would use such terms in writing to you, unless she was forced to it."

"You have exactly expressed my own opinions," she said, as I finished speaking. "Laura never wrote that letter of her own free will. If I were to act as I feel inclined I would answer her husband's letter in terms that he would not soon forget, and begin by telling him that he only carries out the old saying, that 'listeners never hear any good of themselves.' But then there is Laura to be considered. I suppose we shall have to ingratiate him so far as to accept his invitation, if only for her sake. You see I take it for granted that you will be willing without even consulting you," and she looked at me again with her old frank smile as she spoke.

"Yes, I suppose it is the best policy to accept the invitation," I replied, "and you may rely upon my accompanying you. I must be off to the school for a short time," I added, taking out my watch and consulting it.

"And I too must return to the house," she answered. "Adieu until next we meet."

And, so I am to pay my second visit to St. Kestor this evening.

CHAPTER VII.

SIR PETER FAIRBAIRN, KNIGHT.

IT was evening, and Grames, the butler, was as usual engaged upon the arrangement of the table, looking with a critical eye upon the result of his handiwork, first from one corner of the table and then from the other.

There was still some little time before the dinner hour and yet two of the guests were already met in the drawing-room, each arrayed in the costume which the rule of society lays down, and in conformity with which she insists with relentless mercilessness. The form encased in the regulation black cloth trousers and swallow tail coat, was that of a tall and heavily-framed man, well built, and with a pompous bearing. His glossily-starched collar and white muslin tie encircled a somewhat corpulent neck, which was surmounted by a head and face of absurdly small dimensions for so ponderous a body. He possessed an abundance of hair, which was of a disagreable drab colour, of a fluffy texture, brushed right off from the forehead, without leaving any parting visible, and reaching almost to his collar at the back,

Seeing him from behind, one naturally expected that the hair brushed back in so picturesque a fashion would reveal a broad intellectual shaped forehead, but instead of that, it was both low and narrow, with hollow temples. His little bead like eyes, were of the same colourless, lifeless hue as his hair, and set very close together, but standing out with almost repulsive prominence. The lower part of the face was almost perfect in contour, the features being regular and soft in outline; the only covering was a long drooping moustache, and a little bushy growth of whiskers on each side of the face, leaving the chin bare. To gather any idea of the character of the man from his face was exceedingly difficult, if not absolutely impossible, for though the eyes and forehead imparted a forbidding aspect, there was a gentleness and simplicity expressed about the mouth and dimpled chin that seemed to contradict any opposite conclusion which might have been arrived at. The person so described was distinguished from his fellow men by the appellation of "Sir Peter Fairbain, Knight." He was of Scotch parentage and descent, and had spent the greater part of his life over the border. In his youth he had started as an errand boy to a large Scotch firm of distillers, and owing to his diligence and precocity was a few years later taken into the house as a clerk, from which position he had by degrees, risen higher and higher, and by dint of scrupulous economy, and the natural manliness of his race, was eventually able to put no small amount of cash into the business and get himself taken as a partner.

F

At the age of fifty he found himself the sole representative of the firm, death having claimed his former masters, and left him in undisputed possession as head of the wealthy and flourishing concern, which just forty years before had received him as a menial, on the lowest rung of the ladder, which ultimately led him to position and wealth. Then a desire for change came over him, and having secured an efficient manager for the distillery, he started for England, and arrived in London at the heighth of the season. Delighted with the society in which he found himself he resolved to leave the business in the hands of his manager, and settle down as a resident in the metropolis. His success so far had only served to inspire him with still more ambitious hopes, and he resolved that his wealth should purchase for him the fruition of his desires. His first step was to ingratiate himself with the Lord Mayor by various munificent subscriptions towards public objects; his next to render this intimacy a means towards gaining an introduction to several needy aristocrats who were glad enough of the aid supplied by his well-filled purse, and who in turn repaid him by getting him elected a member of several of the most exclusive West End clubs.

And thus the wheel gradually revolved, and Peter Fairbairn was finding his way towards the culmination of his highest ambition. At length the time arrived when he considered it advisable to unfold his great scheme, and a few hours afterwards the news had spread through the city that Peter Fairbairn was going to erect an orphanage at a cost of thirty thousand pounds, and furthermore to endow it with a second sum of the same amount.

The site chosen was in a rapidly increasing suburb, and in a wondrously short space of time the workmen had almost completed their task. Everything in connection with the undertaking had gone smoothly. The foundation stone had been laid by a duke, and now a prince of royal blood had consented to open the building. After the ceremony, plain Peter Fairbairn received the honour of knighthood, and felt himself fully repaid for all his hard scheming and expenditure, when at last he could declare, " that he had shaken hands with royalty."

But Scotland was a many miles away, and his English admirers and worshippers never knew on what rigid lines that house of business was conducted, in order that he might not suffer for his generosity to themselves; how his work people were compelled to toil so many extra hours for less wages; or how the rents of the houses were increased and every farthing was screwed out of the poor tenants who had already found it difficult enough to keep a roof over their heads. That was a page in the book of his life's history which he had kept carefully concealed.

The other guest, who was Sir Peter Fairbairn's companion, was a fine, handsome woman about thirty years of age, handsome with that fully-matured sensual beauty, which to some people offer such charms, and inspires others only with feelings of aversion. Even the heavily-fringed silky lashes did not serve to veil the natural boldness of her coal black eyes, and there was an unmistakable voluptuousness in the full red lips and rounded chin which told its own tale of the passions slumbering beneath the outwardly fair exterior. Nor were her charms entirely the gift of nature, for artifice most liberally supplied whatever Dame Nature might have intended to bestow but cruelly omitted. In the darkened eyes and classically-arched brow there was more than a suspicion of *kohol*, while the exquisite rose tints which so admirably heightened her dusky beauty were never seen either to increase or fade, the carmine of her lips being equally lasting in its brilliancy.

She was tall, with a fully developed figure, almost too pronounced to suit a fastidious taste, and her costume was such as it is our misfortune to come across only too frequently amongst the fashionable women of the day. Her dress was a rich black satin, elegantly embroidered in gold. It fell in long sweeping folds from the waist and lay a tremendous heap of drapery around her as she stood. The bodice or corsage fitted so closely that not a crease or wrinkle was discernable. It was cut quite low in a square, both in front and at the back, narrow shoulder-straps taking the place of sleeves. There was not a vestige of lace or trimming to relieve the severity of outline occasioned by the sombre black against the warm flesh tints of the skin, and save for a few gleaming brilliants her neck and arms were entirely bare. What can appear more anomalous than the custom for a supposed delicate, modest woman to outrage common decency by the assumption of such apparel, either in a public ball room or assembly? Such exhibitions should be enough to cause the blush of shame to mantle on the brow of every pure-minded Englishwoman. Surely it will be early enough to talk and preach about the indecencies of the stage when all similar indecencies are banished from those higher circles whose actions the multitude are but too prone to copy!

"Now do be upon your guard this evening," the lady was saying to Sir Peter in a half pleading, and yet decisive, manner. "Don't flaunt your wealth before their eyes any more than you can possibly help. I can see Sir Hardress flush and wince beneath it, even when he is trying his utmost to be polite and agreeable towards you."

"Humph!" ejaculated his companion shortly. "If he don't like to hear about it, he don't object to the feel of it, at any rate," and suiting the action to the words, he plunged his great fat hands into his pockets, making a great jingle of gold and silver while he looked at her with a knowing wink.

"Ah, well, you know, Uncle, that's a different thing, altogether," and she tapped him playfully on the shoulder with her fan, as she spoke. "A man may thank you for lending him money, but he won't thank you for reminding him of it. As regards business or bargains, I will acknowledge that you possess an unlimited amount of tact and shrewdness; but—from a social point of view—well, all I can say is that you are unwarrantably deficient in both commodities."

This time Sir Peter gave vent to a low chuckle, and raised himself at full length in his capacious chair.

"You're a straight one, Mathilde, and no mistake," he laughed, looking at her from out of his bead-like eyes, which seemed to be rolling from side to side with almost lightning-like rapidity. "Perhaps you think my lady's testy little sister is sharp enough to be a formidable enemy."

"Oh, no, I don't!"

The tone in which the words were uttered seemed to carry with it a peculiar sort of meaning. Sir Peter raised himself in his chair, and for a second his eyes ceased their restless rolling as he fixed them upon her. "Then what the dickens do you think?" he blurted irritably.

"I think that the worst of Mary Haldane lies upon the surface. She is simply an ugly, satirical woman, without even the tact to hide her own weapons. The person whom we have to guard against is that melancholy silent curate. The man has a history—and an uncommon one, too—and what's more, I don't like the look of him."

Sir Peter slowly rose from the depths of his luxurious chair, and surveyed her with a quizzical sort of gaze. "Yes, my dear, you are a sharp one, too," he said, "and I shall certainly keep my eye on that young gentleman."

The second dinner gong sounded as Hugh Penwood, with Ashley Dallas, entered the drawing room, followed almost immediately by Lady Laura and

Miss Haldane. It was five minutes past the dinner-hour before Sir Hardress appeared, then followed a general exodus in the direction of the dining room.

CHAPTER VIII.

THE APPLE OF DISCORD.

LADY St. Kestor's gaze instinctively fell upon her sister, so soon as her attention was directed towards Miss Fairbairn. The colour, as if in sympathy, suffused her own face, as she noticed Mary's look of astonishment which soon gave place to that of indignation and scorn, amounting almost to loathing at the *bizarre* toilette of the woman who sat as an honoured guest at her sister's table.

Sir Peter Fairbairn monopolised most of the conversation, much to the disgust of the others, but after his first few glasses of wine, he was totally irrepressible, and waxed long and eloquent on his own virtues, and the position and wealth to which he had attained. His rise in the social scale by his own energy and enterprise was his favourite topic, and one on which he indulged on every occasion when he had the chance of making himself heard.

"It was a proud moment for me, my lady, when his Royal Highness took me by the hand," he was repeating for about the sixth time, "and highly honoured I felt when he first addressed me by the title which her Gracious Majesty had bestowed upon me. It becomes the duty of each of us to thank you for your noble gift to the little ones of our great city, Sir Peter," said he, "and I'm proud to remember that I answered him in words as good as his own, and all the swells that he had brought with him standing by to listen to them."

His reminiscences were, however, cut short by the pressure of a foot upon his own beneath the shelter of the table, causing him to pull up suddenly and seek his niece's face. As their eyes met he read the ominous look in her's which seemed to say, "You have said enough"; but she only made some laughing remark, and commenced a spirited conversation with Sir Hardress.

Contrary to their usual custom, the gentlemen rejoined the ladies in the drawing room after but a short delay, Sir Hardress making his way across the room to a couch upon which Mathilde was ensconced in a half-reclining attitude. Drawing aside the folds of her rich satin drapery, she at the same time invited him by an arch glance to the seat beside her.

"How considerate you are to take pity on us so soon," she said, as he seated himself beside her. "I was already feeling bored and out of humour with myself. You see, Lady St. Kestor and her sister have so much to speak about in which I cannot share, that really I am out in the cold."

A dark frown gathered on his brow, which deepened into a scowl as he noted how absorbed Lady St. Kestor and Mary were in their conversation.

"Laura's conduct is unpardonable," he replied, "to neglect you who are her guest; but, bah! I can promise you it shall not occur again."

Mathilde had unfurled her large feather fan and used it to conceal her features.

"Oh, Sir Hardress, you don't understand me, indeed you do not." The low musical voice was tremulous with emotion, and she coyed with the fan sufficiently to draw him also within the radius of its shelter. "Indeed I did not wish to imply that Lady Laura was anything but kind to me. You have mistaken my words. I only meant to say that all is so—so different when you are here."

Her bosom heaved with her agitation, her eyes were lowered with a sort of conscious shame at her avowal. As she lent slightly forward, and placed one soft white hand upon his own, he felt it tremble as it rested against him.

"Promise me that you will say nothing to your wife, or, indeed, I shall be most unhappy. You will promise?"

Her face was so close to his that he felt the blood surging to his temples and rushing to his head. She had cast a spell over him, and he could resist her no longer. "My darling I will promise you anything."

With a quick horrified gesture Mathilde snatched away her hand and withdrew to the furthest corner of the couch. Again she used her fan to conceal her features, and behind it Sir Hardress could hear every quick gasping breath that she drew.

"Forgive me, Miss Fairbairn, for the moment I was mad, and I hate myself for speaking the words which have given you pain. Have you no pity to pardon me, then?" he pleaded, as she neither moved nor spoke.

"I blame myself," she answered, in tones which seemed to have grown harsh and unmusical. "I must have merited such strange forgetfulness on your part." She still kept her face resolutely hidden from him, the only view of her that was obtainable being a glimpse of her soft, plump, white shoulder and arm.

"Nay. Now you wrong yourself without exonerating me," he replied. "But if you desire to punish me still more I will leave your side, and thus endeavour to prove to you that I am really repentant."

Once again she slowly lowered her fan and met his gaze, "You win me over in spite of myself," she said, and the new shyness which crept into her manner only served to render her all the more fascinating to the man upon whom she was practising all her arts of coquetry, before the wife to whom he belonged, and whose ruin and misery she was plotting.

"Are we not to see the dear children this evening?" Miss Fairbairn asked, as soon as their truce was settled. "Poor little mites, I noticed they were not in the drawing-room last evening; their mother guards them very carefully."

"Where are the children, Laura?" Sir Hardress asked, crossing over to the window were Laura still stood conversing with her sister.

"Archie is not so well," she answered. "He has a feverish cold, and I thought it the safest plan to keep him in the nursery for a day or two."

"Nonsense," snapped Sir Hardress, "you coddle the boy a deal to much. You are going the way to make him susceptible to every breath of wind that blows, by such foolish pampering. Is Barbara also condemned to the sick list?" he continued with an ugly sneer.

"No! but she did not care to come down without Archie," Lady St. Kestor answered in the same patient manner as before.

"You can ring the bell and request Simmonds to bring them down. I will not have them banished in this manner."

"But Hardress—!"

"Not a word," he said, interrupting the protestation which was trembling upon her lips. "Miss Fairbairn has expressed a desire for them, and I insist upon their presence."

Into Lady St. Kestor's gentle blue eyes, there flashed a look of scorn and contempt. "I might have guessed it," she said, unable to master the indignation which possessed her so strongly, "but I refuse to send for my children at that woman's bidding."

Sir Hardress spoke no word in reply, but gnawed fiercely at the ends of his drooping moustache, and stroked his chin and pointed beard with a nervous hand. His expressive dark eyes also gleamed with an evil look which was ugly to see.

Immediately afterwards Grames entered in response

to the ringing of the bell. Sir Hardress turned and looked at his wife. For once she met his gaze with a look of defiance.

Grames waited in silence for his orders, but Lady St. Kestor never even looked in his direction or testified that she was aware of his presence.

"Tell Simmonds to conduct the children here without delay." It was Sir Hardress who spoke at last. Lady St. Kestor had remained master of the situation so far, but she was fully aware that even her present triumph was but a poor one, and likely to be followed by most disastrous results.

Miss Fairbairn, though an apparent unobserver had nevertheless watched the little passage at arms between her host and hostess, with an exhilarating sense of satisfaction, which rose to the highest pitch, as she heard Sir Hardress give the order for the children to be sent down. She had paid a visit to the nursery during the afternoon, and knew that they were not to appear on account of Archie's indisposition, but had taken an opportunity for stirring up a little domestic strife, and had succeeded even beyond her expectations.

Ten minutes later, the two children were led in by Simmonds, dressed in their evening attire.

Barbara, who was the elder of the two, was a bright piquant little girl, six years of age. Her eyes were of a deep blue, similar to her mother's, only that they were of a more sparkling brightness. Her complexion was also of the same delicate fairness tinged with the warm roseate hue which was one of

Lady Laura's chief attractions. Her sunny golden hair fell in long natural curls over her shoulders reaching almost to the waist. Archie, her brother, was her junior by two years. There was a strong resemblance between the children, but the boy was of a more fragile build and inherited the dark hair and eyes of his father. As he came forward it was obvious to the most casual observer that he was considerably out of health. A bright crimson spot burnt on each of his cheeks, a hectic flush instead of the glow of health. His little eyes flashed with an unnatural brilliancy, and he hung by his nurse's side reluctant to loose the clasp of her hand.

"Let them come over here, Simmonds," said Lady Laura.

Just before they reached the couch where Miss Fairbairn sat, she leaned forward and selected an apple from a dish of fruit on a table beside her. Dangling it by the stalk she held the tempting rosy-cheeked fruit before their eyes, and thus diverted them from their first purpose of making their way across the room to their mother.

Hastily Lady Laura turned away again towards the window, a look of anguish in her eyes. "And so she tempts even my children away from me!"

"Yes! And with the identical fruit with which Eve tempted Adam."

She was scarcely conscious of having spoken aloud until the sentence was thus supplemented by Hugh Penwood, whom she had not observed standing beside her.

For a moment astonishment held her silent. The next Penwood was bending low before her with the old nervousness in his voice and manner. " Believe me, Lady St. Kestor, I beg of you, that I spoke unwittingly, for an instant, I was oblivious to all around me, save yourself."

Lady St. Kestor indicated her acceptance of his apology by a stately bow. Speech seemed to have forsaken her, and she was destined to see him leave her without having spoken to him a syllable. Every atom of colour had receded from her face, and she still remained standing in the same position almost motionless. Suddenly the hot blood flushed again in her cheeks as she was roused to thought and action by her husband's voice: " You fiend!" he hissed between his teeth as he passed her. " I'll make you suffer for this."

The children still stood beside Miss Fairbairn, who was talking and laughing with them with an air of careless enjoyment.

"Barbara and Archie, come to me." Lady St. Kestor's voice sounded cold and strained, and the children looked round with a questioning surprise in their gaze.

" Mamma is calling you, run to her my darlings!" and Mathilde laughingly pushed them away from her and kissed them as she released them.

As soon as they reached her, Lady Laura took Archie up into her arms and carried him from the room, Barbara clinging to the skirt of her dress. As they reached the door, Mathilde kissed the tips of her fingers and wafted a fragrant caress after them.

When Lady St. Kestor re-entered a short time afterwards, Mathilde Fairbairn and Hugh Penwood were seated side by side, engaged in earnest conversation.

CHAPTER IX.

A DANGEROUS GUEST.

"IF I were you, I'd get rid of that curate fellow!"

It was Sir Peter who spoke. He and his host were sitting together in the smoke-room, a small apartment at the further end of the hall, its distance from the rest of the rooms on the ground floor making it an acceptable retreat for the discussion of all matters of a private character, and thither the two gentlemen were in the habit of very frequently resorting.

Sir Hardress was leaning slightly forward in his chair, his gaze fixed upon the glowing coals, as they crackled and blazed in the broad fire-grate. He simply turned his head and looked at his guest, who was lounging in an easy chair in his favourite attitude, with his slippered feet resting upon the topmost rail of the polished steel fender.

"He is in the way, my dear boy. In our way, I should say, he's one of the rocks ahead, which we must be on the look out to guard against."

"Pshaw?" answered Sir Hardress, impatiently.

"Such a supposition is only the outcome of your suspicious nature; you scent danger even where it is impossible for it to exist."

Sir Peter leisurely uncrossed and recrossed his legs, and settled his position more comfortably before making a reply; then continued in the same cool studied manner as before. "Anyway he takes my lady's part against you, and it strikes me he would continue to do so if even it cost him his means of obtaining a livelihood to do it."

An unbelieving smile still lingered on Sir Hardress's face. "My dear fellow, you are utterly mistaken. My wife is not the sort of woman to stand that sort of thing, and once more I must assure you there is positively not the slightest ground for apprehension on that score."

"You almost make me think I am on the verge of a more important discovery still when you talk in that style; surely you are not going to set yourself up as your wife's champion, are you?" He was lazily watching the blue smoke curling upwards as he puffed at a choice cigar, but he cast a side glance at Sir Hardress in order to note the effect of his words.

Sir Hardress had flung himself back into his chair, and fallen to caressing his pointed beard, an angry scowl darkening his handsome face, but he made no further reply, and the silence remained unbroken for several seconds. His guest was again the first to break it. Slowly, as if the exertion was almost too great an effort, he raised himself to an upright position, and pushed the chair backward on its castors, until he was on a level with the table, then fixed his elbows upon it and supported his chin between his hands. The former look of indifference faded from his face, and gave place to an entirely different expression. Into the gleaming close-set eyes crept a determined sparkle, which might have been termed defiant, and the heavy dimpled chin seemed to have developed hard and cruel lines which had before been hidden by his mock urbanity.

" You don't seem much inclined for conversation," he commenced; "but its no use cutting up rough about trifles. You are ambitious to get M.P tacked on to the rest of your title, and to see your way clear towards becoming both popular and wealthy. Ah, what a pity that you are not free to secure a rich wife; the rest would be comparatively easy, but as it is your eight hundred a year is a mere flea-bite, and all these wretched farms on the estate like so many vampires fastened upon you! Now, if it were only invested in whisky, why it would be the basis of a colossal fortune for you."

" You would convert the world into one gigantic distillery if you could have the planning of the universe, I do believe," said Sir Hardress, with a mixture of contempt and amusement.

" Perhaps I would," assented Sir Peter; " you may have your laugh, but I am ready to wager that even then we should find some stragglers had been left out, who would be clamorous to consume enough to keep us prosperous even under those conditions."

" Well I leave that to you," Sir Hardress answered.

I don't care about whisky under any circumstances, and though it may represent money to you, I should always imagine my gold and silver stunk of it. But, as you say, I am ambitious, and so far as I am able I am willing to pay for the attainment of my ambition. Have you fixed your price?"

"Well, what I desire is of so trival a nature that it is scarcely fair to call it a price. I should like you to make me the testamentary guardian of your children."

In blank astonishment Sir Hardress fixed his gaze upon him. "Are you mad?" he asked him at length, and he brought his hand down upon the table with a heavy thud as he put the question.

"No, not exactly," answered Sir Peter, a gleam of amusement flashing in his eyes. "Only like yourself—ambitious. But, you see," he went on, "I have no need to be ambitious in a monetary point of view; mine is entirely of a social character, and I wish it to be known that we are more than ordinary friends. It will sound well and soon be in everybody's mouth that Lord St. Kestor, of St. Kestor, in Devonshire, has appointed Sir Peter Fairbairn guardian of his children. It's deuced hard work mounting the social ladder, I can tell you, but I've sworn to get to the top, and I will."

"If even I were to consent to your proposition, you would soon discover that you had attached a thoroughly false value to the thing; nobody would care one jot more for you on that account."

"Well, we'll call it a whim if you like. I've taken a fancy to the children, and surely you won't hesitate about gratifying it."

Sir Peter waited for a moment, watching his host, who had lapsed into a deep reflection.

"Haven't you foresight enough to see that this may be the first step towards accomplishing a separation from your wife; she's not likely to stay with you if the children are out of the way."

The bored expression gradually faded from Sir Hardress's face, and the dawn of a new interest began to break upon it. "I would do anything to gain Mathilde. I have but to think of her and in one breath I both bless and curse you for ever bringing her across my path."

He spoke with an intense passion ringing in his voice, and in an excited manner rose from his chair, and strode rapidly across the room, backwards and forwards down the narrow space left between the window and the table. Sir Peter watched him with quiet content. He had been exerting every means to kindle something like passion or interest within him, and he had almost begun to despair of being able to do so. But the name of Mathilde acted like magic. All his apathy vanished—his reserve melted like snow before the sun.

"And yet your wife is fair enough to look upon."

"She is like milk and water by the side of Mathilde's peerless beauty. She is a statue—but Mathilde is warm responsive flesh and blood!"

"But you thought you loved her once!"

"Pshaw—don't mock me with reminders of that foolish infatuation. I thought I loved her till she proved a hindrance and a burden to me. While I remained plain Hardress Carew, with no particular ambition to aspire to, she contented me. Was it likely that I should ever suppose it probable that the St. Kestor inheritance would fall upon me while three good lives stood between me and its possession? But I'd married the parson's daughter when I came in for my good fortune. I who might have chosen—"

"Whom?" The Scotchman leaned still further over the table and anxiously scanned Sir Hardress's countenance.

"Mathilde!"

Sir Peter dropped back into his old position and shaded his face from observation. Simultaneously Sir Hardress ceased his rapid march, drew up his own chair close by the table, and addressed his first voluntary question to Sir Peter.

One and two o'clock had both chimed, and yet their conversation had not lagged for a single moment. The atmosphere of the room was gradually becoming chilled, the fire had long since died out, leaving no trace of its former cheery comfort, save in a few charred embers, but the conference still continued, and when Sir Hardress at last drew out his watch, and wound it up preparatory to concluding the interview, the hands pointed to the hour of three.

When they at length separated, each stole noiselessly to his own apartment rather like a guilty marauder than as host and guest.

And the pure and gentle wife slept on calmly and peacefully while her husband and his vile colleague sat into the early hours of the morning, plotting and intriguing how best they might acomplish the destruction of her hopes and happiness, by robbing her of those who were dearer to her than life itself.

CHAPTER X.

A SIMPLE FUNERAL.

THE following day Archie's cold had developed so considerably that it was deemed necessary to have the doctor called in. Lady Laura was therefore, enabled on that plea to absent herself almost entirely from her guests, and to remain in the nursery without fear of molestation.

It was with no little surprise that she heard from Sir Peter, just before retiring for the night, that he and his niece had completed their preparations for leaving St. Kestor early the next morning. A sudden feeling of relief and thankfulness rushed to her heart, and so spontaneous was the emotion that it flashed in her eyes and was instantly read by Sir Peter.

He took a cruel pleasure in quenching the glad light which for a moment his words had raised. "We are to stay at our town house, which I rented for the season. Then we purpose spending some weeks at Craig-Feldie, where Sir Hardress has promised to join us, with yourself and the little ones. I hope your ladyship will allow us to return your liberal hospitality, so long extended towards us, in our poor way. My niece will be only too glad to second the invitation."

"I certainly hope that we may have the pleasure of Lady St. Kestor's company at Craig-Feldie."

In response to her uncle's words, Mathilde rose languidly from her chair, and smiled upon her hostess as she supplemented her own honeyed phrase, and again retired to her chair with a mock respectful bow.

Sir Peter indeed had gained his revenge, for the invitation had fallen upon Lady Laura with a crushing weight, and her eyes sought her husband's face with a helpless, wistful look. But he only answered with that calm, impenetrable reserve, which, as she had already learned, it was impossible to pierce. They were waiting for her reply, and though her lips seemed to have grown stiff and speechless, she just managed to articulate, "I thank you! you are very kind," and answering Miss Fairbairn with a bow as sweeping as her own, she left them to return to her place by the sick child.

But her heart was heavy with a foreboding of some ill to result from the proposed visit, and she gave herself up to devising some scheme which would render its non-fulfilment feasible. An event occured, however, which for the time being dispelled all other thoughts, though it was destined to accelerate the realisation, and convert the shadow into the substance—the shadow which had so long been hovering over the house of St. Kestor.

During the same night the household was disturbed by the ringing of the great bell at the principal door, and Sir Hardress shortly afterwards entered the night nursery, where his wife was sleeping by the side of the child. She soon learned from him that her father had been seized with paralysis, and that she must hasten to him without delay. A very few moments sufficed to call the nurse to take her place, and to prepare herself for the visit. When she reached the entrance hall, she found her husband already there awaiting her. As they stepped out into the darkness of the solemn, silent night, he drew her arm within his own, and though he addressed very few words to her, still there was more of tenderness in his manner than he had allowed to be apparent for a dreary length of time. Even the grief and agitation which she was experiencing on her father's account could not enable her to subdue the momentary feeling of joy, engendered by his altered manner, and hope, sudden and swift, was once more born within her.

From the first moment of the seizure the rector had remained unconscious, and as several hours passed without any sign of returning animation, the watchers began to fear that his last words had already been spoken. With mingled feelings of hope and suspense they awaited the physician who had been summoned from Exeter by the family doctor. But when he at length arrived, the Reverened Archibald Haldane had passed beyond the reach of all human aid. Without a word or a sign of farewell he had crossed the slender rubicon which divides us from "the great majority."

And thus it happened that Sir Peter Fairbairn and his niece departed without again bidding adieu to their hostess, but leaving various sympathetic messages to be delivered by Sir Hardress who had only arrived in time to see them to the carriage.

Perhaps a more impressive service had never been witnessed than on the occasion of the old rector's funeral. The church was filled to overflowing with the parishioners and simple village folk, amongst whom he had ministered for so many years. They had not learned the necessity of repressing their emotions, and gave unchecked and audible vent to their tears and lamentations, at times altogether drowning the voices of those engaged in conducting the service. But there was no unseemly rushing or crowding, and all fell back with respectful sympathy to allow the bereaved ones to reach the grave. " Poor young leddy—poor young leddy," was whispered from one to another, as Mary Haldane stood listening to the solemn words of the burial service, " What'll she do without her father ? "

"Eh, but she a plucky one ! " retorted some one standing by. " Come what may, she'll meet it with a smile. Her heart might break, but nobody 'ud ever know it."

A reverential hush ran through the crowd. The service was over. A couple of minutes afterwards and the faithful flock were bending over the grave taking their last look, some of them holding the children whom he had christened, in their arms, to drop a bunch of daisies or a tiny flower upon the polished coffin, which held the remains of their pastor and friend.

So soon as the mournful little *cortége*, which consisted of Sir Hardress and Lady St. Kestor, Miss Haldane and Mr. Penwood, the lawyer and the doctor, reached the parsonage, they repaired at once to the late rector's study. He had left a will with the lawyer, but it was only a simple document, for he had little to bequeath, and there were no conditions or formalities introduced. There were a few small cottages and the sum of one thousand pounds, all of which he left unconditionally to his second daughter, Mary Haldane, Sir Hardress St. Kestor being appointed trustee. To Lady Laura he left his watch, a gold hunter, to be given to her son Archibald when he should be old enough to wear it. For the little Barbara was to be preserved the handsome Bible and Church Service, which had been presented to him by the Archbishop on his ordination, and for Laura a diamond ring, which had been her mother's betrothal gift from himself. A trifling remembrance for each of the servants completed the contents of the last simple testament. In death, as in life, he had been just to all. Lady Laura, by her marriage, was provided for, but her sister was alone and dependent upon whatever he might provide for her.

As far as Miss Haldane was aware, she had not, except her sister, a living relative in the world, and the only one with whom she could think of taking up her residence for any time was her god-mother, an old lady who had been a friend of her mother's in her youthful days, and stood as sponsor to each of the girls in turn.

"Of course, you will return with us," Sir Hardress had said to her, after the meeting in the study on the day of the funeral, "and you must make your home with us for the present." At the time she consented willingly, but after remaining several weeks decided that it would be better to make an early departure.

Though Lady Laura was as affectionate as ever, there was a strangeness in her manner which Mary could not fail to perceive. If they happened to be alone or conversing together, she would start uneasily at the slightest sound, or appeared to be on the *qui vive* for some interruption, and there was a nervous constraint which never vanished, unless it was that she was sure of her husband being absent from home for some considerable time.

When Miss Haldane last broached the subject of her departure, Lady Laura's distress was keen and bitter, but she used no endeavours to persuade her to extend her visit. "Oh, Mary, Mary! I cannot bear to think of your going out into the world, cast adrift from the dear old home which sheltered us both. Would that we might go forth together and fight the battle of life hand in hand!" and the miserable young wife flung her arms round the younger sister, whom she was so powerless to help, and to whom she seemed to cling for consolation and support in her own behalf.

At the request of Sir Hardress, Hugh Penwood had decided to continue his curacy, at any rate for some little time, or until it could be ascertained what arrangements the new incumbent might deem it advisable to make.

It was a foggy, cheerless day early in the month of November that marked the separation of the two sisters. On the morning of her departure, before any of the household were astir, Mary had taken her farewell look at the grey-stone parsonage, and paid a visit to her father's grave, over which the newly-placed turf still lay brown and bare. Lady Laura and Ashley Dallas were to accompany her as far as Exeter, but their real leave-taking took place before quitting the Hall.

"Be sure and write to me regularly," urged Miss Haldane, "and remember that if ever you are in need of me I will come! I am almost certain to remain with Mrs. de Grey during the rest of the winter months, as she has lost her companion."

Mrs. de Grey was the woman who had been her mother's friend, and who had written to her goddaughter immediately upon hearing of the rector's decease, inviting her to join her as soon as possible at her residence in Eaton-square, London, urging her speedy acceptance in the kindest of terms, and adding that having recently lost her friend and companion, who had left her for the purpose of being married, she was then feeling more than an ordinary amount of loneliness and would look upon Mary's visit as a personal kindness.

And thus was opened the first path which led Mary Haldane from the home of her childhood— from the village of St. Kestor, to the Modern Babylon.

CHAPTER XI.

HUGH PENWOOD MAKES HIS FIRST EXPERIMENT IN "THOUGHT READING."

IT wanted but a week to the advent of Christmas and it was now thoroughly settled that Sir Hardress and Lady St. Kestor, accompanied by their children, should spend the sacred season as Sir Peter Fairbairn's guests at Craig Feldie.

In vain had Lady Laura hoped and pleaded that her recent bereavement might be put forward as an excuse for the postponement of the visit. But her husband had remained obdurate and insisted upon her acceptance. He had also evinced a decided disposition to treat her more kindly and generously ever since the night of her father's death, and she dreaded to anger him by an obstinate refusal or resistance. Unwillingly, therefore, she consented, rather than be the means of stirring up the old strife and misery.

As their departure was fixed for the following day, it was arranged that the new rector, accompanied by Hugh Penwood, should spend the evening at St. Kestor, in order that he might become better acquainted with his patron before the latter left for his visit into Scotland.

The Rev. Eric Lennard was a genial and entertaining man, not much over fifty years of age, and yet one who had seen a great deal of life, posessed a fund of stories and anecdotes, and could talk well on every conceivable topic.

Sir Hardress was delighted to meet with someone with whom he could argue. Politics were freely discussed; theology and its various doctrines were speculated upon; and then their conversation, having wandered on to science, led to the expression of their opinions concerning some of its professors.

" Talking upon this subject reminds me of a book which was brought before my notice just recently by a friend of mine," said Mr. Lennard, " entitled ' Occultism,' or ' Occult Forces,' I forget which ; but it is a most extraordinary production, opening up an entirely new field for thought and conjecture. There is something fascinating about it too, which would render such a study intensely interesting. I have only read about half way through it at present, but I shall be pleased to place it at your disposal if you would care to have a glance at it."

Sir Hardress inclined his head, and thanked him, at the same time continuing the conversation as though he found pleasure in the subject.

Mr. Lennard, who was enthusiastic in everything in which he took an interest, now thoroughly roused, launched off into a recital of wonderful and mysterious events which had occurred to persons with whom he was acquainted, and about which there was not a shadow of doubt to be entertained. "I have one friend," he went on to say, "who nine times out of ten will succeed in telling you your actual thoughts by simply placing the hand of the person upon whom he is experimenting upon his own forehead. I have been a witness of it repeatedly. And yet he can't account for the ability or perception himself," and the rector held up his hands as if to demonstrate his words.

All had grown interested alike in the converstion; Lady Laura was listening eagerly to every word as it fell from the rector's lips and Hugh Penwood sat and gazed at him in a manner which seemed to imply, " What sort of man is this ? "

"Most extraordinary!" ejaculated Sir Hardress. " How would it be to try it—do you think any of us here would prove likely subjects ? " and he smiled at his own proposition as soon as it was made.

The rector glanced around at the little group.

"The number is almost too select for much choice," said Sir Hardress. But the rector did not reply. His gaze had settled upon Hugh Penwood's face, and he was studying him with a new earnestness mixed with a strange fascination, which also riveted the attention of their host and hostess.

"It has just flashed upon my remembrance that Mr. Penwood bears a very striking resemblance to the friend of whom I spoke," he said, at length. " Not only a resemblance in form or feature, but in manner and disposition, and that accounts for my

H

previous feeling of familiarity towards him which I have hitherto been unable to explain. Yes, I think Mr. Penwood would be the most likely subject amongst us. What do you say to our experimenting upon you, eh?" asked Mr. Lennard, with a laugh.

"Oh, I am far too stupid to be at all impressionable," stammered out the curate, colouring furiously at thus being made the centre of observation.

"You would be far more likely to succeed with Mr. Dallas or Sir Hardress," he finished, looking across at the latter as he spoke as though begging of him to extricate him from the position into which he was being forced.

"My dear fellow," interrupted the enthusiastic rector, "it is the highly sensitive and shrinking nature such as yours, which invariably responds to the operation; in fact, its very responsiveness creates the required conditions."

His listeners looked up at him in some astonishment.

"Well, so my book says!" he hastened to add, as he read the surprise expressed on their faces. "'A nature susceptible as an Æolian harp is to the breath of the wind is the one best suited for the purpose'; remember, I am only quoting," he added. "Now, Mr. Penwood, out of the room you go! I will think of some public person just to simplify the matter, and then you shall try and find out the name, using the same means as those adopted by my friend;" and acting upon the impulse, he laid his hand upon Penwood's shoulder, and led him from the room, and left him to wait in the same apartment into which he had been ushered on his first visit to the Hall.

Five minutes might have elapsed ere he was recalled. With almost breathless interest they watched and waited for the result.

" Have you any inkling ? " the rector asked, as they stood together for fully three minutes.

" None," Hugh Penwood replied, as he dropped the rector's hand from his forehead. " I foretold my failure, and you see that I was right."

" Oh, wait a bit—wait a bit," answered Mr. Lennard, still undaunted. " The fault may rest with me. ' If at first you don't succeed, try, try, again.' You may be more fortunate with Sir Hardress."

So once more Mr. Penwood was hurried from the room to wait until a fresh name had been fixed upon.

" Be sure and keep your mind entirely concentrated upon that one idea," Mr. Lennard was saying to Sir Hardress when Penwood again entered in answer to their summons.

In about two minutes Penwood removed Sir Hardress's hand from his forehead, and looked about him in a half-dazed manner. " No, I can gather nothing," he said, and, as he spoke, he shivered as from cold. " I am evidently not susceptible," and he smiled at Mr. Lennard as he walked over to the fireplace and stretched out his long slender fingers towards the blaze.

" And I am convinced that you are susceptible, and very susceptible, too," persisted the rector. " You have failed with your first and second subjects ; the third time decides it. Lady St. Kestor shall be your third subject."

Mr. Penwood turned suddenly from the fire as though to negative the proposal, but the words he was about to frame were never uttered. "Why shouldn't I?" he muttered to himself, and passed out of the room a third time.

"Mr. Penwood!"

He had allowed himself to sink into a reverie, and was aroused by his name being called.

"We thought you must have fallen asleep in consequence of our keeping you waiting so long," said Mr. Lennard, as he appeared.

"I had not noticed the length of time," he answered, "and my thoughts were so engrossing that I did not hear your first call."

Lady St. Kestor stood on the hearth-rug facing him, her face flushed and her eyes sparkling with nervous excitement.

"Perhaps it will be only fair to tell you—"

"No; tell me nothing," answered Mr. Penwood quickly, raising his hand in a gesture of dissent.

Mr. Lennard was silent, and a keen look of pleasure and interest was in his eyes as he watched the firm, rapid strides with which Penwood crossed the room.

Without the slightest hesitation he took Lady Laura's soft, white hand within his own, and pressed it to his forehead. In an instant a convulsive movement seized his frame from head to foot, a spasm as of pain for a moment contorted his features, his eyes closed, and his face looked white and rigid.

Lady Laura's hand dropped heavily by her side.

"You were thinking of your father," he said, and sinking into the nearest chair he drew out his cambric handkerchief, to wipe away the cold sweat which had gathered in great beads upon his brow.

"I told you that you would succeed," exclaimed Mr. Lennard excitedly, clapping him on the shoulder, "You were bound to—it is written on your face."

"Do you think the success in this instance can be taken as an absolute test?" queried Sir Hardress. "It might be urged that Lady Laura's thoughts would naturally revert to the parent whom she has so recently lost, and also that Mr. Penwood would be likely to assume that she would do so. I advised her to fix upon some other person," he concluded, addressing Hugh, who still looked agitated as he sat tugging with restless fingers at his steel chain.

"Perhaps it might have been better," his guest replied somewhat laconically.

"I could not help dear papa's memory being uppermost in my thoughts," interrupted Lady Laura. "Even had I decided upon another person, Mr. Penwood's presence in itself would remind me always of him, I suppose in consequence of their connection."

"Let us convince ourselves by again putting our friend to the test," suggested the rector.

The curate looked up quickly with a deprecating glance. "No don't ask me," he said, impulsively; "I would rather not."

"Nonsense," laughed both Sir Hardress and the

rector, simultaneously, "You're not nervous, are you? Upon my word if you are going to take it seriously I shall be sorry that I introduced the subject."

"I defer to Lady St. Kestor," answered Hugh, rising from his chair and pushing it abruptly away from him. "If she is willing, I will try again, if only to oblige you."

"Hear, hear!" exclaimed the enthusiastic rector. "I am sure Lady St. Kestor will not disappoint us."

Lady St. Kestor looked very much as if she would like to refuse, but with her usual good nature, combined with her customary deference towards her husband, she somewhat nervously assented.

"Now, Laura, this time you shall not fix your thoughts upon any particular individual, but on some object or occurrence," said her husband, and his glance wandered around the room in search as he spoke. He pointed to a picture suspended from the wall. It was an oil painting, representing Handel seated at the organ, the young Prince George beside him.

"How will this do, Mr. Lennard?"

"Very well. What say you, Lady Laura?"

"Yes, anything!"

Again Mr. Penwood was called, and his glance also wandered around the room. Directly that his hand came into contact with Lady Laura's. His eye rested upon the picture, and he was on the point of speaking, when, as if acting on a secondary impulse, he placed her hand upon his forehead. Suddenly he started backwards and almost staggered. There was a dazed look of perplexity in his eyes. "I think I read your thoughts this time, Lady Laura," and he seemed unable to withdraw his gaze from her face.

"Yes, you have guessed it," she replied, but her voice trembled, and her face and neck were both suffused with a crimson flush. She tried to laugh, but the attempt only culminated in a hysterical sob. "You see it is the only oil painting in the room," she went on rapidly, addressing Mr. Penwood, "all the rest are water colours."

Hugh looked at her in the same half bewildered way before replying. Then his rare, gentle smile overspread his face, and his perplexed expression gave place to one of relieved thankfulness. "I observe that it is so; still I hope that may not again disqualify us."

"Oh, no, nothing of the kind," interrupted the rector. "I may say that we are satisfied, may I not?" he asked, addressing Sir Hardress.

Sir Hardress bowed assent. "Yes, I am fully satisfied," he added as an after thought. He, too, was absorbed in his own reflections and had scarcely heeded the rector's question.

"If you would care to have the book that I mentioned, I will send it on to you early to-morrow." The rector was shaking hands with his host, preparatory to departing as he spoke.

"I shall be much obliged to you," Sir Hardress replied, "and if you don't mind just stepping into the library I will shew you a somewhat curious old volume which I came across the other day."

As the two men, followed by Ashley, passed out of the room, Lady St. Kestor cast an imploring look at Hugh Penwood. He advanced towards her. "You wondered, Lady St. Kestor, what could be the subject of my conversation with Miss Fairbairn?"

They had changed places for once. She was nervous and abashed, while he was surprised and inquiring.

"I cannot imagine what you will think of me," she commenced. "It was decided that I should fix my attention upon the picture, and I thought I had succeeded in doing so, but as soon as ever I felt your hand upon my own, the remembrance flashed across me—of yourself and Mathilde Fairbairn as I had last seen you together. I tried to banish it, but could not; and you may guess at my dismay when I felt that you had divined the thought which was uppermost in my mind. How am I to thank you for your discreet silence?"

"If you will let me answer your unspoken query I will ask no more," he said, speaking hurriedly, and proceeding to his explanation without a pause.

"Miss Fairbairn told me of her own and her uncle's departure on the following day, and urged me to accept from her a donation of twenty pounds, to be distributed among the poor of the parish, or at my own discretion in any case of need which might arise. It was a generous gift, and I assured her that it would be the means of cheering many homes and brightening many hearts, and I also promised to acquaint her later on with some of the objects or persons whom it had benefited.

A look of unmingled surprise was expressed on Lady St. Kestor's face as she heard his explanation, " And you believe that—that Miss Fairbairn is a well intentioned generous woman ? "

The question was put with a curious hesitancy.

But Mr. Penwood answered readily enough. " Indeed, I believe her to be all that you have said."

It might have been that she had borrowed a flash of her sister's sarcasm ; it was certainly not with her usual charity and goodwill that she next spoke, " Miss Fairbairn has been fortunate in gaining your good opinion."

Immediately she turned to bid him a courteous adieu, for Sir Hardress and the rector had already reached the threshold, and were waiting for Mr. Penwood to join them.

CHAPTER XII.

DRIVEN INTO EXILE.

CHRISTMAS had come and gone, and the New Year was already three weeks old—three weeks which would long be remembered for their extreme severity. Jack Frost was abroad early and late, chilling alike the aged and the young with his icy breath. The rich shivered beneath the weight of their costly furs and by the side of blazing fires. God only knows how the poor fared beneath their rags and paltry coverings, crouched and huddled by their empty grates. Perhaps the fathers and even some of the mothers deserved no pity, if all were judged by strict and merciless justice; but the poor pinched and starving children had had no hand in bringing about their hapless fate. Mere accident of birth was alone responsible for their heritage of poverty, squalor and, perhaps, crime.

In one of the poorest and meanest parts of the city of Edinburgh was situated Bannockburn-square. It was in reality an intersection of short, dismal streets, all bearing such strong uniformity as to render them to a stranger almost undistinguishable. This difficulty made it a pretty safe hiding-place for the rogues and vagabonds which more or less infest all cities. The buildings were of considerable height and let off in flats, or merely double or single rooms as the case might be, the proprietors caring little or nothing for the characters of the occupants so long as they paid up regularly. For the rest they might come and go without any fear of questioning.

It was towards one of these wretched tenements on the night in question that a woman clad in garments that were pitifully thin, wended her staggering footsteps. Just as she was passing the liquor vaults, mid-way down the street, the light from its bold flaring lamp fell full upon her, and revealed a white haggard-looking face which must have been comely once upon a time. The hollow cheeks and sharp-pinched features told an eloquent tale of poverty, while the dark lustreless eyes bore in them an almost unearthly look. She was carrying a bundle in her arms, pressed tightly to her bosom, and covered entirely by the thin shawl around her, which she held in position with her white attenuated hand close to the throat. On the third finger of that hand, gleamed a slender hoop of gold; alas it was but the badge of her slavery and of her shattered existence.

She had just passed beyond the glare of the lamp when the heavy door was swung open and the sound of men's and women's voices raised in drunken hilarity fell upon the still calm of the outer air. A big-boned, brawny-looking Scotchwoman emerged from behind the swinging door and stepped on to the pavement, followed by her husband, a little shock-headed fellow, whose habitual custom it was to appear a few paces in the rear whenever in his wife's company.

"Here's Jess Cameron!" she called out, her voice raised to the highest pitch, "and looking fit to drop wi' that precious bairn in her arms too. Jess! Jess! You've have no need to hurry home, for my Sandy here is only waiting to invite you to a glass o' steaming whisky."

The woman addressed as Jess Cameron halted on hearing her name called, and a weary smile flitted across her face as she replied to the good-natured offer: "You are very kind, Nance; may the Almighty bless you for speaking a kind word to me; but I fear I am too weak to stand the sort of eomfort which your Sandy would be good enough to give me. My poor head!" And again the pitiful smile stole across her face, as she raised her hand to her head, and once again pursued her way staggering along as best she could.

Crossing over to one of the smaller side streets, she turned under an archway, which was a passage or side entrance to one of the numerous lodging-houses. It was not until she had reached the top of the third flight of stone steps that she paused, though it was with the utmost difficulty that she was able to breathe. At the summit she sank down upon the topmost step to regain her exhausted strength, and to brace herself for the interview that would follow.

A faint moan from the infant beneath the shawl

reminded her that she had already been seated several minutes. After waiting to hush its cries, she proceeded down the narrow little passage towards a closed door, from under which a light was streaming. With a nervous trembling hand she turned the handle and slowly pushed the door open. It was a small square room, poorly and barely furnished, but clean and neat in all its details. There was a wooden bedstead in one corner, and a mattress with a rug thrown loosely over it in another.

A bright coal fire burned in the small grate, casting a warm cosy glow over the apartment. A large empty box, turned bottom upwards, served for a table, and at it was seated a man who, to guess roughly by his appearance, could not be more than thirty-three or four years of age, while at a glance it was evident that his companion was a girl scarcely out of her teens. The improvised table was supporting what appeared to the famished woman standing on the threshold, a most sumptuous repast. There were two cups filled with steaming coffee, which scented the room with its delicious aroma. There was also a tin containing rashers of bacon, which emitted a most appetising odour. The feast was crowned by a plate of griddle cakes, which the two were just in the act of discussing when the wife and mistress's presence caused an unwelcome interruption to the enjoyment of the good things provided.

At the sound of the latch they each turned their faces towards the door. For a second the woman hesitated, and cast an eager look of curiosity at the girl who was her husband's companion, but his voice quickly roused her from her abstraction.

"Well! are you daft—standing there as if any one was likely to want to eat you! This is my sister Meg—a lass you'd do well to imitate. She knows what's good, does Meg; and, better still, how to get the money to buy it."

Jess advanced without making reply, her eyes fixed with a hungry stare on the viands spread so temptingly before her.

"A drink of coffee, Rob, just one drink!"

She stretched out her hand with a pleading gesture. In an instant the man dashed it away with a brutal force that almost sent her reeling backwards, causing the infant to again give vent to its bitter plaint.

"None o' that Jess!" he sneered. "What you work for, you shall eat, but so long as I am here you don't fatten on what Meg provides. How much have you earned to-day? Come, toss up!" he continued in the same brutal strain.

Jess slowly and sadly shook her head.

"Nothing! Nothing! There are always so many on the same errand as myself. I seem to have no chance amongst them all."

"All right, my girl," he answered. "You don't come that tale over me. If you don't get the money one way you must in another. You shall take the child in the street, and sing for it. They shall have a cup of coffee ready for you by the time you come back."

"Oh, Rob, Rob! you'll never think of turning me

out into the streets again to-night; you can't mean it. Since nine o'clock this morning I have tramped the city trying to find work. I am worn out, hungry, and nearly perished. No, you are trying to joke with me!"

The man listened to her passionate appeal with an evil smile playing over his face. She would have pleaded with him still further, but that he rose from his seat with all the instinct of his savage nature fully aroused against her.

In an instant Jess shrank away, and stretched out her disengaged hand as though to shield herself from an expected blow.

"Don't 'ee hurt her, Rob! She looks cold and tired. Let me give her some coffee, there's a good fellow," and Meg took up her own cup from the table and offered it to Jess.

But an almost wild look had crept into Jess's eyes as she kept them fixed upon her husband in mute terror.

"Not now! It would choke me," she said to the girl who held the coffee towards her, and the words came in quick gasps— "but I—I thank you."

"Take it away, Meg. You see my wife's saucy— what's good enough for us would choke her," and he gave vent to a burst of laughter which sounded to the woman's overstrained nerves little less than fiendish. With the courage born of despair, she turned upon him—

"Strike, Robert Cameron! and show your sister what a coward is capable of doing. Tell her also that as you do not choose to work yourself you send your wife instead, and beat and starve her when she fails to provide the food and money to keep you in idleness."

There was an upheaval of something beneath the rug on the mattress, and two little curl-tossed heads were visible; two pairs of sleepy, wondering eyes looked up in affright, awakened by the loud voices and angry tones which had so rudely aroused them. Then great, glistening tears stole down each sorrowful little face, as they listened to the mother's broken faltering voice.

The slight movement had been sufficient to attract her attention. Instantly she ceased to upbraid her husband, and rushed to meet the two bright-eyed urchins, who had sprung towards her immediately they saw themselves observed. But a heavy hand fell upon her shoulder, and pulled her fiercely back.

She looked up swiftly, and met her husband's gaze. There was something in it so evil and repellant that she shuddered, and tried to hide her face from him.

"You've had your say—now, go! Here, Meg, take the child," and he pointed to the infant, "and I swear that you shall never set eyes on it or any one of them again so long as I live to prevent it."

For a moment a dead silence ensued. Jess fixed her eyes upon her husband's face; unfeigned astonishment held her dumb.

He took a step forward as if to carry out his threat, and with a wild cry memory and realisation burst upon the faculties which had been almost numbed. In her frantic terror she pressed the babe with a clutch so tight that he commenced to struggle and scream.

"You would snatch my babe from me," she went on, scarce heeding its cries. "Part me from my children? No, no! I will appeal to the law. I have borne almost every cruelty that you could practise upon me and been silent, but now the world shall know what a monster you are."

By this time the two boys had crept from their bed, and were clinging to her skirts, their piteous sobs falling like a mournful accompaniment to their mother's words.

Cameron had gradually drawn nearer to her while she had been speaking, but Jess no longer shrank from him; the anger which was blazing in her eyes must have swallowed her former fear. She scarcely flinched from the blow which descended upon her from his clenched fist, as he wrenched the screaming child from the close clasp of her sheltering arms.

"You shall go to the law," he said, taking her by the shoulders to eject her from the room, "and let the law teach you what you are. Perhaps you'll be able to earn money for that. But in case you shouldn't I can save you a little expense by telling you that the children are mine, not yours. I may allow you to nurse them, to work for them, to live with them; or I may take them away from you. Ask the law to give them back to you, and it will tell you that they belong to their father, and that a woman has no

I

rights. You'd better have left well alone and kept your place."

He had reached the door, and stood with it held open in one hand, with the other one he pointed for her to leave the room.

A terrible fear had taken possession of her while he was speaking. Ignorant as she was of the laws of her own country, she had only looked upon them as a means of obtaining justice and help in her sore need, but that they should prove the means of depriving her of her own flesh and blood, of robbing her little ones of their natural protector, she could neither believe nor realise.

But his words had shaken her faith to a certain extent and already her heart was sinking as the idea forced its way into her mind that possibly he had spoken truthfully.

The babe's screams were gradually hushed as Meg paced to and fro with it in her arms. The two elder children had thrown themselves upon their mattress and buried their faces in the rug to suppress the sobs which shook their little frames in so heartrending a manner that the despairing mother, with a wild cry, turned and fled down the stone steps, out again into the frost and snow of the cruel winter night.

But the mental agony which she was enduring rendered her for the time being almost unconscious to any outside influences. There was a horrible something tugging at her heartstrings and racking her brain, which she had never before experienced. She seemed to have forgotten that she no longer carried the child, but still kept drawing the thin, well-worn shawl more closely around her, holding her arms in the same position as if she still retained it in her embrace. The pangs of hunger were unnoticed, and the lagging weariness forgotten. With swift, almost flying footsteps she pursued her way along the streets without heeding any particular direction. At last she paused from sheer exhaustion. The wild excitement which for a short time had endowed her with superficial strength was gradually abating, and giving place to the misery of comprehension and reflection.

The snow, which for a time had ceased to fall, was again rapidly descending in large feathery flakes, which enveloped the struggling woman in a covering of shroud-like whiteness, as with difficulty she sought to retrace her steps. After half-an-hour's weary tramping she again found herself in front of the tavern which she had passed on her way home. It was the one spot of brightness amid the gloom of the dark deserted streets which she had been traversing so long. Involuntarily she stopped in front of it and listened to the sounds of life and mirth from within. Somebody was singing an old Scotch ballad, which she had sung often enough in the happier days so long gone by. Uproarious applause followed the conclusion of the song, and as she listened her husband's words suddenly recurred to her mind—" You shall take the child into the streets and sing for it."

The next instant the heavy doors had swung to after her receding form, and she was standing before the bar importuning the portly hostess of the Bannockburn Arms to permit her to carry out her suddenly-formed project.

"Here's Robert Cameron's wife wants to go into the parlour to sing, so as to get a bit of money to take her to Craig-Feldie," she said, addressing her husband, who was just entering.

"The brute's turned her out at last," she added, in an undertone. "If she tries to get to Craig-Feldie to-night, it's my opinion he'll have her murder to answer for."

The "gude man" of the Bannockburn Arms eyed her narrowly for a moment before replying. He was wondering whether his guests would approve of such a half-starved, poorly-clad woman, from whose garments the clinging snow was gradually melting, being thrust in their society, her poverty and her wretchedness would seem so incongruous an element in their joyful midst.

Meanwhile the genial hostess had retired behind the rows of fanciful barrels, and a minute or two later emerged, with a cup of steaming coffee, brought to her by the most rubicund of maids. "Drink it off," she said to Jess as she passed it under the half raised partition, "and then we'll talk about the parlour."

Jess faltered out her thanks in broken but grateful words, which the landlady cut short by bouncing off into the parlour to acquaint her patrons with the request which Jess had come to offer. When she returned Jess was draining the almost empty cup, and the warmth and strength had brought a faint tinge of colour to her cheeks. The hostess beckoned to her, and opened the door of the parlour for her to enter.

"They're rather a rough company, but you needn't fear them; they're honest and good hearted, and'll be sure to give you something."

There were little pools of water left just where she had been standing, which had slowly dripped from her dress and shawl.

With the landlady's words of encouragement to sustain her, Jess entered the parlour of the Bannockburn Arms. She was aware that the room was large and brilliantly lighted, and that there were a number of people seated around a long table, but she was too confused and nervous to look about her at all.

At one end of the room a huge fire was burning in the grate and there were wooden stools placed on each side of the fireplace. Seating herself on one of these, and partially lowering her head, she was not forced to meet the curious looks of observation which fell upon her from the guests assembled at the table. Without any preliminary notice she commenced in a faltering tremulous voice to sing from memory the charming pathetic ballad "Auld Robin Gray." There was a singular purity and sweetness about the tremulous voice, which seemed to gain strength and confidence as she gradually lost the self-consciousness which rendered her task so difficult to undertake. There was a force and intensity, too, in her expression which unwittingly commanded the attention and sympathy of her hearers. When she commenced some of the men were smoking, while others were carrying on whispered conversations, but by degrees the pipes were laid aside, and not a word or sound broke the silence. The host and hostess had deserted their posts and stolen in quietly, amazed to hear poor Jess Cameron singing "like an angel," as they afterwards declared, while the rosy-cheeked maid, standing on tip-toe in the rear, looked on in open-mouthed astonishment.

But Jess sang on, apparently oblivious of all around her. Her tattered old bonnet had fallen back, revealing the glistening drops of wet upon her jet black hair. She had reached as far as the last verse—

"I wish that I were dead, but I'm not like to die." when great tears welled into her eyes, and sudden sobs rose so fast and thick as to almost choke her. Her head dropped upon her hands, and for a minute or two she swayed to and fro with the awakened agony conjured up by the words of the song she had chosen.

"Don't'ee take on so, my gude woman," said one of the men, who had been first to set the example of laying aside his newly-filled pipe. "You'll soon be having your bairn in your care again; ye canna make me believe that the law o' bonnie Scotland wad be so cruel as to tear a helpless bairn from the arms of its mother. Noo, noo, my lass, cheer up. Here's a saxpence towards helping you on your road to Craig-Feldie, and good luck to ye."

"Drop this wee bit of silver in for me, Colin!"

The last speaker was a bonnie lassie who was

seated at the table in the company of her lover, a big brawny fellow, whose great soft heart was beating in quick response to the tearfulness expressed in his Jeannie's eyes and voice. A minute later a shoal of coppers, interspersed with several gleaming bits of silver, were swept into the metal plate upon the table.

"Here, Jeannie shall give it to her," said the first spokesman, handing it over to her. Jeannie took the plate, and poured the contents into Jess's lap as she sat upon the stool, her face buried in her hands as she rocked silently to and fro. Impulsively she snatched the girl's hand and pressed it to her lips. "God bless you and them for their goodness to me to-night. Let them know that I am grateful." With her vision blinded by tears she made her way out of the room.

"Poor thing, poor thing!" ejaculated the girl, the tears streaming down her face as she spoke. "To think that the man she loved and married should have the power to make her suffer so. I'll know the rights of it though, and if the law lets him rob her of her bairn, then me and my Colin must say good-bye, or may-be some day I might stand in her shoes."

"Nay, nay, lass," said Colin, "It's no fair to measure all by a man like him."

"You're right there, Colin," she answered him, "but if women were not so ignorant about their own position I'm thinking they would not so easily rush into marriage as they do now. Why, what is a wife more than a slave, if she can only keep her children by her husband's permission, and be turned off as he'd turn off a hired servant? It's wrong, and any woman who thinks at all will say the same, and rebel against it too!"

"Hear, hear! Hurrah for Jeannie," cried the company one and all. "Let's drink to woman's pluck before we part," and bumpers were filled and drunk with hearty gusto. But poor Colin sat apart, looking glum and dissatisfied at the new colour which affairs had so suddenly assumed.

CHAPTER XIII.

A MOTHER STEALS HER OWN CHILD.

NO sooner had Jess Cameron quitted the parlour than she was hustled by the landlady into her own cosy apartment, and a substantial meal placed before her. But she could not be induced to share the comfortable bed which was offered to her by the sympathetic, rosy-cheeked maid, at her mistress's suggestion.

"I should go mad if I tried to sleep," Jess repeated over and over again. "I must keep on the move. If you will only tell me what time I can take the train to Craig-Feldie you will do me the greatest kindness possible."

It was soon ascertained that the only train which would be available left at 3 o'clock a.m., and without the slightest hesitation, Jess decided upon travelling by it. Once more she stepped out and faced the piercing wind and and biting cold, but the meal of which she had partaken, served to fortify her with a new reserve of strength for the carrying out of a hazardous and daring project which had formed itself in her busy brain; a project which, if successful, would entail a frightful amount of risk, and which, if unsuccessful, might result in (she shuddered as she owned it to herself)—in death.

Jess Cameron had resolved to *steal her own child !!*

Hastening towards the home from which she had been pitilessly excluded, she turned down the familiar passage. The windows were all darkened, and not a sound broke the silence of the night. The household had evidently retired to rest. For a second her hand groped along the stonework, which abutted somewhat around the door, until it came into contact with the object for which she had been seeking. It was the latch-key of the door, which it was customary for the keeper of the house to leave there for the convenience of several of his tenants, whose occupations necessitated their remaining out until the early hours of the morning, this arrangement being contrived in order that his own sleep might not be disturbed by being called up to admit them.

Neither was it the first time that the arrangement had proved of service to poor Jess Cameron. On more than one occasion she had been compelled to absent herself from home on account of her husband's brutality, and had used the same means to creep in steathily, and lie by the side of the children, when she had assured herself that their father was sleeping.

Gently closing the door behind her, she noiselessly ascended the steps, halting frequently to listen for the sound of anyone moving. But as no such sound met her ear, she would start again with new vigour in her steps and fresh courage in her heart as she drew gradually nearer to the fulfilment of the task which she had set herself.

The last flight of steps was already reached. The door of the chamber which meant *home* to her, was in sight. She could see that the light had been extinguished, but there were occasional flickerings, which shone beneath the door with a sort of lurid glow, by which she guessed that the remnants of the fire still remained, or it might be that it had been replenished.

Kneeling by the door, she placed her ear close to the keyhole to listen for any sounds from within. She pressed her hand over her heart to still its tumultuous beating. Her breath came in such quick convulsive gasps that she even feared it might arouse the sleepers should their slumber be but light. But no such contingency occurred, and she soon gained confidence enough to enter the room. Her knowledge of the fastener upon the door enabled her to gain an ingress without the betrayal of the slightest noise. Once more she stood, a silent sombre figure, upon the threshold.

The flickering light cast by the fire, enabled her to see from her post of observation that her husband was lying back asleep, in an easy chair which he had evidently coaxed his landlord to lend him. The two boys had fallen asleep, closely clasped in each other's arms. And on the large bed lay Rob's sister Meg, still wearing her ordinary apparel, while one arm was under the sleeping babe, who, after a couple of hour's unceasing sobbing, had at last succumbed to Nature's sweet restorer, from sheer exhaustion.

The mother advanced with trembling footsteps towards the bed on which the babe reclined in a stranger's arms. At the same instant a startled sob broke from one of the sleeping boys, and in a tone of piteous wailing his cry of "Mother! Mother!" fell upon the hitherto unbroken calm. Oh, how the sorrowful cry stabbed the mother's heart, as she knelt in the shadow, fearful of being discovered beneath the roof of her own home. With eager, dilated eyes, she watched her husband start uneasily, as the sound disturbed him. He raised his head. Was he going over to the child? If so, she was lost. For he could not fail to see her in passing. An unspoken prayer rose to her lips, that her presence might be shielded from his knowledge.

He listened for a second, then his head sank back into its old resting place; his arm hung loosely over the side of the chair. The flames from the remnants of the fire gradually died away, and the embers had fallen to ashes in the little grate, ere Jess dared to venture upon her perilous undertaking. The boys were both sleeping soundly, undisturbed by any ugly dreams, while her husband's heavy but regular respirations proclaimed that he, too, had fallen into deep unconsciousness. Several times she learned over Meg before daring to touch the child. At last satisfied that it was her first deep sleep, and that unless the infant should happen to wake she might be able to take possession of it without disturbing her, Jess raised the child by its garments.

It was an awful moment : upon its issue everything depended !

So far she was safe. The next instant the babe was in her arms. Hastily snatching up a portion of an old blanket she took it to wrap the child in, before leaving the house. As she reached the door, the babe commenced to move about uneasily, and ere the second flight of steps was gained had burst into a fit of crying which all her endeavours were powerless to subdue. Terror-stricken, she rushed from the house, not knowing whether its cries had been heard and its abstraction discovered. On, on, she went in her wild flight, pursued by the haunting fear that she was being followed. Breathless and panting she arrived at the railway station just half-an-hour before the train was timed to start.

In an agony of suspense—that half-hour was passed. A couple of other passengers turned up about five minutes before the departure, but they took no heed of Jess, and in safety they steamed out of the station.

The village of Craig-Feldie was situated at a distance of about twenty miles from Edinburgh, but the nearest station was at least fully four miles from the village, so that when Jess left the train there would still be that distance to traverse before reaching her destination. But after the risks which she had incurred, the weary tramp across four miles of unknown country seemed as nothing, for she had never been in the vicinity of Craig-Feldie before, and, thanks to the generosity of the friends at the Bannockburn Arms, she possessed the wherewithal to provide her little one with nourishment, at least for one day, and for the rest she must leave it to Providence, who had hitherto provided, if with a sparing hand.

CHAPTER XIV

CRUELTY AND TREACHERY.

SIR Peter Fairbairn's residence at Craig-Feldie was an old-fashioned mansion, with craigs and turrets which had been the delight of many a generation born beneath its aristocratic shelter. But gradually its proud scions had deserted the crumbling pile, and for years it had remained empty and forsaken, save by the bats and owls, or by wandering quadrupeds, which were in the habit of making it their headquarters. It was situated amidst the wild splendour of uncultivated forest scenery, backed by a thickly-wooded plantation which abounded in game, though it was many a long day since the crack of a rifle had sounded to disturb its inhabitants.

There were times when Sir Peter's tongue, having been loosened by a liberal amount of wine, he would confess to his friends that he would have preferred building a mansion after his own heart, which would have embraced all the modern appliances and inventions of the day, combined with the most lavish decorations which art could have supplied. He would have marble and glass and gilding *ad libitum*. But Mathilde had heard of Craig-Feldie, viewed it, and declared its decayed grandeur, backed by its illustrious ancestors, to be the essence of the perfection which Sir Peter required in his selection of a country residence. The prestige enjoyed by its previous occupants could not fail to shed a certain amount of its lustre upon the titled distiller and his connections.

And thus his own desire had been overruled. The purchase was completed, and the place soon patched up and put to rights. But Sir Peter had insisted upon the interior arrangements being conducted by himself, and the result was that the exterior and the interior of the mansion presented a most incongruous contrast.

The party from St. Kestor had been located at Craig-Feldie nearly three weeks. From the first evening of their visit, a change had been perceptible in Mathilde's manner and bearing towards Lady St. Kestor. There was no longer the slightest attempt towards ingratiating herself with her guest, but, on the contrary, she sought every opportunity for the display of her caustic wit and familiar relation towards Sir Hardress.

At first Sir Hardress had the grace to somewhat deprecate her advances in the presence of his wife, but latterly, on more than one occasion, Lady St. Kestor had been compelled to vacate the room, for the preservation of her own dignity. By Sir Peter she was invariably treated with deference and respect, in consequence of which she began to think that she had misjudged him. There were times when she found him looking at her as though he pitied her, but this always roused her resentment, and caused her to shun his society more than she would otherwise have done, for she could not bear the idea of his broaching to her the subject of her unhappiness.

So far Lady Laura had not breathed a word to her husband concerning the daily and almost hourly insults which he was offering to herself by his attentions towards another woman. He, too, had altered strangely, and for the worse, since the commencement of their visit to Craig-Feldie. He was continually complaining of something she had either done or not done. It seemed as if he tried every means to goad her into retaliating against his taunts and tyrannical treatment.

But Lady Laura had determined to avoid any disagreeable recriminations or open quarrel, so long as they remained Sir Peter's guests, though she had decided that it would be impossible to continue her existence with her husband under the same conditions as before the disgraceful occurrences of which she had been so frequent a witness. As the time passed on, however, without any apparent likelihood of their removal, she ventured to ask him when they happened to be together in their dressing room, which had now become a very rare occurrence if he did not think they had already made their visit long enough.

"Now you are surely not commencing to badger me again about that, are you, Laura?" and he at once assumed the air and expression of a martyr. "I tell you candidly that I intend to remain here for an indefinite length of time, so the sooner you make up your mind to it the better. What you have to be dissatisfied about I can't imagine," he continued; "you must be the most ungrateful woman on the face of the earth to quarrel with quarters such as these."

The tears filled her sad, blue eyes at the result of her appeal. The sight of them incensed him still more, and fanned the flame of his irritability still higher.

"For Heaven's sake stop those theatrical tears, you snivelling idiot, or, by Jove, I'll turn you out of the room. I swear it!"

"That would be no more of an indignity than plenty of other things which I have had to submit to since we came here," Lady Laura replied as well as her tears and agitation would permit. Fearfully she glanced across at Sir Hardress to note the effect of her somewhat daring speech. He was looking thoughtfully down into the leaping flames of the bright turf fire. As the light played upon his face, she thought that it bore a milder, softer expression, as though the anger had died away and sweet and gentle pity had stolen in its place.

Instantly her anger and her wrongs were forgotten. Encouraged by his silence and his apparent contemplation, she advanced to where he stood. "Hardress! Forget all that I have said as I will try to do, and let us live as husband and wife should. If you will let me, I will live for you, work for you, and find my happiness in ministering to your comfort. Only take me away from here, away from the woman who has enslaved you by her fatal charms, and come between those whom God hath joined together."

In her earnestness she had forgotten that it was her calm impassive husband to whom she was uttering such an appeal; again, he appeared to her excited vision as the lover who had wooed her in the simple rectory garden in the " sweet spring time." For the time being the events of the past years were all blotted out, she had forgotten the children who called the man before her " father," and linked her name with his in parentage, She would have clasped her arms around him, and laid her head upon his breast. With clinging soft caresses, she would have wooed him back to loyalty and love.

Her hand was laid upon his arm, her face was dangerously close to his own. For an instant his pulses throbbed the quicker. A peculiar something at his heart stirred and thrilled him, as he little guessed his wife's influence had power to do. His better nature fought boldly for an instant to find its way to the surface, but only to be crushed by the demons which had so long held him in possession. It was a crucial moment for them both; the husband and wife looked into each other's eyes, as though each as trying to fathom the secrets of the other's soul.

The tones of a woman's voice broke the silence. It must have been the arch-fiend's last trump, which he had reserved, and it brought down the trick. As

Hardress listened to Mathilde's rich full-throated melody, the glamour which his wife had almost succeeded in casting around him was instantly dispelled. The arch-fiend had conquered.

With the rapidity of a lightning flash his former expression changed to one of repulsive fierceness. His dark eyes gleamed with a dangerous light, which spoke of hate and abhorence towards the woman whom he had sworn " to love, honour, and protect." Quick as Lady Laura was, to note the change in him, she resolved to chance her last stake to thwart the woman who had ruined her life. " Hardress, listen to me, oh, in pity listen," she implored, " for the sake of our little ones ——"

She was close to him ; the tears were raining down her face ; she caught one of his hands between her own to raise it to her lips ; her head was bent, and she did not see his upraised hand. The next instant it fell upon her with a terrible violence, and she felt herself pushed with such force that the walls seemed spinning around, and closed upon her as, with the faint echo of his curse ringing in her ears, she fell stunned and unconscious to the ground. At the same instant a low tap sounded on the door, and immediately afterwards it was opened by someone outside.

" You did not hear me knock, I think ? " said Mathilde, stepping forward ; " and yet I called to Lady Laura several times. I did not know *you* were bearing her company."

All the answer that he made was to point to the

prostrate figure of his wife as she lay stretched upon the floor.

Mathilde started backwards as though in affright, then slowly advanced and knelt beside the unconscious woman. "She has fainted," she said; "but what is the meaning of this?" pointing to an ugly livid bruise upon the temple.

The blood rushed to Hardress's face in one great crimson wave as Mathilde directed her attention to the horrible disfigurement of the pale, pure face. Blunted as were his finer feelings, he could still feel his degradation, and with it was mingled a certain degree of remorse. Without making any reply to Mathilde's query, he also went and knelt beside her. "I'm a brute," he muttered between his teeth. "Begad I am."

"Give me a pillow to place beneath her head, and then go to my room and ask Colins to give you my vinaigrette and some sal-volatile," said Mathilde in a matter-of-fact way, affecting not to notice what he had said.

Mechanically he rose to do her bidding. As he reached the door, she called him softly back again. "You had better go about it as quietly as possible," she said. "You don't want a crowd to see this," pointing to the bruise. "Tell Colins that Lady St. Kestor is unwell, but you don't wish Simmonds or the children to be alarmed, so she had better not mention it."

He simply bowed assent, then his gaze again rested upon the inanimate form and marble features of his wife. Mathilde saw the look, and, as she interpreted it, a spasm of jealousy passed across her face.

"I will remain with her until she recovers," she said, and there was a look of relief in his eyes as he went in search of Colins to procure the remedies suggested by Mathilde.

Hardly had Sir Hardress disappeared from view when a vindictive, cruel thought flashed in her large brilliant eyes. Hastily rising from the kneeling position which she had at first assumed, she placed one daintly arched foot upon the fallen victim at her feet, and raising her arms triumphantly above her head, exclaimed with a mocking laugh, "Ah, my Lady Laura, you may be beautiful and good, but you are no match for me. You little guessed how near I was when you tried to win him over to you so short a time since. Bah! my voice can win him from your side, even when you are suing for his love. I'm glad he has struck you. He hates you now, but I will teach him to loathe you before I have finished!"

Sir Hardress returning a couple of minutes later with the vinaigrette and the sal-volatile, found Mathilde still kneeling beside Lady St. Kestor, chafing her limp white hands between her own. When Lady Laura recovered consciousness some time later and discovered who was her attendant, a strange feeling of dread crept over her and her first inquiry was for Simmonds, who, since their stay at Craig-Feldie had acted in the double capacity of nurse and lady's maid.

"When Sir Hardress told me that you were unwell

I thought it was a pity to alarm Simmonds or the little ones," explained Mathilde, in her most amiable tones, "so I have nursed you myself since yesterday."

Lady St. Kestor closed her eyes and shuddered, but if Mathilde noticed it, she made no comment, but busied herself with some preparation in the form of nourishment which she afterwards administered to her unwilling patient, who at first most resolutely refused to partake of it. But Mathilde undauntedly insisted, until from sheer weakness Lady Laura at last obeyed.

"If Sir Peter does not object I should very much like to have my sister with me," she said, for the first time voluntarily addressing Mathilde, during several hours.

"I am certain that he would be only too pleased to consent to anything which would add to your comfort," she responded with alacrity, "and I will speak to Sir Hardress in time for him to send a letter by to-night's post."

"If you will give me a pencil and paper, I will write myself," her patient replied, "then there will be no necessity for troubling Sir Hardress."

Mathilde cast a hasty searching glance at her face, but she read nothing there. Did Laura wish to convey by that remark that she did not desire any communication with Sir Hardress? Although he had not visited the room since she had regained consciousness, she had not expressed a wish to see him or even mentioned his name. Mathilde wondered if she remembered all, or how much, of what had taken place between them.

And as Lady St. Kestor, after sealing the note in the envelope, handed it to Mathilde, she wondered at the marvellous change which the last few days had wrought in her hostess. She could hardly realise that the woman whom she had so despised could be the untiring and devoted nurse, who had acceded so readily to the request which she had scarcely dared to proffer.

When Sir Hardress first avoided his wife's apartment, it was because he could not bear to look upon the suffering which was the result of his own ungovernable temper, and felt ashamed and unable to meet the reproach which he expected to see in his wife's eyes.

But Mathilde soothed and sympathised with him, deplored the stupidity of Lady Laura in aggravating him so far as to render him desperate, and hardly conscious of his acts, and thus she soon managed to make him view his own conduct in a defensive light, so that he now looked upon his wife as the aggressor, and blamed her and hated her the more for the very helplessness which he had brought about.

With all his genius, his sparkling intelligence, and other gifts which fortune had lavished upon him, he was as malleable in the hands of the designing adventuress, as clay in the hands of the potter.

CHAPTER XV

A TERRIBLE DISCOVERY.

BY the end of the third day, Lady Laura felt so much better and stronger that she expressed her determination to rise as usual on the following morning, and though Mathilde did not entirely negative the proposal, she stipulated that she must be content to remain in her own room for at least one more day.

On the following morning Lady Laura rose accordingly, and not wishing for Mathilde to come or to send her assistance, proceeded with her toilet unaided. It was the first time that she had seen a mirror since her indisposition, and she looked incredulously at the discolouration on her temple. Suddenly it flashed across her that it was the mark left by the blow inflicted by her husband. Horrified and ashamed, she buried her face in her hands. She understood now why Mathilde had waited upon her, and kept every one else away. They wanted nobody to know or to see her, she was in league with Sir Hardress, and was anxious to screen his shameful conduct.

And Lady Laura, too, resolutely made up her

mind that not even the children should see her until every trace of the degrading mark had faded from sight; she felt as if she must hide her shame from all the world.

As yet no reply had been received from Miss Haldane, and in that reply lay her only hope. It was the one gleam of sunshine amid the darkness surrounding her. Wearily the day dragged along. Books, needlework, writing were each attempted in turn, but all alike failed to interest.

The snow had been falling almost continuously for two days, and the park, viewed from the windows, looked like a great white wilderness. By four o'clock in the afternoon the daylight was fast giving way to the gloom of night, and Lady St. Kestor shuddered at the thought of the long evening still before her. Then suddenly she resolved to seek the company of her children and brave the questions which their childish curiosity might prompt them to put to her, relying upon her own ingenuity to fence with them, and Simmonds also, if need be. Proceeding to act upon her impulse, she started at once for the nursery. As she passed along the corridor leading to the rooms, which had been apportioned to the children, there were none of the sounds which are usually heard proceeding from juvenile headquarters. Lady St. Kestor listened for the shouts and laughter, the romping and stampede of little feet, or even the childish cries at some unexpected tumble or broken toy. But no such welcome sound greeted her.

"Perhaps they are asleep," said Lady St. Kestor

to herself, despite the strange and ominous silence, which affected her so strongly that she hesitated before entering the room. Flinging the door wide open, it was disclosed empty and desolate, and bearing an appearance of general neatness absolutely appalling to the mother looking wildly around for the traces of occupancy. There was no fire in the grate, and the high nursery fireguard was no longer in its place. A number of toys were packed neatly on a shelf. A broken drum and a three-legged horse lay side by side in a corner as though waiting to be removed. In the fading light of the dying day, and the solemn stillness which appeared to have usurped the clamour of children's voices, Lady St. Kestor stood, with clasped hands and a horror-stricken gaze, taking in every detail with eyes that saw and understood beyond the present.

It was but an instant's work to rush into the second inner room, used as the children's sleeping apartment. Again that horrible neatness prevailed. The little bed whereon those precious forms had rested, were stripped of all the linen, and the carpets and rugs had been taken from the floor, and rolled up, into a corner.

Lady St. Kestor imagined that she had suffered mental torture in its worst degree from her husband's insults and humiliations, and that its culmination had been reached by the latest indignity which she had received at his hands. But all that had gone before was as nothing compared with the agony and despair which she now endured. The feeling which possessed her during those first few moments was so nearly akin to madness that she was neither conscious of what she said nor did. But a few moments later the occupants of the billiard-room, who were amusing themselves by a game before dinner, were startled from their serenity by the vision of a wild-eyed, white-faced woman rushing into their presence and demanding in frenzied tones the restoration of her children, at the same time hurling reproaches and taunts upon her husband for his vileness in robbing her of them. There was no trace of the calm, high-bred Lady St. Kestor in the furiously-angry woman, who had forgotten her fears as she denounced her lord and master in terms which at first held her hearers speechless with astonishment.

At length Sir Peter chuckled as if he very much enjoyed the scene, while his little black eyes rolled unceasingly in his merriment. But Sir Hardress had grown white with rage, and his black arched eyebrows met each other in a heavy scowl. His chest heaved painfully as the wife, whom he had hitherto looked upon as his slave, hurled her reproaches at him, and it might have been that he would have repeated his recent violence and again brought her low at his feet, had not Mathilde interposed between them.

The sound of her voice, so calm and dulcet, seemed to Lady Kestor's strained and excited imagination, like the pouring out of the oil amid a seething torrent, and impatiently she wrested herself from the grasp of the hand which Mathilde had laid upon her.

"Gently Hardress!" she was saying to him, "you know Lady Laura is an invalid. This is simply hysteria brought on from extreme weakness; you must not for a moment treat it seriously. I warned her not to leave her room too soon, and you see I was right in doing so. Come Lady Laura," she went on, turning to her guest, "let me conduct you back to your room, and then I can explain to you this little matter which you have evidently taken so much to heart."

"No, Miss Fairbairn, I will not return to my room, nor will I listen to any explanation from you concerning my children. If there is any explanation forthcoming, their father is the proper person to give it."

As Lady Laura concluded, she turned from Mathilde, and confronted her husband, "Hardress, I am waiting!"

Involuntarily she started back a few paces for a horrible expression was gleaning in his eyes and its very repulsiveness startled her. He was standing by the side of a small table containing glasses; he brought his hand down upon it with a crash that sent the glasses shivering to atoms at his feet.

"Perhaps to-morrow, or some time when you have regained your senses, I may, if you come to me in a proper frame of mind, and apologise for your unpardonable behaviour, consent to discuss the subject with you, but as it is, I positively decline to have anything to do with a mad woman. Let me recommend you to take Miss Fairbairn's advice, and retire to your room until the paroxysm has exhausted itself," and with that parting shaft, he turned on his heel and walked out of the room.

Lady St. Kestor's glance had not before been turned in Sir Peter's direction, and as yet his voice had not been heard in the discussion. Remembering the pity which he had so frequently silently evinced towards her, she turned to him as a last resource— as a drowning man clings to a straw. Falling upon her knees, with outstretched hands before him, she implored him to exert his influence over her husband, and bring him back to listen to her.

Perhaps in that moment Sir Peter enjoyed the sweetest triumph of his life: he only wished that all the world was present to witness Lady St. Kestor's supplication.

"Come, come, my lady!" he remonstrated, raising her from the floor, and placing her in a capacious chair close by; "You really must not give way in this fashion. To-morrow you'll laugh at your own fears. The little folk are safe enough, but the fact is, we thought you were in for an attack of fever, scarlet or typhoid, or something of that sort, and your husband took the alarm, and at once packed Mrs. Simmonds off to St. Kestor with them, where I should think they are all safe by now, so you can't wonder at the master being a bit vexed when you took on so."

As Lady St. Kestor listened to Sir Peter's explanation, incredulity, wonder, and hope were chasing each other through her mind, expressing themselves in her large blue eyes. Sir Peter hardly liked the look with which she answered his story, and shifted his eyes somewhat uneasily. "Will you swear that what you have told me is true?"

Her voice sounded strained and hoarse, perhaps from the intense excitement under which she was labouring. Her fingers nervously interlaced themselves backwards and forwards, as she eagerly awaited his reply. The charming pink flush and roseate hue had entirely disappeared from her face; she looked fully ten years older as she sat there with the light from the lamp falling full upon her haggard face.

"I only know that Sir Hardress was away all day yesterday, and told us on his return that he had seen them safely started on their home journey. If your ladyship wishes me to do so, I will ask Sir Hardress for further particulars."

"No! No! I will not trouble you further. To-morrow I will ask him myself. And now, if you will excuse me, I will retire to my room. And thank you for your kindness."

Despite Sir Peter's assurances, Lady Laura still felt far from satisfied, and yet the explanation was sufficiently plausible to render a refutation difficult. For the first time it occurred to her that the letter which she had written to her sister might have been tampered with or probably withheld altogether, and she resolved to write a second without delay, and place it in the post bag herself when she could do so without being observed. She even thought of writing at the same time to her husband's cousin Ashley

Dallas, who had remained behind at St. Kestor.

Mr. Dallas, who was a briefless barrister, had not been altogether loath to accept Sir Hardress's suggestion to join him at St. Kestor, and fulfil the position of steward on his estate, at any rate until he could meet with someone upon whose efficiency and honesty he could rely. But up to the present time Sir Hardress had either been unable or unwilling to fix upon a substitute, and Ashley liked the free and easy country life so well, and managed the estate so admirably, that it seemed highly probable that the Temple and the law courts might know him no more. To Lady Laura he had been a true friend and a pleasant companion. But on further consideration, she decided that the circumstances were too uncertain to justify any appeal to him. She would await the result of the second communication to Miss Haldane.

CHAPTER XVI.

FURTHER CONSPIRACIES.

"WELL, is it decided?"

It was Mathilde who addressed the question to her uncle. She had entered the breakfast-room, where Sir Peter sat enjoying his morning repast at a liberally spread table.

He looked up from the luscious steak he was just in the act of consuming, and lazily scanned her appearance. "Yes, we decided it finally last night. I am to stand for Exeter, with my lord's support. All St. Kestor will have to back me up, I'm bound to win—the other chap won't have a leg to stand on." He threw himself back in the chair, rubbing his hands together with a triumphant satisfaction.

"And you have no fear about getting Sir Hardress returned for a Scotch division?" Mathilde continued, a suspicion of anxiety in her tone.

"Fear be hanged!" he replied, casting a contemptuous look at her as he spoke. "What have you got there?" and he nodded his head at a letter which she was holding in hand. Without replying to his question she placed it beside him.

" Humph ! Miss Haldane,
        c/o Mrs. de Grey,
                Eaton-square,
                        London."

He read the address slowly and again looked up at his niece, who had seated herself opposite to him at the table.

" It was a clever story you concocted for her yesterday, but she dosen't quite believe you for all that. I told you she would not trust her letters to me again, and I was right."

" What shall we do with it ? " and Sir Peter turned it over in his hand from one side to the other, studied the back, held it up to the light, and propped it against the silver cruet in front of him.

" Oh, give it to Hardress, as you did the last one," she answered, snappishly, at the same time drawing her chair closer to the table, and fixing her elbows upon it. " I've something more important to talk about just now than that paltry letter. Has it ever occurred to you that in the game we have been playing I might not rest contented with simply driving this woman from her husband and unsurping her place through their separation. You know that I have loved Hardress since the first hour of my acquaintance with him, and I thought once that so long as I gained his love in return I should be satisfied. But now all that is changed. I want to be his wife! I want to bear his name and take the place which she occupies in society. I cannot be content with simply thrusting *her* out of it. I must have it for myself!"

There was no excitement in her manner. She made her statements in a perfectly cool and unhesitating style. There was a coldness and hardness in all that she said, which was positively repelling. But her listener did not shrink at hearing her give vent to such cold-blooded treason, nor did he even expostulate with her concerning it. On the contrary, he rather seemed to admire her audacity, for a peculiar smile played around his mouth and dimpled his heavy chin as he answered her.

"Well, my dear, if we had the ruling of each other's lives, it might occur to us to say that Lady St. Kestor had seen enough of this life; as it is, however,——" He did not finish the sentence but shrugged his shoulders, lifted up his hands and fixed a questioning glance upon Mathilde's face, as if looking for its conclusion there.

"As it is, however," Mathilde took up the last words and finished the sentence, "we have not the courage to say so!"

Though she spoke sarcastically she still kept her eyes upon her uncle with a look of serious earnestness in their depths which implied that she did not intend the subject to be dismissed without a fair amount of discussion. Sir Peter was conscious of the gaze, and tried to elude it by altering the position of his chair, until he obtained a view of the snow-covered park from the window, which he pretended to be deeply absorbed in studying.

But the *ruse* was not successful. Again Mathilde turned to the attack and forced his attention. This time she was plainer than ever.

"I have made up my mind that I will be Lady St. Kestor," she said, "and I only want your advice and co-operation, for my scheme to succeed."

"Oh then you have a scheme already laid," said Sir Peter, suddenly wheeling round in his chair, and again facing her. "Are you going to tell Hardress of this new freak?" he asked, bending towards her, and lowering his voice as he spoke.

"No!" she answered sharply, and decisivly, "he is too much of a coward. He won't mind if even he suspects that foul play has been resorted to, but if he were sure—well—I doubt whether he dare risk the consequences of a marriage with me no matter how safely the secret was guarded."

It was evident that Mathilde had thoroughly gauged the character of the man for the sake of whose name she was anxious to dare and risk so much, and she forthwith began to unravel her plans to the unscrupulous creature beside her, who listened in open-mouthed wonder and admiration at all the elaborate details of the deeply-laid scheme, as they were gradually unfolded and revealed to him.

Late that same afternoon, Lady Laura took up her position at the window of her room, to watch the departure of the postman who called at Craig-Feldie for the bag containing the letters to be sent from Edinburgh in the evening. She watched him ride down the road until a turn in the park hid him from sight. " He carries the means which will lead to the restoration of my little ones and happiness," she said to herself, sinking back into the chair so recently vacated.

Lady St. Kestor little guessed the letter from which she hoped so much, instead of being on the road to Edinburgh and England, lay snugly ensconced, by the side of its fellow, in the breast pocket of Sir Hardress's coat.

CHAPTER XVII.

LADY ST. KESTOR DISCOVERS SIR PETER'S FAMILY SKELETON.

THREE more long and weary days had come and gone without bringing to Lady St. Kestor the letter which she so much desired, or any further knowledge concerning the childrens' departure. Besides which, she was experiencing such a strange feeling of lassitude and general langour that she began to fear something serious concerning her health.

Sir Peter fussily insisted upon a doctor being called in, who pronounced it as his verdict that his noble patient was suffering from the effects of the very severe and depressing weather which had so long prevailed, and gave it as his humble opinion that by a return to England and home, in conjunction with his valuable treatment, a thorough and speedy cure might be hoped for.

When the fourth day arrived without bringing any reply from Miss Haldane, Lady Laura was almost beside herself with suspense and despair, and as there was no other alternative, she forced herself to ask

Miss Fairbairn if she knew whether any letter had come for her, or if Sir Hardress had heard any news of the children. Mathilde knew nothing, but promised to make inquiries and bring her whatever letters might have arrived. Half-an-hour later she returned. "Sir Hardress has no letter for you," she said, sympathetically, "and I was to tell you that the children are well."

"I am much obliged to you," Lady Laura answered, with an expressive sigh, and again Mathilde withdrew, turning her head to cast one lingering look at the thin white face, lying in almost painful relief against its background of crimson velvet.

Once more the conviction forced itself upon the unhappy wife that her husband had voluntarily fixed her abode among a camp of traitors, and that her precious missive might not after all have travelled in the post-bag to Edinburgh on that snowy afternoon three days ago, when she had stood to watch it from her window.

The library, which was situated on the ground floor, was one of the cosiest and yet perhaps the least-used rooms in the house, and thither Lady Laura was in the habit of repairing whenever she could muster strength enough to venture downstairs. It was a large room, but one half of it was apportioned off from the rest by an immense screen, which rendered that part near the fire-place, quite a cosy retreat for the student or reader in search of comfort and amusement.

It was just about the luncheon hour when Lady Laura entered and drew her favourite chair towards the great wide hearth and fixed her slippered feet upon the fender. Of late, it had been her misfortune to spend her nights tossing restlessly from side to side until long after the dawn had broken in the sky. And as she lay back in the chair, soothed by the warmth and quiet, sleep must have stolen on her unawares, for when she opened her eyes, she listened for a moment startled and surprised. The room was empty when she entered it, but now there was someone talking in subdued but apparently agitated tones. Lady Laura's first impulse was to declare her presence and apologise for her accidental intrusion, but her purpose was arrested by a remark which held her chained to the spot with fear and horror; she believed herself to be on the brink of a terrible discovery. The speaker was a woman, evidently belonging to the poorer class of society, but there was a rugged eloquence in her words which touched the listener's heart, and forced the great scalding tears to her eyes.

"Have ye no mercy—no pity?" the woman was saying. "Think of the poor innocent bairn dying from cold and want of food. And he was such a bonnie laddie, but it was that cruel night that did it, wandering for hours in the snow until his little body was so chilled; he's never been the same since."

Every vestige of colour receded from Lady Laura's face as she listened. Even her lips had grown bloodless, and her eyes looked wild and strained. She never doubted for a moment but that they were speaking of her little son Archie, and that Mathilde had some reason for wishing to get rid of him, and had deputed the task to the woman, who was too tender-hearted to carry it out. By some means or other she must see and follow this woman, and at all hazards, effect her child's rescue. Scheme after scheme flashed through her busy brain with lightning-like rapidity; she felt herself imbued with almost superhuman energy to do battle for her child.

"I consider you acted very foolishly by taking the child away in such an insane fashion. I've no doubt by the next day your husband would have taken you in just as usual; besides, what was the use of encumbering yourself with a sickly baby?"

Lady Laura recognised the brusque cruel voice of Mathilde, but wonder and surprise held her in possession. Mathilde was speaking of some other child; not Archie, after all.

There was a sob in the woman's voice as she answered: "You don't know, Rob; I can't earn the money I could once, and he'd rather kill me than keep me now I'm of no use to him. You've never been a mother, Matilda, or you wouldn't have insulted me about leaving my baby behind; but there, you was always hard-hearted, even as a little one, and I might have known you'd no pity to give me."

"Hush, hush!" interrupted Mathilde. "You will let the servants hear you if you speak so loudly."

"Well, I thought perhaps your money and your

grand house might have softened your heart a bit, but it seems I was mistaken." And Lady Laura imagined that there was just a spice of contempt mingled with the despair in the woman's tones. "If it were not for my bairn's sake, I'd scorn to ask for the money which you grudge me, but I tell you," raising her voice and speaking with a ring of determination, "that I will have it, and I'll find my way to your uncle now, in spite of all your fine servants, knowing that I'm his poor sister and your aunt."

"You will do nothing of the kind," hissed Mathilde between her set teeth, and planting her back firmly against the door to prevent her egress. The two women eyed each other for a second or two, then Mathilde gave vent to a low mocking laugh. "What a spitfire you are, *Aunt* Jess," with a sarcastic lingering on the "aunt." "If I go to Sir Peter I really don't know how I am to plead your cause. When he gave you the fifty pounds four years ago he expected to be rid of you entirely, and my advice to you is, keep out of his way altogether. Besides, how are we to know that your scamp of a husband will not be pouncing down upon us, if he discovers your whereabouts?"

"Oh, he'll not do that, you needn't fear," answered the woman whom Mathilde had called Aunt Jess. "He doesn't know that Sir Peter Fairbairn is any kin to me. I wouldn't have let him guess it for the world, or it's little peace that me or brother Peter would have had either."

By this time Lady St. Kestor felt very uncomfortable at the position in which she found herself. A mistake in the first instance had supplied the disclosure of the family skeleton, and her interest had been aroused to such an extent for the unfortunate woman with whose story she had accidentally become acquainted, that she had assured herself she was bound to take some means to befriend her, and simultaneously the idea flashed across her mind that by this very agency she might get a letter conveyed to her sister, by giving it to the woman to post for her, and paying her well for the service.

"I will order some food to be prepared for you and brought in here," Mathilde was saying, "and while you are refreshing yourself, I'll talk the matter over with Uncle Peter."

Lady St. Kestor trembled from head to foot as she listened to the closing of the door as Matilda left the room. Here was the very opportunity presented to her which she had been desiring, but which seemed so improbable. Lady Laura took a cautious glance round the screen before indicating her presence. The poor unfortunate woman whom she had thus discovered to be Sir Peter's sister had seated herself in one of the handsomely-upholstered chairs, her dingy and threadbare garments looking sadly out of place amid the luxury of her surroundings. She sat with her back turned partially towards Lady Laura, her elbow upon the table and her head leaning upon her hand. Her very attitude was suggestive of hopeless dejection, and enlisted Lady Laura's sympathy afresh. With a quick, firm step Laura advanced towards the table. Jess suddenly raised her head and started from her chair, a terrified look in her eyes. Her lips parted in affright, but before she had time to raise the alarm which Lady Laura saw was trembling upon them, her hand was laid with a soft, caressing touch upon her shoulder, and her blue eyes were looking down into the woman's face with a pitying tenderness in their depths, which the terrified woman was quick to read and understand.

"When you entered the room, I must have been asleep there," pointing to the screen. "And though I do not know your story, still I pity you and I know your trouble is connected with a little child."

Lady Laura scarcely spoke above a whisper and most of the time kept her eyes fixed upon the door. "Tell me your trouble in as few words as possible," she said, "and I will do all in my power to help you."

Just as she was concluding, footsteps were heard along the outer hall coming towards the door. Lady Laura quickly raised her hand, pointed towards the door, and again retired behind the screen. The next instant one of the under servants entered with a well filled tray, and placed it before the half-famished woman. "Cook's cut you a prime slice of beef, Missis," he said, as he hovered fussily about her; "and here's something that'll warm ye and mak' the blood dance in ye veins—a glass o' real homebrewed. Now, if ye want anything else, just ye tinkle and I'm your man," and with a reassuring nod and smile in parting, he left her to partake of the viands sent up for her delectation.

When Lady Laura heard the door safely closed behind him, she again stepped from her place of concealment, and stood by the table.

"And do you mean to say," she asked, "that the law of this country permits your husband to deprive you of your children? Oh, no, no! There must be some mistake," and Lady Laura shook her head incredulously.

But the woman answered in the same hopeless tones, "I have made sure of it, and those who know, have told me that he could snatch my baby away from my arms, and it would only be by going to law and spending money which I could never get that I should have any chance of getting it back even for a few years or until seven years old. I've lost my other two boys, and God only knows how I shall keep this one."

Suddenly Lady St. Kestor held out her slender taper fingers and clasped the thin but roughened palm of her companion in a long close hand-shake. "Your name is —— ?"

"Jess Cameron," answered the woman in some surprise and confusion as she noted the distress in Lady Laura's voice and manner.

"And mine is—Laura St. Kestor. My husband is Sir Hardress St. Kestor, of St. Kestor, in Devonshire, but for aught I know, the tie which exists between you and me Jess, is a strong one—the tie of one common trouble. Like you—I am unhappy. Like you," and her voice grew trembling and husky, "I have lost my children—I firmly believe taken away from me by my husband."

Trouble, and the great debt of nature, which we are all called upon to pay sooner or later, are sad and ruthless levellers of rank and all social distinctions. Although, between the two women, yawned the great gulf which separates aristocracy from democracy, the despair in each of their hearts had spanned it at a bound and bridged it indissolubly.

"I dare not keep you any longer," Lady Laura continued; "but if you will be here at seven o'clock to-night outside the window of this room, I will give you a letter to post for me; but be on your guard lest you are discovered."

Jess Cameron pressed a kiss upon the hand which Lady Laura had offered to her in friendship. "Anything that you command me I will do, my lady; all that I ask is to let me serve you."

"Hush!" she answered her. "I have done nothing to deserve such gratitude. Here is money; take it," she urged somewhat peremptorily. "Doubtless you may have to use some of it in my service. When you come to-night, I will explain to you what I wish you to do. Now there is one thing more that will require your courage and mine—will you do it?" and she fixed a steadfast look upon Jess's face, as if trying to measure her strength and fortitude. "When Miss Fairbairn returns to you, as she may do any moment, I want you to draw her attention to my presence here."

Jess started, and looked in blank astonishment in Lady Laura's face.

"When you are gone, she may find me here, or

she may discover my absence from my room, and suspect me of spying and listening. But if you call her attention to my being here, she will never dream that we have spoken to each other, or that I could by any chance make you the means of assisting me. But all that, I must tell you another time; now you will have to take it upon trust."

Jess was beginning to understand, though the perplexed look still lingered on her face, "And you will pretend to be —— ?

"Asleep!" answered Lady St. Kestor. "Yes, I shall pretend to be asleep."

Footsteps were heard coming along the passage. There was not a moment to be lost. Jess had scarcely time to coax her features to wear their old expression or to banish the new light of excitement from her eyes, when the door was opened by Mathilde. "Here is what I have been able to get for you," she said, flinging down some coins upon the table; "and a nice half hour I have had of it I can tell you. My uncle says I am to warn you to pack up and be off directly, for if you or your husband should ever attempt to extort money from him again, he'll have you prosecuted as vagrants."

"Did you tell him, Mathilde, that it was only for my child's sake I came to beg from him now?"

"No! of course I didn't. He wouldn't have believed it if I had."

"I might have known," Jess said. "It's just about fifteen years ago since he left his own brother, your poor uncle, to die, in the workhouse. And he begged with tears in his eyes that he would let him see his neice, that he'd made a lady of, just once before he died. But poor fellow, Peter took no notice and let him die a pauper's death."

"That's years ago now," Mathilde answered, "and it's no use reaping up old scores. He should have been grateful to him for all that he had done for him."

Jess gathered the money from the table, and transferred it to her pocket. Then lowering her voice to a whisper, she said, "Are you sure that we are alone in this room?"

"Quite sure," Mathilde replied sharply; but why do you ask such a question?"

"Because," and there was a faint tremor perceptible in her voice, "I thought I heard something move behind that screen when you were out of the room."

"Nonsense!" snapped Mathilde, but nevertheless, she walked rapidly towards the fireplace, and turned the screen aside. In a capacious easy chair Lady Laura reclined, her head partially inclined to one side. Her eyes were closed, and the lips slightly parted as if in deep slumber. One arm hung loosely over the chair, and her slippered feet were supported on a large crimson-covered hassock.

Mathilde looked down upon her, half-scornfully, half-angrily. Then suddenly she stooped and gazed closely at the closed eyelids, bending low until her face was almost on a level with that of the apparently sleeping woman.

Jess scarcely dared to breathe so great was the

tension on her nerves; but Lady Laura never flinched from the scrutiny brought to bear upon her. As her inquisitor withdrew her face from its close proximity, she heaved a half sigh, and slightly turned her head, but in the most natural manner possible.

Miss Fairbairn quietly replaced the screen before making any comment as to the discovery.

"It's nobody who would take any interest in your concerns," was the only explanation which she thought it necessary to offer to Jess, "even if she had heard any part of our conversation, which evidently she has not; so in either case you have no cause to fear."

CHAPTER XVIII.

SIR HARDRESS IS BRUTALLY CANDID.

LADY Laura remained in the library for fully an hour after their departure believing that Mathilde would be sure to return, but when she had not appeared by that time, she concluded that she might go back to her own room without comment or suspicion being excited.

Once there, she would set about writing the letter which Jess had promised to come for that evening. But first, it was necessary to hear from her husband whether the reason stated to her concerning the removal of her children was the true one.

Contrary to her expectations, Sir Hardress responded to her request, not only in person but immediately. They had not met since the last fatal outburst, and both felt more than their usual amount of constraint. Sir Hardress, however, was the first to regain composure. "You have honoured me by the request of an interview," he began, in tones of icy politeness, "excuse me if I ask you to make it as brief as possible."

Lady St. Kestor hated herself for the foolish tears

which she could not repress, and for the choking sobs which she vainly tried to stifle. She had determined to be so calm and cold, but in the presence of the man who, but a few years before, had wooed her as an ardent lover, she could only think of him at his best—as what she had believed him to be. Until that moment the wife had thought her love was killed, but she had not fathomed the depths of her own devotion.

"I sought this interview," she commenced "because I wish you to set my doubts at rest concerning our children. Think what a shock it was to me to go to the nursery, intending to surprise them at their play, and to find the room empty—the children gone! I might—I ought to have been made aware of it."

It was with the greatest difficulty that she managed to keep from breaking down altogether, but steadying her trembling voice as best she could, she still continued: "I want a thorough understanding from you, Hardress, as to how long I am to be kept apart from them, and as to why I receive no information concerning them, either through yourself or from Simmonds. I have a right to ask and to be answered!"

Sir Hardress had seated himself in a low chair by the side of a small table, upon which his elbow rested. His head was lowered, and not once had his wife been able to catch a glimpse of his face during the whole time occupied by her appeal. If she had understood him better, she would have been aware that his unwonted patience in listening boded no good. She waited some seconds for his reply, before he even altered his position. Then slowly wheeling round his chair he sat so as to face her. Carelessly running his fingers through the luxuriant mass of dark curls which covered his head, he leaned back, and with an insolent stare surveyed his wife from head to foot. She had become painfully thin and hollow-eyed of late, and during the last few days had grown wonderfully aged and haggard. The simply made robe of black velvet which she was wearing served rather to increase her pallor, and give effect to the slight hectic flush which had risen on the tear-stained face. She stood before him with one slender hand resting for support upon the table which stood between them.

"Let us dispense with heroics; and, for Heaven's sake stop those theatrical tears," was his first comment. "Hadn't you better be seated? It annoys me excessively for people to be standing about," and he waved his hand peremptorily towards the chair into which Lady St. Kestor sank without objection or reply.

"Thank you, that is better. It is not because you have thought well to adopt the domineering tone that I reply to your questions, but because I deem it expedient to be candid with you."

In a nonchalant manner he drew a cigar case from his pocket, and took out a cheroot, which he set about lighting, ere he proceeded. It was so much extra torture for the wife who was waiting in agonised suspense for each word that fell from his lips. She was leaning slightly forward in her chair, her slender fingers locked nervously together in her lap. There was an expression of defiance, strangely mixed with supplication, in her attitude and gaze; the pensive blue eyes were fixed upon his face, with a hungry yearning look, which met with no more response, however, than does that of the hunted deer upon the huntsman who seeks its death.

"For once I am inclined to agree with you. I also think it better that we should fully understand each other, and, as I stated before, I am prepared to be candid with you."

Lady St. Kestor's breath came in short, quick gasps as again he paused to enjoy several long whiffs from his cheroot. "In the first place, Laura, I considered that while you were confined to your room, it was a good opportunity for removing the children, and I am thankful to have accomplished my object so easily, for I congratulate myself that I have avoided a scene!"

"A good opportunity for removing them!" Lady Laura repeated, rising from her seat, and looking around her in a half vague, half excited manner. "What do you mean, Hardress?"

Sir Hardress was reclining in his chair apparently engrossed in watching the ascent of multifarious blue rings of smoke, as he emitted them from his mouth. Without looking at her, he answered, "When you conduct yourself in a rational manner I will proceed, but I am in no hurry, and can wait until you are seated."

An angry retort was upon her lips, he exasperated her almost beyond endurance, but once again she smothered her resentment and reseated herself without a comment.

"I was about to explain to you when your foolish interruption occurred," he resumed, "that I consider it advisable that the children should not be subject to your influence or guidance, as I have formed other views for them, contrary to those which I am aware you would seek to inspire them with."

He paused for a moment, but as Lady Laura did not speak, he went on, "I have been educated to reverence and espouse the doctrines of the Romish Church, which is the religion of my country. I have the greatest contempt for your milk-and-watery Protestantism, and I refuse to have my children inculcated with its tenets."

"And yet you pretended to embrace its faith, and led my father, who trusted you, to believe that you had done so!" She could not stifle her contempt: it crept into her voice in spite of herself.

"That was simply diplomacy on my part," he answered, with one of his old cynical smiles, "and the old fellow really was so easily gulled."

"Can you have forgotten the solemn promise which you voluntarily gave to me—that in the event of our having children they should be reared in the Protestant faith; or was that, too, but a part of your diplomacy? I have no doubt you flatter yourself that you *gulled me* (as you are pleased to term it) as easily as you did my father—the father who, I am proud to know, was too upright and honourable himself to be a match for you."

"Take care, my lady!" and there was an ominous glitter in his eyes, which his wife had learned to dread, "I thought it was decided that there were to be no heroics, and yet you are taking upon yourself the airs of a stage queen."

But Lady Laura had too much at stake, to care about sarcastic words or inuendos, and once more she put the question, but in tones as icy and as studied as his own. "Do you wish me to understand that it is your intention to wilfully break that promise?"

Carefully withdrawing the half-smoked weed from between his lips, and fixing it upon the outstretched arms of a little brass figure, he amused himself by balancing it backwards and forwards. He took a delight in thus manifesting his utter unconcern at the suffering which he was inflicting upon his wife, shewing by so simple an action how easily his attention was diverted from the important topic under discussion.

Lady Laura could not decide in her own mind whether he had absolutely forgotten her, or whether he was simply trying to torture her. She would have demanded a reply had he not at that moment turned to address her. He evaded her question by putting another. "Did you ever suppose that I had any serious intention of keeping it?"

Lady St. Kestor met the mocking light in his eyes, which were fixed upon her, with the first flash of real hatred which had ever shone in her own. "Nevertheless it was a promise, and I will call upon the law to hold you faithful to it, should such a course be necessary," she answered as she rose and stood before him, her whole frame trembling with indignation.

But he only laughed again as he answered, "If you were not an ignorant fool you would know that such an agreement made before marriage would be held null and un-enforceable, as derogating from the paternal rights which *I cannot* forfeit."

"You tell me so in order to terrify me, or perhaps dissuade me from attempting any redress, but you cannot make me believe the truth of such a statement. I have far too much faith in the wisdom and integrity of the statesmen who direct the government of our country, to believe that they would sanction a law both unjust and cruel—a law which would place a mother in the position of an unpaid nurse to her husband's children—a hired servant, liable to forfeit her position at any moment, from either malice or the sheer caprice of their father! I say a thousand times No!! Such a law as you might wish to enforce would be an outrage upon the sacred and natural rights of motherhood! It is a law against which every English wife and mother would cry shame, and at which every right feeling and thinking man, too, would fight against, for England would cease to feel proud of her sons who tried to make her daughters slaves!"

So great was the amazement of Sir Hardress at

the eloquent outburst from his wife, that for a moment he was hardly prepared to answer. There was a spice of admiration in his glance as it rested upon her flushed face and flashing eyes; and the thought occured to him that he had never seen her to better advantage. But the idea of her daring to tell him that she did not believe his statement, raised the very demon of anger within his breast, and stirred afresh the fury which he had previously tried to hide beneath his cynicism. Lady Laura was equally surprised at her own daring, but in her enthusiasm and indignation she had scarcely been conscious of her own words.

"So, madam, you think well to defy me, even after my warning," her husband commenced, and she saw that he was white to the lips with rage. "But you made a mistake when you thought to combat your will against mine, and upon your own head will fall the consequences. It is quite time that you should be fully acquainted with your own position, the position which the English law assigns to you. To start with your legal position is almost a fiction, inasmuch as it depends entirely upon the position which I choose to give you. Your rights as a mother are *nil*. The children in the eyes of the law belong solely to me. I alone have the power to direct their education, either secular or religious, and to decide their place of residence. I can remove them from you during my lifetime, and I can separate you from them even after my death, by leaving them in the custody of a guardian appointed by testament."

"But, Hardress, hard as you may be, you would never—never—take such an advantage if even the law empowered you to do so!" The old affrighted look had crept back into her eyes, and her face had paled almost to the hue of death.

"On the contrary, I mean to enforce every advantage which the law gives me to the very uttermost, and as there is a Heaven above us I swear that so long as I have the power to prevent it you shall never look upon their faces again!"

Without giving her time to reply, he turned fiercely upon her, "And now I have done with you, never accuse me again of not being candid. Any other information that you may require upon the subject I would advise you to obtain from a qualified legal adviser," and with the sarcastic smile still playing upon his features, he was about to leave the room, but Lady Laura felt that it was her last chance, and hastily pushing her way in front of him, planted herself firmly against the door to bar his progress.

There had been defiance, and there had been terror, but now it was despair that rang in her voice, as she once more confronted him, with hands outstretched, pleading for her children as she would never have stooped to plead even for her own life. "Hardress, hear me, oh, listen to me if only for one moment. If you take away my children you take from me the very essence of my life, and you rob our children of a mother. Who can love and care for them as I can? Who would have such patience and tenderness as I—the mother, who never knows pain or weariness in ministering to her little ones? See, Hardress, husband, I will kneel to you, at your feet I plead for mercy and pity for all our sakes. If you will not part me from them, I will be content to be your slave. I will do your bidding, obey your lightest wish, and always remember that you heard my prayer and granted it!"

If she had once looked into his face she would have seen that he gloated over her humiliation, though her words touched him, and caused his heart to throb so violently that he was obliged to press his hand upon it in the effort to still its tumultuous beating. If he could have avoided this contretemps he would have done so, for he had a natural shrinking from anything approaching a scene, but he pitied himself for having to bear the reproaches, which he looked upon as the outcome of his wife's selfish conduct. If she had treated the matter philosophically, he argued to himself, he would have been spared the ordeal to which he had been subjected.

Lady Laura still knelt, waiting for a word to fall from his lips—a word of pardon or reconciliation. But none came. Only an oath broke the silence For the second time he raised his hand to strike her, but with a cry upon her lips, she caught it in its descent. But he was only foiled for a second—the next instant he hurled her away from him, and mercilessly pushed her aside from the door with his foot. Without another glance at her as she lay extended from the result of his violence, he left the room, and shut the door upon her.

Never more could Sir Hardress St. Kestor lay claim to either self-respect or manliness. Henceforth he must slink through life bearing the odium of a savage and a coward, for whether as a popular leader of men or the flattered favourite of society, in the innermost recesses of his heart and conscience would burn his guilt and treachery and the shame of his broken vows pledged before the sacred altar of God!

CHAPTER XIX.

LET ME BE YOUR FRIEND.

FOR a minute Sir Hardress stood outside the door and listened, but not a sound was audible, not even so much as a moan or a sob. In spite of himself there was a something within him which urged him to enter, and offer some atonement for his brutality. The white haggard face and reproachful blue eyes seemed to haunt him. Behind that closed door, he could still see the prostrate form stretched in its cruel agony, perhaps senseless and inanimate, the form of the woman who bore his name and who was his wife; the woman whom he had held in his arms, who had lain upon his breast, whose lips had clung to his in the purity of devotion—of the wifely affection which she had showered upon him. But into their garden of love the serpent had found its way, and planted its insidious sting in the very heart and root of its verdure until by degrees it had become a mere wilderness of weeds, which were choking even all remembrances of that fairer past. With a muttered curse upon his lips, Sir Hardress turned away from the door, and walked hurriedly down the corridor to the smoke room. Without the slightest hesitation he proceeded to the buffet, reached a spirit decanter and poured from it about half a tumbler of neat spirit, which he drank off without stopping to dilute it.

"There, that will pull me together." he said to himself as he replaced the tumbler on the sideboard. "Curse her; she shall pay for this!" and he flung himself into an arm-chair and dragged it noisily towards the fireplace. His face had assumed a greyish pallor within the last few minutes, and there was a blueness about the lips also. He shivered as if from ague, and it seemed to him as if his blood had turned to ice in his veins, and yet he had to mop the perspiration which had come out in great drops on his head and face and even on his neck. Usually a very abstemious man, the quantity of raw spirit that he had taken was telling its tale upon him. He began to wonder what was going to happen to him, and laying his hand upon the bell, rang a violent summons for someone to be sent to his assistance.

Almost immediately Mathilde entered, evincing the most violent concern. "Whatever is the matter?" she exclaimed, hurrying across the room to where he sat, and noting with dismay the alteration in his appearance. "You must have some brandy," and as she would have turned aside to reach it, he grasped her roughly by the arm.

"No, no! I have had a draught of that cursed stuff already, and it has almost done for me! Feel here!" and he placed her hand over his heart.

It beat so feebly that it was almost impossible, except for an occasional fluttering, spasmodic sort of action, to believe that it was beating at all.

"I want warmth," he said, "and for God's sake be quick."

In a very short space of time, Mathilde, with the aid of Sir Peter's valet, had enveloped him in rugs and supplied him with heated appliances, chafing his hands and rubbing the moisture from his head and face. To their satisfaction, the remedies resorted to were not long in bringing about the desired effect; a more natural colour stole into his cheeks and lips, and the respirations grew stronger and more regular. When almost a quarter of an hour had elapsed, Mathilde intimated to the valet that he might withdraw, as Sir Hardress seemed inclined to sleep.

For the following half-hour she sat and watched beside him, and once, when he stirred uneasily and would have flung one of the rugs aside, she took his hand and held it within her own. She was still holding it when he awoke, and as their eyes met she made no attempt to withdraw it, but smiled upon him and drew her disengaged hand with a gentle touch across his forehead.

"You are feeling better?" she said, slowly and softly.

"Have you not brought me back to life? How can I feel otherwise?" he answered, insinuatingly, as he returned the pressure of her hand and almost imperceptibly drew her nearer towards him by the couch to which they had managed to convey him.

"I have so much to thank you for—so much, indeed, that words fail me. What can I say, Mathilde?"

Her head drooped lower, her eyes looked into his with a long steady gaze, as she answered him:

"Say that you will always be my friend! I am a lonely woman, with no friends and but few acquaintances. You are lonely, too, and misunderstood. It would be hypocritical for me to pretend I did not know it. When you suffer, I suffer also. Let me be your friend, sharing alike your joy or sorrow. If you are ill, let me wait upon you; if you are in trouble, let me minister unto you; don't let us be separated, for my life is bound up in yours."

Her voice trembled with emotion, the bold flashing eyes glistened with tears—tears which, however, failed to dispel their usual hardness of expression.

"Mathilde you madden me when you talk like this." Sir Hardress interrupted her, suddenly assuming an upright position and drawing her still closer to himself, "you ask me for my friendship as if it were a favour. Oh Mathilde let me beg for yours. Let me be towards you what you have asked from me. Give me the right to care for and protect you against the world!"

"Hardress!" The name was uttered almost beneath her breath, she caught his hand and laid her lips upon it in a kiss which set his pulse tingling, and sent the warm blood to his face in a feverish glow.

"Do you mean this?" and she held his hand as if in a vice until he answered, "Mean it—my—friend!"

as he hesitated before finishing the sentence, she almost held her breath; she knew that he had been on the point of using a stronger term of endearment, but had checked himself in time.

"Can you doubt it?" he continued, "have you not seen! have you not known that from the first moment that I saw you, you were more to me than any other woman. Answer me Mathilde!—was it —is it not so?"

He had slipped his arm around her and drawn her head back until it rested against his breast and lowered his head until his face was almost on a level with hers. He forced her to look into his eyes while he questioned her.

"I know that you were kindness itself," she said, lowering her eyes with a newly born reserve which rendered her still more charming in the eyes of the man beside her "and" she added, "I know that you are different from all other men!"

With a sigh, it might have been of despair, Sir Hardress suddenly loosed his embrace. "Oh Mathilde!" he said, "fate has dealt hardly with us. Why did she let us meet now instead of years ago— now—when it is too late!"

"Not too late, Hardress! We can be friends; we are friends!" and again she pressed her lips upon his hand.

He snatched his hand away from her with a low mocking laugh and rose from the couch, leaving her still kneeling beside it.

"No! No! Mathilde," he said, "we can neither

of us deceive ourselves with platitudes. You are no ignorant school girl, nor am I a fool to be gulled with friendship."

It was the man's nature to be thus brutally candid. He had not even the civility nor the instinct of refinement which alone may be responsible for the glossing over of guilt. Coarse and blunted as were the feelings of the woman who had tried to entrap him, perhaps it was that her woman's finer nature held sway in spite of herself for she winced beneath his words, and involuntarily lowered her head.

"I tell you I will have all or nothing! I love you! I love you Mathilde! There—now you have the naked truth, shorn of all its sham. Have I shocked you! Will you send me away from you—or—"

Mathilde, by a sudden movement, turned away from him and supporting her elbows upon the couch buried her face in her hands.

The next moment Sir Hardress seated himself beside her, and once more drew her towards him by gentle force. "What have you to say to me Mathilde?" and he looked into her eyes with all the love and passion burning in his own undisguised and un-repressed.

"Hardress, what will you think of me?" she said, meeting his gaze with one as passionate as his own. "I can only bid you stay. I cannot let you go!" and the next instant her arms were clasped around his neck. The barrier of secresy which had hedged around their guilty love was broken down, their reserve melted like snow before the sun, and the injured wife was doomed by that fatal embrace

"My love! my darling!" he exclaimed, "Oh God! this is my punishment for fettering myself with those hateful ties in the long ago!"

"You will promise, Hardress—promise me!"—Mathilde commenced in a nervous manner most unusual for her, "that should the opportunity ever arise in the future—you will make me—your wife?" and something like a sob convulsed her frame.

"I promise!" Sir Hardress answered.

"Swear it!" she continued vehemently, "swear it!"

"Swear it!" he repeated, and then added "I trust to Heaven the day may not be far distant!"

A malicious and yet triumphant smile flashed into Mathilde's eyes, though she pretended not to have heard his last remark, it seemed to say, if interpreted, "I will take care the day is not far distant!"

CHAPTER XX.

MATHILDE OFFERS HER SUGGESTIONS.

IT was the evening following the day upon which Sir Hardress had openly avowed his affection for Mathilde. Dinner had been over about half-an-hour, and he was waiting in the library in response to a note which she had slipped underneath the door of his dressing room an hour or two previously. Ever since the morning it had seemed to him that she had avoided him, and by the evening he had worked himself into a thorough state of nervous irritation, and now he waited with the note twisted in his fingers, glancing at the timepeice and watching the door with a furtive gaze. At last his enforced patience was rewarded, as the door opened his heart beat with a great bound; the very sound of her draperies trailing around her seem to add to his excitement. He rose hurriedly to meet her with both hands outstretched, and would have placed his arm around her, but that she made a sudden backward movement and shook her head, while a half sad smile played upon her lips.

"Mathilde!" he exclaimed, "What has changed

you so suddenly? Have you already repented of your—of our compact? Is it true that you have avoided me to day—and why?"

With a haughty and somewhat defiant setting of the head she advanced to the upper end of the room and took up a position in front of the fire, keeping her face partially concealed from him.

"Yes! I have avoided you!" she said, answering his last question first, " you have not been wrong in supposing so, and I have avoided you because I thought it policy to do so!"

The hard cold tone in which she spoke was unmistakeable, Sir Hardress had, at her first words, become visibly paler, and he gnawed fiercely at his moustache as he watched and listened.

"Policy indeed!" he interrupted her, "is it not rather late in the day for a discussion of policy between you and me?"

"Last night I allowed sentiment to overcome my better judgment," she replied hastily, "deliberation has taught me that I am placing myself in a false position—I want you to give me back my promise!" and for the first time she turned and faced him.

For an instant they looked upon each other in silence, she cold and majestic, but to the eyes of the thwarted man, more beautiful and desirable than ever. It was an entirely new experience for him to have his wishes opposed in ever so slight a degree, he looked upon her in almost incomprehensible astonishment. "Have you so little courage that it has oozed away so soon?" he asked in a voice of suppressed emotion, and there was a dangerous glitter in his eyes which was not lost upon Mathilde. She was playing her game skilfully though it was a difficult one that she had set herself to play, but she had unbounded belief in her own powers and she watched him with extreme satisfaction.

"It is hardly a question of courage," she replied. "If I had been lacking in courage, I should not have dared to admit that I cared for you. I begged for your friendship—that was my safeguard, and you refused it! And so," her voice faltered, her expression softened, "and so," she continued, "we must part, part until you can fulfil the promise which you made to me."

In an instant Sir Hardress was beside her. Once more he held her in a passionate embrace. "Mathilde!" he said, "you shall not leave me like this; I swear you shall not! You have told me that you love me, that your life was bound up in mine. What can it matter whether we are together or miles apart? the fact still remains the same. Don't mount the marble pedestal of virtuous propriety now—it is too cold and hard, and will serve no purpose, for you are mine!—mine!" and he kissed her lips and forehead between each word as he spoke. "What more can you want? What more can I say or do that will satisfy you?"

"What do I want?" Mathilde once more withdrew herself from his embrace as she repeated his words. "I want to be your wife now! Nothing less than that will satisfy me! How can you expect me to wait upon a mere speculation in the vague future? Wait very likely until my hair is grey, and old age has set its seal upon me—you would want a younger, fresher bride then, perhaps, one in the spring-time of life to brighten your own winter. And who can tell that Lady Laura may not outlive both of us? She certainly has the advantage so far as years are concerned. No, no, Hardress, our romance savours too strongly of the ideal; we have been foolish, very foolish, but—we can end it!"

But even as she made the proposition, she took one of his hands within her own and pressed her lips upon it, in a long gentle caress.

"I cannot give you up, you know I cannot!" Sir Hardress exclaimed, snatching his hand away from her. "You insist upon looking on the dark side of affairs—oh, my darling, won't you have a little patience? We don't know how things may turn at present!"

Mathilde fixed her eyes upon him with one of those bewildering glances which almost seemed to bewitch him. "Can't you find some means of getting rid of her?" she said, and the question was asked in the softest and most dulcet of tones. Thus it was that the cat-like treachery of her nature evinced itself. When she was most dangerous she sheathed her claws in velvet, and hid her fangs behind a smile. As Sir Hardress gave an involuntary start of dismay or surprise, she gave vent to a low laugh.

"Have I shocked you very much?" and she laid her head against him confidingly and looked up into his face with an arch smile.

"Get rid of her! What do you mean, my love?" he asked.

"Could you not get her locked up in an asylum? That would soon kill her—she is such a poor nervous creature!" Mathilde answered in a most matter-of-fact style.

Sir Hardress slowly shook his head, but expressed none of the horror at the proposition which Mathilde had reasonably expected he might show. All that he said was, "Almost impossible! It's deuced hard to do anything of that sort now-a-days!"

For a minute or two there was silence between them; both had their eyes fixed upon the great red glowing coals in the huge grate before which they stood, as if they might be finding a solution to the problem by which they were perplexed in the living embers which were so soon to be reduced to ashes of the past. It was Mathilde's voice which broke the silence. "Couldn't you take her abroad and leave her—desert her?" she said. "Oh, I am sure you could do something to be rid of her if you really wished to!"

"Oh, you women! how cold-blooded you can be towards each other!" but he laughed as he took her face between his hands and looked into her eyes as if trying to read what was really upon her mind; her openly-expressed desire to appropriate him to herself entirely flattered as well as gratified him.

But Mathilde was not to be put off by either reproaches or laughter, and persistently returned to the subject. "You—you would not regret—if—anything happened to her, would you?" she said, once more looking into the leaping flames and tapping her foot upon the bar of the fender as she spoke.

"My darling! how can you ask?" he answered. "You know that I should hail with delight the removal of any obstacle which served to keep us apart—come to me, Mathilde!" and he held out his arms for her to nestle against him in a long close embrace.

"Then it is only the theory and not the principle that you object to?" Mathilde said, as she allowed him to kiss her.

"What are you talking about?" he said.

"A little while ago you accused me of lacking courage," she answered, "but don't you think, my dear Hardress, that we might cry quits? Never mind," she added, "don't take any notice of what I say. After all, you are right, and we must wait patiently to see what turn events will take!"

"Spoken like my own sensible Mathilde," he said, in a tone of considerable relief, "and, in the meantime——"

"And in the meantime, sir, we are friends!" she concluded the sentence, and playfully tapped him on the cheek as she spoke. "Now come and have some coffee before my uncle sends in search of us."

CHAPTER XXI.

"I DON'T WANT YOUR LOVE."

AS the door closed upon Sir Hardress's retreating form, a low moan escaped Lady Laura's lips, she had not believed it possible that he could leave her without, at any rate, having ascertained whether she had lost consciousness or not, and every sense was strained in listening for some sign of his return. And so the moments dragged along until nearly half-an-hour had passed away and still she lay without having altered her position, though the boon of unconsciousness was denied her. After a time, however, she raised herself to a half sitting position, leaning against the wall for support, for though keenly alive to the mental suffering, she experienced a peculiar sensation of numbness in her limbs which almost deprived her of the power of movement. "What have I done? oh! my God what have I done that I should suffer so?" she repeated to herself as in a dazed mechanical sort of fashion, she kept brushing the hair back from her forehead with one delicate blue veined hand. Her face was white as marble, even to the lips, which seemed drawn and parched, and the blue eyes looked larger, and had lost their wistfulness in a sort of wild hunted expression which was entirely foreign to them. She had latterly become gaunt and haggard and bore but a slight resemblance to the Lady St. Kestor of but a few months previous.

After one or two unsuccessful attempts she at last succeeded in rising to her feet and by the aid of one or two articles of furniture reached an easy chair into which she sank thoroughly exhausted. And as she sat with closed eyes, the tears trembled upon the heavy lashes, and chased each other slowly and silently down the cold white face, occasionally falling with a splash upon the hands inert and nerveless upon her lap—she might indeed have sat for a Niobe, so calm and motionless she appeared. But after all it was but the calm which precedes the storm. As the physical condition became restored, all the horrors of the situation burst upon her afresh. With an exclamation of despair, she rose from her chair and paced the room like a caged animal—"oh Hardress! Hardress!" she cried—"do you want to kill me—or drive me mad! Oh my poor little children—in what way have we injured you that you should bring this cruel suffering upon us? Why, why have you separated us? and with a hysterical burst of sobbing she buried her face in her hands, upon the table. Then in a little while, misery again gave way to the courage of desperation, "I will make one more appeal to him," she said to herself, rising and crossing to the mirror, over the mantelpiece.

She looked long and earnestly at the ravages which her late experiences had wrought in her appearance but she made no effort to remove any traces of her agitation. "He must see that my heart is breaking" she thought as she turned away from the contemplating of her own features "perhaps he will have pity." Her hand was upon the bell, when a knock sounded upon the door. A maid entered carrying a tray with some light refreshments upon it, which she set upon the table in silence.

Lady Laura stood by the window, looking down into the park in order to keep her face concealed from the maid's scrutiny.

"Will you tell Sir Hardress St. Kestor that I wish to see him when he can spare me a few moments?" she said as she was about to withdraw from the room.

"My lady Sir Hardress has been very ill!" And the maid waited, fully enjoying the situation; she had been lucky enough to be the bearer of the bad news entirely herself.

"Very ill?" repeated Lady St. Kestor, suddenly wheeling round, forgetful of her own desire not to be criticized.

"Yes, my lady!" answered the girl, "Mortal bad he was for a little while, so Sir Peter's valet says, but he's better now, and asleep, and Miss Fairbairn is watching by him! Shall I take your message my lady?"

"No!" answered Lady Laura, and even the maid noticed how cold and strange her voice sounded,

"I will see him when he awakes if he is well enough!"

Once more Lady Laura resumed her position by the window, and the maid withdrew. She had no further excuse for remaining, though she departed somewhat disappointed that her news had been received so quietly. She had anticipated that the wife would probably have insisted upon forcing an entrance to the husband's side, thereby dethroning his self-constituted nurse.

"It seems there aint much love lost on either side," she informed her compatriots of the servants' hall, a little later. "I know whether I should stand anybody nursing my husband and driving out with him every day, while I was left at home shut up, little better than a prisoner!"

"Its very likely her own fault!" chimed in a red faced, stolid looking kitchen maid, "I've always heard as how those pink and white sort of women can be terribly aggravating!"

"Yes, she upset the poor gentleman something awful to day!" said the valet. "It took me and Miss Fairbairn all our time to pull him round, I can tell you; if he happened to have gone off," and the valet lowered his tone to the most confidential of whispers, "I won't say as it wouldn't spell manslaughter for my lady!"

"Oh my! you don't say so!" with various other similar ejaculations, was heard in chorus round the table, and eager questions were poured forth upon the valet, who suddenly found himself a person of importance.

"And just fancy her never going near the poor gentleman, when for all she knew she might have killed him with her nagging and bad temper," said the cook, its positively shameful!"

"May be she didn't know he was ill!" meekly suggested an under housemaid, who had been but a short time at Craig-Feldie, as was apparent by her daring to offer an opinion contrary to that expressed by the cook whose word was law in the establishment, and who ruled all offenders with the proverbial rod of iron.

"Not know he was ill indeed! Just hark at that!" and the confused girl suddenly found herself encompassed by so many scowling brows and black looks that she reddened and stammered out some excuses. "How dare you try to teach your betters, an ignorant chit of a girl like you!" demanded the wrathful cook, "p'raps another time you'll keep your opinions to yourself till you're asked for them! Not know he was ill, how could she help knowing when it was her own doings?—the only wonder is, that the poor gentleman ever got down stairs alive!"

By this time the under housemaid had sought refuge in tears behind a volumnious pockethandkerchief, gaudily printed with a view of Edinburgh Castle. And thus were the affairs of Sir Hardress and Lady St. Kestor discussed and enlarged upon. What did it matter how much was false or how much was true? The world forms its opinions, and sets them forth. Imagination merges into belief and the victim in many cases bears the brunt of the offender's delinquencies, especially if the victim be—a woman

When the maid had left the room Lady Laura turned away from the window, her hands were clasped tightly in front of her and a slight tinge of colour had returned to her cheeks.

"Then perhaps that accounts for; for his leaving me so suddenly! It must have been the result of our painful interview. He regretted his harshness, and perhaps remorse upset him. After all he is not so bad as I imagined!" And so the wife deluded herself with more fair false hopes, while the husband was bartering away his soul to another woman.

She had been some hours without food, and though still feeling no desire for it, she forced herself to partake of the refreshment brought to her by the maid. "I must fortify myself to see Hardress again," she said, pouring out a glass of wine and drinking it with difficulty. In a few moments, however, she experienced the benefit of the food and stimulant combined and her courage rose accordingly. Taking a sheet of paper from a stationery cabinet, she wrote upon it, "I am sorry to learn that you have been ill. If you are well enough to grant me a few minutes' conversation I shall esteem it a favour.—Laura."

It was just at the conclusion of that fateful interview with Mathilde, when that impious prayer had escaped Sir Hardress's lips and "I trust to Heaven the day may not be far distant," and which had found the responsive echo in her heart, that the wife's note was handed to him.

His first impulse was to fling it into the fire

without taking any further notice of it, but Mathilde intercepted it. "May I read it?" she asked, with the note held between her fingers.

An ungracious nod was the only assent he gave, but he restlessly stroked his moustache, and kept his eyes upon her face while she scanned the few words which the note contained. Without making any comment she placed it right in the centre of the fire, and watched the blaze rapidly consume it.

"You will see her?" she said, as the last vestige was lost to view.

"See her!" he repeated. "No, confound it, why should I? What does it mean? More clap-trap and fool's nonsense! No, you had better go, Mathilde, and tell her that I refuse to see her again."

"Do you hear?" he continued, imperatively, when Mathilde made no sign of fulfilling his request. "I tell you—I will not see her!"

"Oh, yes you will," she answered in a low, decisive manner. "See her and have done with her. Whatever you may have left her in doubt about before, settle now! Tell her she will never see the children again, and, if you think it will cause her to leave you or make an end of herself, tell her they are dead!"

Sir Hardress winced and slightly shivered as he looked nervously around, but the cold hard voice of the woman went on relentlessly, "Tell her that she is mad, and that when she leaves here it will be for the shelter of a safer place, where she will be so well taken care of that she will never be able to escape. Oh, if only I were in your place, I could say so much

—and you—you say nothing!" and Mathilde ended almost with a sob. "Are you going?" she asked, suddenly ceasing her march across the room and facing him, anger and mortification shining in her eyes.

"Yes, I am going," he answered, the old, cynical, cruel smile playing about his lips and the corners of his mouth.

She had just succeeded in sending him to his wife in one of his most dangerous and cruel moods. It was useless for Lady Laura to match herself against such an adversary, for there could be no equality between them. An honest foe any of us may grapple with, but we might as well try to caress a serpent or coax a wild animal as to cross swords with a combatant who cannot lay claim even to his own code of honour. Lady Laura's self-raised hopes fell instantly as her eyes rested upon her husband's face when he entered the room. She had retired to her own chamber, which looked wonderfully attractive and cosy. There were large sconces on the walls suspended from brackets of crimson plush, and in these wax candles were burning, as they were also on the toilet table, and on either side of the mirror which hung above the mantel-piece. By the side of the fireplace a large couch was drawn up, covered with an immense striped rug of Italian silk; while opposite to it stood a capacious easy chair upholstered in purple velvet. She had changed her tight-fitting velvet dress for a long loose robe—half dressing, half tea gown. It was of some flimsy material of a peculiar

O

shade of blue, and profusely trimmed with creamy lace. She had been standing by the toilet table, but crossed over to the hearthrug when her husband entered.

"I am pleased to see that you are better," she said, at the same time inwardly noting his unusual pallor and the discolouration which still remained about the eyes and mouth, signs which doubtless rendered her still more gracious. "Won't you be seated?" she asked him, drawing the easy chair nearer within the radius of warmth, and pointing to it as she spoke.

But he curtly shook his head. "No! What have you sent for me for?"

Lady Laura laid one trembling hand upon the plush-covered mantel-board, and gripped it tightly in order to steady herself before replying. When she did so, the words were far different from what she had intended to speak. "Are you still so hard and pitiless?" she said, "I had hoped when I heard of your illness that perhaps it would soften your heart towards me."

"Then you thought wrong," Sir Hardress answered turning upon his heel to leave the room, "and if that is all you have to say to me, I will wish you a very good evening."

"No, no! Hardress, in Heaven's name I implore you to wait one moment; for God's sake don't leave me like this."

With a half smothered ejaculation he flung himself into the chair which she had previously indicated, throwing his head back with a weary gesture and languidly closing his eyes. His attitude and apparent indifference made it extremely difficult for Lady Laura to re-open the conversation. After a short pause, Sir Hardress partially unclosed his eyes and drew his watch from his pocket.

His wife interpreted the action as he had intended she should do. " I won't keep you any longer than I am obliged," she remarked half apologetically and yet with a certain tinge of grievance in her tone.

" Hardress, will you be honest with me and tell me in what way I have offended against you so far as to forfeit not only your love, but your esteem ! for that such is the case I can no longer doubt ! "

" I am glad you are satisfied on that point ! " he answered, without even unclosing his eyes, it may, perhaps, save a lot of bother, and at any rate, useless argument ! "

" Hardress, you are inhuman. What do you— what can you mean ? "

" I mean that I am tired of you. I hate the tie which fetters me, and if I could be rid of you, I would wish never to see your face again ! There, at last I am honest with you ! " He leant forward in the chair, a ferocious gleam in his eyes as he fixed them upon the trembling woman before him.

" Another woman has come between us ! " she said, in a voice hoarse and strained ; the dazed expression again in her eyes.

" Yes ! you are right again," he answered, " another woman has gained what was never yours—my love !

and you,"—he almost hissed the words, "are the stumbling block to my happiness. I curse the day that I ever saw your face!"

With a low cry of intense pain she stretched forth her hand as if mutely begging of him to desist, and sank upon her knees before him.

"Have mercy! have mercy!" she cried, "it is more than I can bear! If I have lived too long for you, I will go away. Restore my children to me and we will never trouble you again. Do anything but separate us, I cannot live without my little ones—indeed I cannot!" and the supplication ended in a sob. But again she continued as she still knelt, "if only in memory of the love which I have given you; of the love which even now will not be crushed, I implore you to grant my prayer!"

"I don't want your love!" he interrupted her angrily at the same time rising from his chair. "As for the children, they are under proper care, and I do not choose that they should be under your guardianship." Once more Lady Laura rose to her feet with a cry of despair, as she flung her arms above her head.

"Are you mad? Sir Hardress asked, fixing a coldly enquiring gaze upon her—"pray try and calm yourself."

"Mad!" she repeated, you are driving me mad indeed. But perhaps that is what you have been striving for—well, you will succeed, perhaps you have succeeded already—yes I think I must be mad, my brain seems on fire" and she laughed hysterically, holding her throat and swallowing rapidly as if there was something choking her.

For the first time her husband watched her in in some alarm, "perhaps I had better say goodnight," he said "you will be better alone."

"Yes, perhaps so," she answered in the same hysterical manner in which she had previously spoken.

"You will say good night to me?" he asked her, at the same time offering her his hand.

"Oh yes, I will say good night!" and she held his proffered hand in a feverish clasp, but her eyes seemed to look beyond him as she said " and may God forgive you for your cruelty to me and mine, for I cannot!"

There were no more tears or reproaches or pleadings; she recognised that all her endeavours were futile, and for the time being it seemed that she had lost even the power to suffer and yet as she stood there, cold and passionless, rigid and motionless in her dumb despair, a peculiar thrill of shame and remorse seized upon Sir Hardress and he turned quickly aside in disgust at his own weakness. Not a word was spoken on either side, the situation grew more painful as each moment passed, once more he turned and looked at his wife, who still stood in that same statue-like rigidity, his heart beat faster and the question would force itself through his mind. "What concession can I make to her!" Then the thought of Mathilde arose to combat his better judgment, and, as before, Mathilde conquered!

"I am only distressing you by remaining," he said at last "perhaps you will allow me to see you to-morrow?"

He added the latter part of the sentence, thinking it would be a means of pacifying her and allow himself a better means of escape.

His wife simply bowed her head in response, but never removed her eyes from his face until the door had closed upon him.

And Sir Hardress drew a long breath of relief as soon as he found himself safely outside his wife's room and in the corridor. He drew his hand across his forehead with a weary gesture, his head ached and there was a peculiar uncomfortable sensation which he could not get rid of, and which might be described as conscience, and which bad or unprincipled as one may be, is still singularly persistent and difficult to dispose of.

"By Jove! she almost made me feel ashamed of myself," he ejaculated, "egad, if I had remained much longer she would have got the best of me, and I might have given in to her. How she looked at me with those eyes of hers, their expression has made me feel quite eerie," and he quickened his steps in the direction of the library to acquaint Mathilde with the result of this second interview.

And Lady St. Kestor still lived and moved, like one in a dream. When she found herself once more alone, she first of all extinguished the various candles, leaving the room simply illumined by the fire-light, drew the easy chair to the centre of the rug, and seated herself within it. For the time being, not only her physical but her mental capacities had become numbed, and before long she succumbed to the exhaustion which was the outcome of her suffering, and slept as soundly as a tired child. When she awoke several hours later, and dragged herself to bed, the fire had died out and she was shivering from cold. But even then no recollection dawned upon her of the terrible to-morrow which awaited her—a wife without husband, and a mother without children!

CHAPTER XXII.

HESTOR BANFORTH PLAYS HER PART.

"IF you please, Miss, there's a person in the hall inquiring for Lady St. Kestor's nurse; says she's her sister, and that she's come all the way from London expecting to find her here. She won't believe me when I tell her that Mrs. Simmonds has gone away."

Miss Fairbairn was closeted with one of the maids in the store room, and listened with an air of impatience as the servant explained his errand. An angry frown puckered her brow, and she hesitated fully a minute before making a reply

" Is Sir Hardress in the house ? " she asked him.

"No, Miss, he and Sir Peter have gone out together, and won't be in again before luncheon."

Mathilde drew out her watch and consulted it. It wanted fully an hour before the time for luncheon. "Take her into the library," she said, as she transferred the watch to its resting place, "and I will see her before troubling Lady St. Kestor."

A few minutes later Mathilde entered the library where the woman was already seated. As soon as

Mathilde closed the door, the woman rose, dropped a low curtsey before her, and remained standing in an attitude suggestive of the deepest humility, with her head inclined rather low upon her breast, and hands meekly folded in front of her waiting for Miss Fairbairn to address her. Her dress was of a dark material of the coarest texture, and made to fall in heavy pleats from the waist. She wore a large black shawl folded from corner to corner, and pinned across the chest with a big cameo brooch, and on her head was a rather large bonnet of rusty black with a neat little white border inserted beneath the brim. Her hands were encased in thick woollen gloves which appeared to be several sizes too large for her. All these little details seemed to be taken in at a glance by Mathilde, but she had not yet had a chance of gaining an idea of her personal appearance.

"My servant tells me that you are a sister of Lady St. Kestor's maid. May I ask what led you to seek her here, and also your name?"

The woman slowly raised her head, and Mathilde had an opportunity of better observing her. Her face was anything but prepossessing, and there was something altogether incongruous about her appearance. Her complexion was of the very ruddiest type, the skin coarse and roughened as if from exposure. She appeared to possess an abundance of hair of a fiery red, brought down low upon each side of the face, entirely covering the ears. The eyebrows were thick and of a corresponding colour, but, strange to say, the eyes, instead of being grey or blue, as is usually the case with such adjuncts, were large and wonderfully dark. The effect of those eyes was remarkably peculiar. In such a face they appeared altogether weird and uncanny. As Mathilde met their gaze she instantly averted her own from some cause inexplicable even to herself.

The woman leaned slightly towards her, and in a voice partially lowered, said, " Excuse me, m'arm, but I am deaf—very deaf ! "

A look of annoyance passed over Mathilde's face. This time she only put one question : " What is your name ? "

The woman hesitated for a second, and fixed her eyes upon the floor as though trying to seek the information there. Then quickly raising her head she replied in the same half-whispered tones—" My name is Mrs. Barnforth—Hester Barnforth ! "

" What have you come here for ? " was Mathilde's next question.

A half vacant expression crept into Hester's eyes —she had evidently failed to catch the words. She was rather under, than over the medium height, and appeared unusually small as Mathilde stood towering above her. Looking very much as if she would like to shake her, Mathilde repeated the question in a still louder voice, articulating each word slowly and distinctly.

As Hester Barnforth opened her lips to reply, Mathilde noticed how large and white were her teeth and immediately began to wonder where she had seen teeth like those before, and to whom they could have belonged. Meanwhile, the mysterious woman was speaking in the same hushed tones which it seemed customary for her to adopt. "I wrote and told my sister that my mistress was dying, and asked her to be on the look-out for a situation as sewing maid, or nurse, or something of that kind for me, as I expected I should have some difficulty in getting suited, owing to being so deaf. She wrote back to me direct, saying as how kind her mistress was, and the lady and gentleman, too, where she was staying, and she was sure if I came right away when anything happened to my mistress, as how her ladyship would let me stay with her for a few weeks and help with the children, or it might be that the other lady would find me something to do. But I stayed on for a week after my poor mistress died. The master sold up the furniture and started for France the day I left for here, and now the servant tells me my sister isn't here, and her never to let me know as she was going away. I can't believe it, m'arm!" and Hester trembled on the verge of tears.

Mathilde had seated herself in a large arm chair, drawn close up to the table. She held up her finger and pointed for Hester, who was still standing, to advance nearer to her. "How am I to know that what you say is true?" she asked.

The woman slowly shook her head as an indication that she had not heard.

Mathilde grew furious, and stamped her foot upon the floor in her vexation. Suddenly snatching up a pen from an inkstand on the table, she drew towards her a sheet of blank paper, and wrote upon it in text hand the question which she had failed to make her understand. " Can you read ? " she asked, directing her attention to the paper.

The woman nodded her head, but did not seem to resent the question. Perhaps she was used to proving her statements before having them accepted, and looked upon doubt as a matter of course. Anyway she answered without hesitation, " If you want to inquire about me, m'arm, I can give you the address of my late mistress's niece. She could speak to my character and all that I've told you, too, for she spent a great deal of time with her poor aunt, especially at the last."

Mathilde remained thoughtful, without making any reply.

" Perhaps you'd be so good as to let her ladyship know that I am here, m'arm," Hester suggested, when several seconds had passed in silence.

Mathilde roused herself from her abstraction, and looked at the woman with a critical survey from head to foot as though she was debating within herself what course to adopt. In point of fact the sewing maid had turned up most inopportunely, but Miss Fairbairn was exercising her ingenuity to find out whether she might not utilise her services for her own advantage. After thus taking mental stock of her, Mathilde reached a fresh sheet of paper, and wrote upon it in smaller characters than before. " Your sister has been sent away with the children because their mother was ill. If you like to stay for a few days and wait upon Lady St. Kestor, you may do so. But mind you keep a still tongue in your head, and do my bidding!"

Hester Barnforth's grim features relaxed for the first time into a broad smile as she perused the written words. Laying the paper again on the table, she dropped another stiff little curtsey, but the only words which she uttered were, "You may rely on me, m'arm!"

Mathilde's next act was to collect the various papers which she had written upon, and tear them into fragments before consigning them to the waste paper basket beneath the table. "You had better follow me and see her ladyship at once," she called in her loudest tones, as she led the way from the library up the staircase to Lady St. Kestor's apartments.

Mathilde rapped somewhat sharply at the door. The nurse was breathing heavily, and she turned round to look at her. There was an eager look in the large dark eyes, and her hands, which she kept folded in front of her, were unquestionably trembling. Mathilde hesitated before opening the door, and eyed her suspiciously. "You are not nervous, are you?" she asked in angry tones.

The nurse shook her head, and whispered, "I was only wondering if my lady will care to keep me."

"Psha! don't be a simpleton," Mathilde shouted in her ear, and preceeded her into the room.

Lady Laura was reclining upon a couch in front of the fire, but on their entrance assumed an upright position.

"Don't disturb yourself," Mathilde said. "I have brought Hester Barnforth to see you. She is a sister of Simmonds, and came over expecting to find her here. She is very anxious to remain and wait upon you, if you will consent to her doing so."

Lady Laura turned and surveyed the new comer with anything but friendliness in her gaze. "Has Sir Hardress sent her to me?" she inquired of Mathilde, and her lip curled contemptuously as she put the question.

"No, he does not know that she is in the house, or perhaps, not even that such a person exists. I brought her to you thinking that you might not like her to be turned out of doors."

"I am indifferent. She may stay if she chooses," Lady Laura said, but without casting another glance in Hester's direction.

"I forgot to tell you that Hester is very deaf," Mathilde told her, as she was about to lead her away to shew her the rooms which she would occupy, and which were *en suite* with Lady St. Kestor's.

Lady Laura replied with a monosyllable, "Indeed!" without raising her eyes from the book in her hand. Evidently she was determined not to be drawn into a conversation with her fair hostess.

But Miss Fairbairn was equally determined not to be non-plussed.

"May we look forward to the pleasure of seeing you at dinner this evening, Lady Laura?" was her next question.

This time Lady St. Kestor not only raised her eyes

from the book, but actually placed it on the couch beside her ere she replied, but when she spoke it was with a decision and firmness which startled Mathilde in no small degree.

"I shall not have the pleasure of dining with you this evening, Miss Fairbairn," she said; "nor is it probable that I shall ever do so again. I hope to be strong enough to travel in a day or two at the latest, when it is my intention to start for England."

"Indeed! you amaze me," ejaculated Mathilde, "your husband has not led us to expect so sudden a move on your part. May I ask if you intend going straight to St. Kestor?"

"That I cannot answer!" Lady Laura replied, "My plans are not fully settled, but I think it likely that I shall call upon my sister first."

There was a sudden exclamation from the sewing maid, whom both ladies seemed to have forgotten. As they each turned instantly to look upon her, she advanced towards Lady St. Kestor in a nervous supplicating manner. "I thought you was asking the lady to send me away," she stammered—"Oh, please let me stay, my lady—I will do my best to please you; indeed I will!"

Mathilde laughed aloud. "I told you she was deaf," she explained, and taking her by the shoulder hustled her out of the room. "I told you not to make a simpleton of yourself," Lady St. Kestor heard her shout to her, as the door closed behind them.

An hour later the maid entered the room again, carrying the luncheon-tray. Her appearance was considerably improved by a starched muslin cap placed on her head, from which long ends streamed nearly to the waist. A white muslin apron partially covered her dark dress. At her wrists and neck were cuffs of snowy linen, but the hands which had before been encased in the clumsy woollen gloves were now concealed by black mittens tightly drawn across them. Lady St. Kestor noticed, however, that so much of the fingers as could be seen were white and well shaped, with rosy-tipped nails such as any high-born dame might envy.

Lady Laura watched her curiously as she flitted noiselessly about the room, deftly arranging with artistic fingers every object as it came to hand. But the woman was strangely silent, performing every little duty without either question or comment, and yet there was no sign of sulkiness; on the contrary, she hovered about her new mistress as though anxious to ingratiate herself by offering every attention in her power.

Lady St. Kestor with her usual goodness of heart, addressed several questions to her, in order that she might give her an opportunity of conversing if she felt inclined, but owing to her extreme deafness conversation was so laborious that the effort was soon abandoned, and Hester withdrew to the room set apart for her, which was in reality Lady Laura's boudoir.

Just before the hour for retiring, the new maid wheeled a small couch bedstead into Lady Laura's own room, and fixed it at the foot of the bed.

" Please allow me to remain here during the night,"

she said; "I shall not hear, if you require anything' if I am in the other room."

But Lady Laura did not like the arrangement, and strenuously opposed it. She would have insisted upon excluding her from the room altogether, had not Hester put forth a plea on her own behalf "Forgive me, my lady," she began; "I have had my orders, and if you will not allow me to carry them out, I shall be blamed—perhaps lose my place."

It was not necessary to say more; the objection was withdrawn, and with a quick movement Hester Barnforth turned away that her employer might not see the gleam of triumph shining in her eyes. A couple of of hours later, when silence and darkness held their reign, Lady St. Kestor was tossing wearily but sleeplessly upon her pillow, her brain racked by the new phase which affairs had assumed in the introduction of the woman whom she looked upon as no less than a keeper or gaoler. She felt that she was a prisoner, and wondered vaguely what would be the upshot of it all. Unconsciously to herself, she gave vent to a low moan, the bitterness of her musings bringing it from her lips.

Instantly the maid sprang from her couch and hastened to the bedside of her mistress. She had caught the sound with wonderful alacrity for one who had recently evinced such signs of deafness.

The room was in perfect darkness, and Lady Laura could hear rather than see her as she advanced towards the bed. The next moment she felt the pressure of a soft, firm hand laid upon her fore-

P

head, with a touch which seemed not strange, but wonderfully familiar, and a wild idea flashed across her mind, which for a moment held her speechless; the next moment she had dashed it away from her as unreasonable. But the figure so darkly outlined was still bending over her, and had taken one of her hands in a warm lingering grasp—and—was she going mad—was imagination playing her some fanciful cruel trick? A voice, which she would have recognized among a thousand, was whispering strange, wonderful words into her ears, "Courage, Laura, for a little while, and trust in me to help you!"

"A light! a light!" she gasped, scarcely daring to believe the evidence of her senses. The figure disengaged itself from her almost frenzied grasp to do her bidding. A minute later it returned to the bedside bearing a lighted lamp. The flame revealed the face and form of Mary Haldane.

The disfiguring red wig had been removed, and her long rich tresses of waving hair which it had concealed fell unfettered below her waist. Scarcely a trace of the hideous but clever make up remained. The coarse reddened complexion had disappeared, and the lines beneath the eyes and at the corners of the mouth were no longer visible, only the eyebrows remained unaltered, save in that respect the metamorphosis was complete. The sisters gazed upon each other, at first with an emotion too strong to be expressed in words, and silently held each other in a long close embrace. But Miss Haldane was the first to rouse herself from the indulgence of giving way, for she feared the effect which it might produce upon her sister, who sobbed and clung to her even as a child might have done, so great was the reaction.

"And now for an explanation of my escapade," said the little lady, when she had succeeded in somewhat calming Lady St. Kestor's agitation. "To begin with, I received your letter the day following the one on which you gave it to the poor woman (Jess, I think you called her) to post, as you expected I should do. Several times I had felt very uneasy at not receiving any answer from you to at least three letters which I had sent."

Lady St. Kestor started up, eager to disclaim, but Miss Haldane playfully pushed her back again on the pillows. "Of course, my dear, I know now that you never received them—they were purposely withheld from you; but let me go on. I tried to comfort myself with the old saying that 'no news is good news,' that the very fact of your not writing proved that you were not in need of my assistance. I never dreamed of treachery such as this," and her brow darkened at the very contemplation.

Lady Laura noticed it, and stretched out her hand in sympathy.

At the slight action, Mary's face brightened, and again she continued. "After reading your letter, I felt almost desperate and unable to decide as to how I should be acting for the best. I hardly dared to trust to your getting a letter conveyed to you by the same means that you employed in writing to me, and

P 2

I thought in case it failed, you might be placed in a worse position than ever. So I resolved that I would come at all hazards and trust to chance to aid me in making my way to you. I hit upon the plan of impersonating a sister of Simmonds, in consequence of your having told me that her whereabouts was a secret. I trusted to their not being willing to furnish me with her address, but preferring to keep me here rather than running the risk of further enquiries. I also made an arrangement with a lady friend of Mrs. de Grey's that in case I might be asked for a reference she would act as a referee, and for that purpose she gave me her address, which I have duly handed over to Miss Fairbairn. I don't think she will trouble to make use of it, but in case she does it will be all right. And now, Laura, what do you think of my scheme? Am I not a regular arch plotter?"

Lady Laura looked upon her sister with wonder and admiration combined, and with something of a puzzled expression too. "You are clever, Mary, and oh so brave," she answered thoughtfully, "and your scheme so far has succeeded marvellously. But," the old frightened look returned to her eyes, " how will it end? If Hardress discovers that you have stolen into the house under the shelter of a disguise, what will he say —what will he do?" and the poor wretched woman wrung her hands in despair at the picture which she had conjured up.

But Miss Haldane was quick to reassure her. "Remember he is not *my* husband," she said; "and if the worst comes to the worst, I promise you that it shall result in his discomfiture, not mine. So dismiss all forebodings from your mind, and rely upon me to outwit your tormentors. And had you really no suspicion, no idea of my identity when I was introduced to you this morning?" Mary asked, in order to divert her mind from dwelling upon the future.

"Not the vaguest!" Lady Laura replied; "and yet as I watched you moving about so daintily this afternoon, and noticed how slim and taper were your fingers, I could not help comparing you with somebody familiar, and yet for whom I could not find a name. But, Mary?" she continued, "what was your reason for simulating deafness?"

"Oh! I have a very good reason for it," Mary replied with a laugh. "You must know, first of all, that I have come with the intention of finding out as much as possible. I may wish to overhear any conversation, plans, or schemes, and I shall be much more likely to accomplish it under the circumstances. They will not be so guarded when speaking before me and I shall be looked upon as *safe* if I happen by chance to be discovered where I have no business to be."

Again Lady Laura expressed her astonishment as the depth of the scheme was gradually unfolded before her. "And the disguise, how did you manage to obtain that?" Lady Laura's curiosity was fully aroused, and she waited with unfeigned interest for the reply.

"You may well ask that," said Miss Haldane,

laughingly. "It was the most adventurous part of my scheme, and I lay awake one whole night wondering and planning until I hit upon the idea which I afterwards carried out—successfully I think I may venture to say—eh, Laura, since a sister's eyes failed to discover me," and she stopped to give Lady Laura another affectionate embrace.

CHAPTER XXIII.

MARY HALDANE'S MAKE-UP.

"BUT to proceed with my story," said Mary Haldane. "As I was saying I suddenly hit upon an idea. That idea was to procure a theatrical newspaper, which I guessed would contain advertisements from artistes for professionals. The next morning I acted upon the idea, purchased a paper from a railway bookstall, and found the very thing I wanted. I then took a cab as far as Piccadilly, tore out the advertisement, and dropped the paper from the cab window into the street. I studied the advertisement until I knew it by heart. It was worded thus:

" Mons. Pierre, perruquier, costumier, and artist in general, begs to inform members of the theatrical profession or amateurs, that he has had great experience in *making-up* for the stage and may be consulted for advice or practical experiment in the above art. Disguises rendered so perfect that recognition is impossible even by most intimate friends.—Address, 302, Melville street, off Piccadilly "

My plan was quickly formed. I would go to

Mons. Pierre and represent myself as an amateur just adopting the stage as a profession against the wishes of my friends, and consequently anxious to conceal my identity as far as possible. The only thing to be decided was the character which I should assume. So I wrote upon a slip of paper a description of the dress to be worn, as though it were a description from the manager in whose company I was supposed to be engaged. I had hardly time to finish before the cab stopped at my destination. A minute or two later I had turned out of Piccadilly, and was sauntering down Melville street in search of number 302. At last I came across it; a small, dingy-looking shop, with several switches of hair suspended in the one window, and a couple of wigs, which looked as if they had been there for years. I was several minutes before I could make up my mind to enter, the exterior seemed so terribly uninviting, and I looked again to see if I had not made a mistake. But no! there was the name of Mons. Pierre in large black letters printed on the opaque glass which formed half the door. After walking past once or twice, I at last screwed up my courage, and turned in as if quite naturally when I next arrived at the door. A noisy clanging bell proclaimed my entrance, and in response to its summons, a little shrivelled looking grey-haired man emerged from a sort of office at the end of the shop, the window of which was shaded by a closely-drawn blind of faded green.

"I have called to consult Mons. Pierre on a little private matter," I blurted out immediately.

The little old man, whose skin looked like parchment, bowed, and fixed a somewhat curious look upon me as he said, " I have the honour to be Mons. Pierre, at your service Madamoiselle."

Under any other circumstances, I should have had a hearty laugh at the gallantry displayed by the perruquier and costumier, which might have belonged to a courtly beau of ancient times. But as it was, I felt a sudden misgiving, that he might be anything but the right sort of person for my purpose. However, a minute later I found myself behind that mysterious green blind, unfolding my scheme into Mons. Pierre's listening ears. I then handed to him the written description of my costume, at which he emphasised his satisfaction by nodding his head in a a peculiar fashion backwards and forwards as he read. Meanwhile I looked around me. The room was small and square. One side of it was fitted up with a series of cupboards, two rows one above the other. On the opposite wall a full length mirror was fixed then came the fireplace, in a small recess beside it a marble washstand. At the end of the room was a window, looking on to the back of the premises and directly opposite to the one looking into the shop. In front of the back window stood a dressing-table and glass, and there were a number of brushes and combs and bottles containing cosmetics, ranged with great nicety upon it. There was an india-rubber tube fixed in the wall by the side of the mantel-piece communicating with another room. As Mons. Pierre finished reading the description he crossed over, and, taking up the tube, gave a shrill whistle, after which he placed it to his mouth, and called out—" Jacques! attend to the shop." Directly afterwards I heard footsteps descending a flight of stairs, and as they reached the door of the room, Mons. again called out " Jacques! "

The summons was answered by a sickly looking boy, evidently not over twelve years of age, though he wore a white linen slip confined at the waist by a leather belt in which was tucked a pair of scissors and a horn comb, so that he appeared to be a thoroughly fledged barber. All this I had time to notice while his master was speaking to him. " Now, Jacques, for the next half-hour I am engaged—you understand ! " and there was a peculiar intonation in his voice which was not lost upon me. Jacques appeared to thoroughly understand, but could not refrain from casting a glance at me as he said so.

" Then I can see no one remember ! but you may make appointments for every half-hour up to four o'clock ; then you may put up the shutters ; we'll have no more callers to-day." And Jacques turned away to take up his station in the shop, but once more his master called to him. " If Number Three should call, you can ask her to wait, and show her into the green room."

Good gracious. I thought to myself, what an extraordinary man this must be who can reckon upon appointments in such a fashion, and I looked at him with quite a new interest, but what I had heard had also disconcerted me.

'I heard you tell your assistant that you would do no more business after four o'clock; and—and—I must see you again to-day."

"Is it this evening then that you play your part, Mademoiselle?" he asked, and, of course, I answered "Yes!"

"Ah, well, that is all right," he said, rubbing his small thin hands together, which were little more than skin and bone. "I guessed so, and for that reason I see no more customers to-day. Well, now to business; we have a half-hour, and must set to work."

He drew from his pocket a bunch of bright keys, and stood upon a chair to reach the top row of cupboards, which I noticed were numbered One, Two, Three, Four and Five. After unlocking Numbers One, Two and Five, he opened the cupboards and brought out of them three of the most life-like and natural models that it is possible to imagine. He then opened a long centre cupboard which I had not observed, and from which he took three padded figures, or dummies, similar to those used by drapers for showing off their goods. Upon each of these figures he fixed the model heads, and finally wound loose wrappers around them. The first model represented a youthful appearance, the second that of a much older person, the third differed from the other two in complexion, which was very dark, and represented years, the number of which would be difficult to determine. As those three figures confronted me I experienced a most disagreeable nervous thrill.

There was something so altogether weird and strange about the situation and surroundings, and I began to wonder what other vague mysteries might be concealed in the little costumier's sanctum. But as these thoughts chased each other rapidly through my mind, Mons. Pierre invited my attention towards Number One.

"This, Mam'selle, you will observe is intended to represent youth," he commenced, "while this one," pointing to the second figure "gives you an idea of middle age. I have five of these models, which I have named respectively—Youth! Middle Age! Old Age! Blonde! and Brunette! The third figure which I have selected in this case is Brunette, and with these three models to work upon, I think we shall eventually arrive at satisfactory results. Number One represents your age, minus a few lines of age and thought which, perhaps, with the addition of another five years, reckoning this young lady to be twenty," and he patted "Youth" affectionately on the shoulder as he looked at me with quite an arch glance. "I believe I have fixed it accurately have I not?" he said, and of course I had to confess that he had judged even to a year.

"So far so good," he replied. "Well now we will say that Number Two is what you wish to represent as a sewing maid and nurse to an invalid lady; so Numbers One and Two remain in conjunction as youth, converted into middle age. Now for number Three, which I have selected as the model upon which our experiments must be based. You will observe that she is a brunette of a more decided type than yourself, yet supplying the necessary conditions for building up a counterfeit."

I now began to see what the little wig-maker was driving at, and that my identity was to be merged, in some mysterious fashion, into this odd trinity of half-human dummies, that I was in reality to lose my characteristics in the assumption of theirs. I looked at Mons. Pierre, perhaps with some such expression in my eyes, for he laughed a sort of suppressed wheezy chuckle, and immediately commenced with deft and nimble fingers the manipulation of the creatures of his art.

So far I had remained standing, but now he brought a comfortable arm-chair and asked me to be seated, and, perhaps, Mam'selle will oblige me by removing her hat and veil," he said, with another of his grandiose bows.

Mechanically I obeyed, and waited for what was to follow. He next filled the marble basin with water, and soaking a large sponge, commenced to wash the face of dummy number one, until every vestige of her beautiful colour disappeared. He then, by an ingenious contrivance, removed her sparkling blue eyes. For a moment he hesitated, then came and stood beside me. "Mam'selle will excuse me, I know," and he laid his hand upon my head, and twined my hair around his fingers. "Thank you, Mam'selle," he said, as though I had conferred a favour upon him, and then went on with his extraordinary proceedings. Fixing a small table by his side, he placed upon it a number of boxes, one of which he opened and emptied. The contents consisted of a number of glass eyes of all shades and colours, which looked most repulsively peculiar as they lay scattered in various directions. He soon singled out a pair of brown ones, and proceeded to insert them in the place of the absent blue ones. The effect was marvellous. It was like gazing upon quite a different face.

He next poured a few drops of a dark liquid from a small bottle into a saucer, and with a piece of linen rag rubbed it gently over the face and neck so that the lily-like fairness was transformed to a dusky tint. Touching a spring concealed somewhere at the back, the jaw suddenly dropped and displayed a row of white and regular teeth. Placing his forefinger on the palate, he moved the front teeth to greater prominence and again fixed the chin in its old position. The shape of the mouth was entirely altered, it almost formed a square; and I started as I saw the resemblance to my own somewhat heavy chin. The little wig-maker noticed my sudden start with quite a gratified smile. "Mam'selle begins to comprehend," he said, with one of his low wheezy chuckles. "Wait a minute and you will see—you will see," he went on.

I did not know whether he was talking to me, his model, or himself, so I returned no answer.

Suddenly he darted across the room, and raised one corner of the green blind and peered into the shop. As he dropped it, and returned again to his work, he said, " I have to keep my eye on Jacques. You could hardly believe it, but that boy is always going to sleep. I scarcely dare leave him alone for five minutes. I had the chair taken out of the shop so that he could not sit down, but when I went in the next time there he stood, leaning back against the wall, his arms folded in front of him, and his chin fallen on to his breast. He was sound asleep, and I had to give him a thorough good shaking before I could rouse him at all. He's a good lad though, is Jacques—when you can catch him awake."

I couldn't help smiling at the funny little man, he seemed so simple and good-hearted. " But I must get on with my story," said Miss Haldane, as she glanced at the timepiece, ticking along so merrily, " or we shall get no sleep to-night, or rather this morning. It is already four o'clock, and I must resume my disguise, ready for playing my part to-morrow. I mean to find out where the children have been placed, and what their other plans are, and then, my dear, we'll be off. But to go on with Mons. Pierre."

While he had been talking to me about poor Jacques' somnolent habits, he had also been busy sorting a number of wigs in every shade of red from the palest to the deepest fiery, such as you have seen adorning my cranium, and here he offered his first explanation as to his mode of procedure.

" I daresay you will think it strange, Mam'selle," he said, "that I do not choose some raven tresses rather than the conspicuous colour which I hold in my hand, and undoubtedly most persons would do so on account of the lady's complexion. But I say exactly the opposite, and to show you how greatly the disguise is helped by the contrast, I will remove the dark hair from brunette (or number five) in order that you may judge for yourself."

The effect was magical!

He then transferred the red wig to model number one, which was fast assuming my characteristics, and arranged the hair, bringing it low, and covering the ears, partly for the purpose of concealing the natural hair beneath it and partly to impart a narrower appearance to the face. All that remained to complete this transformed image of myself was the painting of the eyebrows, and the addition of the age lines, and the ruddy tint, which was but the work of a few moments. I stood and gazed at the wonderful reproduction of what was, and yet was not, myself, with a fascinated stare. Monsieur Pierre recalled my recollection by asking "if it satisfied me."

I answered his question by putting another. "And is it possible that you can ever transform me as you have transformed this dummy?" I asked.

"It is a positive fact, Mam'selle," he replied. "I can so transform you that you will not know yourself."

Acting in my usual impulsive fashion, I snatched one of his hands in both my own, and I believe there must have been tears in my eyes as I said, "Then I can never repay you or ever thank you sufficiently, for you may be the means of helping me to right one of the greatest wrongs that ever existed."

"Oh, hush, Mam'selle," he replied, " I daresay it will depend a great deal more upon how you play your part; but I wish you success—ah, both success and victory, for I'm sure you deserve it!"

In an instant I felt how foolishly I had acted, but still I did not altogether regret having spoken, for Mons. Pierre had quite won my sympathy and faith.

At that moment the bell rang, and then I heard the footsteps of some person walking upstairs. I wondered if it was the lady they had spoken of as " No. 3," and thought to myself they are fond of numbers here. I wondered what her errand was, if she was a professional, or if she had a reason such as mine for paying a visit to Monsieur Pierre. Then it flashed across my mind that " No. 3 " was perhaps identical with one of the models, and I wondered to myself if I should henceforth be looked upon or spoken of as " Number One or Five," or whatever it might be.

"Will you return by half-past five?" Monsieur Pierre was saying to me, as he stood with a small book and pencil in his hand, and what shall I enter?"

For a second I hesitated, and we looked at each other. "You had better put Mrs. Barnforth," I said.

He made no comment as he entered it, but when he had finished writing, something impelled me to say, " I don't pretend that it is my real name, but it will answer my present purpose."

Again he bowed. " Perhaps it is the name of the

Q

character which Mdlle. is about to assume." he said.

He had suggested the idea, and I resolved to accept it, though I had offered the name quite at random. That was one of the points that I had forgotten, but Barnforth would do as well as any other name to introduce myself by at Craig-Feldie.

Instead of passing through the shop, Mons. Pierre let me out by a side entrance, which opened into a narrow passage leading into the street. "Come in by this door in the evening," he said, and shewed me the bell which I was to make use of. I then drove to Eaton-square, packed what few things I required, told Mrs. de Grey as much of my plans as I deemed it necessary, and afterwards drove to the railway station, where I booked my luggage for " Mrs. Barnforth," and had just time to make inquiries about the trains before I returned to Melville-street.

It was exactly on the stroke of half-past five as I placed my hand upon the bell of Mons. Pierre's side door as he had directed me. Almost before its ringing had ceased to echo, the door was opened by Jacques, who had changed his linen slip for a smart suit of blue cloth, ornamented with scarlet facings and shining brass buttons. A broad smile illumined his pale face when I spoke a few cheery words to him, as he conducted me towards the dingy little room in which I had so recently undergone my strange experiences. There was a lamp burning in the room, but it was turned so low that semi-darkness prevailed.

"Master will be with you in a few minutes, Miss,"

he said, as he raised the light, but I felt an unaccountable aversion to being left alone in that room, and I looked up at the cupboards thinking of the strange things which they contained. So I began to talk to Jacques, anxious to keep him with me on any pretext.

"Have you been with Mons. Pierre very long?" I asked him.

"Ten years, Miss," he answered.

I looked at him in astonishment.

"Then you have been with him ever since you were ——"

"Six years old, Miss," he answered, before I had time to finish the sentence.

"And do you mean to tell me that you are sixteen years of age?" I asked, still more amazed.

"Yes, Miss! And me and the master have lived together ever since. He's been father and mother both to me, and he—well he's got nobody but me."

"Hasn't he a wife?" I asked.

But Jacques slowly shook his head in reply. Then, as if acting upon a second thought, said, "He had one twenty years ago, but she died when the baby, little Dick, was born. Poor little Dick, the master's got him up there in that cupboard, Miss," and he pointed with a thin, stunted finger at a cupboard fixed against the wall in the recess above the marble washstand.

"In the cupboard!" I repeated, and I clutched hold of his sleeve, so greatly was I agitated. Jacques now looked at me in surprise—"Don't be alarmed,

Miss," he said; "of course I mean the model which the master took himself, but we always speak of him as Master Dick, and his father takes on with him as if he was a living child. But I don't know what made me talk to you so free, Miss," he said, looking into my face with a startled expression, "I seemed to forget as you was a stranger."

"Never mind," I answered, "You need not fear my mentioning anything that you have told me, Jacques"; but I resolved in my own mind that I would try and get Mons. Pierre to talk to me about little Master Dick.

There was no time to say more, for the next instant Mons. Pierre entered, and dismissed Jacques with a nod before addressing me, then carefully closed the door and turned the key in the lock.

"Are you quite ready to be introduced to Mrs. Barnforth?" he asked, with no small amount of elation in both voice and manner.

I could only bow my head in assent, for I was far too excited to speak. Until that moment I had not fully realised how momentous was the undertaking. But the strange little model maker was himself too much engrossed to notice any agitation on my part. He did not see that my hands were gripped tightly together as he unlocked the door of the long centre cupboard, nor that my eyes were following his movements with a wild feverish glare. When the door swung back and he triumphantly drew forth the model of—nay, I should rather say the true Hester Barnforth, I started backwards with an exclamation on my lips. So natural and life-like was the figure before me which was, and yet was not, myself. The dress was perfect in every detail, even to the muslin cap and long streamers. It only seemed strange and uncanny that the woman did not speak or heed our presence—that was the only thing to mark the difference between us. As I watched the mute, senseless figure I began to realise that perhaps the absence of these very qualities might also aid me in carrying out my plans still more successfully, and thus I conceived the idea of feigning deafness, and I believe in the end it will turn out to be one of the best cards I hold in my hand.

I think Mons. Pierre must have guessed that some such thoughts were passing through my mind; for when I at last recalled myself to the duties on hand, he led me away from the figure and placed me in a chair as gently as my father might have done. But not for fully a minute did he speak to me.

"I see you are satisfied," he said at last; "and all I can say is, 'God prosper you,' for I'm sure you deserve it."

I can hardly tell you what I answered, for I really felt excited and overstrained.

Then commenced the making-up process, after which he left me to change my dress. I had not thought about a shawl and bonnet being required but he had, and brought them to me.

"Mons Pierre, I should not know myself," I said, when he came in.

"We'll see if somebody else knows you then," he

replied, laughingly, "I will open the side door for you very quietly, and let you out. Return in a minute's time and ring the bell. Jacques shall admit you, he will think you are still with me, and have no suspicion. Do you agree, Mrs. Barnforth?"

Again I shrank nervously.

"Better to get accustomed to it at once," he said kindly, noticing the movement. Of course I assented to the experiment, and a couple of minutes later Jacques ushered me in and requested me to wait while he acquainted his master with my visit. He did not recognise me even when I stood in the little room with the light full upon me, and I already felt my courage rapidly rising.

"Come, Jacques, give Mrs. Barnforth your hand, and wish her good luck, you were talking fast enough to her a short time ago."

Again the broad smile illumined Jacques' whole face as he looked from one to the other of us. "I didn't guess," he said, "but the master is clever, Miss!" and he looked across at him with a world of pride in his eyes, as he spoke.

I held out my hand towards him, and whispered in his ear, "ask him to let me see little Master Dick!"

For a moment he hesitated as though about to refuse, but the next I heard him say, "The lady would like to see Master Dick, sir, if you don't mind, and please don't be angry with me for telling her about him. I forgot as I was letting my tongue run on so."

"Yes, Monsieur. I hope you will not blame Jacques," I said, stepping forward, "it was I who led him on to speak of you—not from curiosity but interest."

"Do not apologise," he replied. "I do not wonder at Jacques talking to you, though I have never known him do such a thing before, and if you take an interest in my little child you may certainly see him."

I could not repress an exclamation of astonishment when little Dick stood before me. I almost doubted whether Jacques had not deceived me, and instinctively laid my hand upon the face to convince myself that the child was not real flesh and blood. The little wig maker sat with it upon his knee, a fond look of admiration stamped upon his face, and beaming in his eyes. It was almost pitiful to see the little old man, pressing his waxen treasure to his heart, and I turned to go.

"Thank you," I said. "May I come and see you and Master Dick some other time, when I hope this masquerade will have served its purpose, and I can tell you what it has accomplished?"

"Yes! Yes! Come again," he repeated, "we shall be glad to see you, shan't we Dick?" and he patted the little waxen face as he spoke, and bent his head, as though listening for a reply.

I turned away with an aching sensation at my heart, and walked to the door with Jacques. The cab which had been sent away was not in sight. As we waited, I asked him, "Why does your master advertise as if he were a foreigner?"

"Oh, because Miss, English people would rather tell their secrets to a foreigner; they feel as if they were safer, I suppose, at least we always find it so."

I was about to say, "But they must discover that he is an Englishman," when the cab came bowling along, and Jacques ran into the shop to fetch my travelling bag.

I turned to take one last look at the old man. He still remained seated, with the child upon his knee, but he had placed the little arms around his neck, and I could just see the long golden curls straying amongst his own grisly locks. Softly I stole away again, rather than bring his thoughts back again to the sordid cares of earth. As I waved an adieu to Jacques, I determined that should I return in safety to London, my first attempt would be to bring a glow of rosy health into his poor pale cheeks and languid eyes.

"And now, Laura mine, you know the rest, and how far my mission has succeeded. I must set about making my toilet at once, so you may look forward to becoming initiated in the mysteries of making up."

"But Mary!" protested Lady Laura, "I dare not let you run this risk for me—it is impossible," and she buried her face in uncontrollable agitation.

"Not another word," said Miss Haldane, peremptorily. "I have already excited you too much, and I am not going to answer any more questions. I shall want your assistance, perhaps, to-morrow, so prepare yourself for whatever may be required."

Half-an-hour afterwards, Lady Laura and Hester Barnforth were both sleeping the sleep of exhaustion, ready to take up their separate *roles* on the morrow, and to act their parts in the great drama of life.

CHAPTER XXIV

HESTER BARNFORTH OVERHEARS A CONVERSATION.

"THERE is one condition I wish to impose upon you Mary," said Lady Laura, the following day. "Do not on any account seek aid from Hugh Penwood. Of Ashley, you may ask any questions you may think advisable, but even him you must bind to strict secrecy."

Miss Haldane's face wore a look of perplexity, but she at once assured her sister that her wishes should be respected.

As if divining her thoughts, Lady Laura went on to explain the reason for her request. "I can't help feeling that in some way or other Penwood will be the means of bringing further trouble upon us, and I shrink from the mere mention of his name. It is foolish and inexplicable, but perhaps I am nervous, and I know you will bear patiently with me, Mary."

But Mary's only answer was to point to the door and place her finger upon her lips. Almost instantly some one knocked, and in answer to Lady Laura's "Come in," Miss Fairbairn entered, clad in a gorgeous morning robe composed of crimson satin plentifully adorned with costly lace. The new maid was busily employed in setting the room to rights, and Mathilde, as she glanced at her, thought she looked even more stolid and stony than on the previous day.

"How do you like her?" asked Mathilde, with a nod in Hester Barnforth's direction.

Lady Laura gave a sneering, impassive sort of smile as she answered, "I don't suppose it would make any difference whether I liked or disliked her."

Mathilde laughed, and walked across the room to where the maid was employed, and touched her on the shoulder. The maid ceased her work and turned towards her, dropping a courtesy as she did so.

"Do you wish to remain here?" shouted Mathilde at the top of her voice, and after a second's hesitation Hester found her tongue, and answered, "If you please, Miss!"

Mathilde made no further remark to her, but as she prepared to depart, told Lady Laura that such a creature was a treasure, as she could not and did not expect people to be at the tronble of talking to her.

Acting upon Lady Laura's instructions, Mary stole quietly into the library soon after seven o'clock in the evening, and had the satisfaction of finding Jess Cameron waiting outside in the hope of seeing her benefactress. Giving her a letter, written during the day to Mr. Dallas, Mary arranged for her to return with the reply as soon as it should arrive.

As Miss Haldane was returning to her own department, the sound of voices talking in subdued tones led her to retrace her steps as far as the great entrance-hall, from which the sounds proceeded. It was like a large square room, and, indeed, was used as such. The tiled floor was almost covered with rugs of various descriptions, and a cheery fire was always burning, beside which were placed comfortable chairs and lounges. The candles had not been lighted, and the ruddy flames alone cast their glow around. As Mary approached gradually nearer she discovered that the voices were those of Sir Peter and his niece.

Sheltering herself behind a large screen, placed to keep off the draughts, she was safe from discovery, unless the servants should enter with lights, and even then she had an excuse, for in her hand she carried a small salver holding a glass of milk, which she would pretend to be carrying upstairs to her mistress.

"Are you sure of winning this election?" Mathilde was asking her uncle.

"Oh, not a doubt of it," he replied; "and if I could only see you Lady St. Kestor I should be satisfied. You've never smitten anyone so far before, and it's a shame you shouldn't win now, for you are not so young as you once were, Matilda."

"You need not remind me of that, uncle," Mathilde remonstrated petulantly. "I tell you I'm determined to win this time, if only because I love him! Only this very day I asked him if he would make me his wife were he free to do so, and he promised me with a sacred vow. I also asked him," and she lowered her voice almost to a whisper, "why he did not find a means of setting himself free. I suggested to him—driving her into the streets—cruelty—desertion; and if those did not answer, locking her up in an asylum for life. But he is too great a coward, and said that he should always live in fear, or some such nonsense!"

"And have you given it up then?" asked Sir Peter, in slightly mocking tones.

"You little know me if you ask me such a question," was the answer, given in a voice ominous of the dark mood of the speaker.

The silent listener trembled as she heard it, and the salver in her hand shook so that she could scarcely hold it safely.

The cruel voice continued—"I told you a short time since that I only wanted your co-operation for my scheme to succeed. Three times I have adminstered the spirit you professed would stupefy and kill."

"Hush! My dear girl, how incautious you are!" Sir Peter interrupted. "How do you know that some of the fellows may not be lurking about!"

"Well, I'm pretty sure they are not," she answered. "Perhaps I was incautions, but if I thought you had been tricking me I should feel inclined to kill you too," and though she finished with a laugh, still it was a laugh in which there was no music.

"Come, come Mathilde!" said Sir Peter, and his tone sounded almost like a coaxing one.

"Why should I trick you? It's not likely. If my lady had swallowed the doses as she ought to have done, they would have done their duty and told no tales. But we'll have another bottle, and you shall try again. You'll have a good opportunity next week, for I and your love will have to be off on our electioneering expedition. You know, my lass, you can easily send him a telegram if anything should happen to her ladyship at all sudden."

A cold perspiration broke out in heavy drops upon the listener's brow, and something seemed to be steeping her very senses in oblivion; her eyes closed, and an involuntary shudder crept over her from head to foot. With a tremendous effort she nerved herself to listen for the rest of the conversation. At the next words she leaned slightly forward, with parted lips and wild dilated eyes.

"How much longer does Hardress intend keeping the children at the Orphanage?" Mathilde was saying. "I never thought she would remain an hour here after discovering they were gone; but, as it happens, it exactly falls in with my plans that she has done so."

"I shall advise him to let them be brought here again under the care of a governess as soon as the coast is clear," Sir Peter answered.

There was a faint sound from behind the screen, but before either had time to speak the new nurse appeared and slowly ascended the stairs, apparently not having noticed the two figures standing by the fire.

"Who the devil is that strange woman," ejaculated Sir Peter: "she is as stealthy as a cat."

"That is Mrs. Barnforth, the woman I spoke to

you about yesterday," Mathilde answered, "and Hester Barnforth is the woman who must administer my lady's next dose of physic. She's stone deaf, stupid as an ass, and obstinate as a mule. Chance did not send Hester Barnforth to Craig-Feldie and to me for nothing."

Perhaps Miss Fairbairn would have expressed some astonishment could she have seen how swiftly and lightly the stolid nurse flew along the corridor with panting breath, until she reached the room set apart for her.

Upon no account must she let Lady Laura dream of the danger threatening her. The only plan that remained was to get her away from Craig-Feldie immediately, and rescue the children from the Orphanage by stealing a march upon the enemy.

CHAPTER XXV

A THREATENED STORM.

THREE months have passed away; months fraught with suspense and anxiety of the most intense description; months which have set their mark upon Lady Laura with cruel distinctness, bringing lines of care upon the pale pure face and sprinkling the red-gold tresses with many a silver thread.

The scene has changed to the season of fair spring-time. The trees have already put forth their verdant buds, which later will burst into leaf. The modest violets and the drooping snowdrops have smiled their welcome, and the garden surrounding a neat little cottage residence on the bank of the Thames is gorgeous with golden daffodils.

In this cottage Lady Laura, Miss Haldane, and the two children have been located for the last three months, and their only factotum, except Simmonds, is Jess Cameron, whom Lady Laura has never ceased to befriend.

Upon the day in question the ladies were seated in their *bijou* drawing room, the two children at play on the hearthrug. Miss Haldane is busy sewing a child's garment, but her sister makes no pretence at employment; her eyes wander wistfully to the window, and with restless fingers she toys with the slender watch-chain suspended from her neck.

For some little time Miss Haldane pursued her work, pretending not to heed her sister's restlessness, but a long drawn sigh at length caused her to lay it it aside. "He is sure to be here directly, Laura," she said in her old cheery style; "don't be down-hearted, dear. Why here he comes." she exclaimed, rising from her seat as an imperative knock sounded on the door.

The next minute Ashley Dallas entered the little room, lowering his head to prevent it coming in contact with the globes of the chandelier. Lady Laura's hands were trembling as she held them towards him, and he noticed how thin, and yet how feverish they felt as he held them for a moment within his own. He noticed too how agitated she was, and immediately proceeded to give her time to recover her composure. Barbara and Archie were soon seated opposite to each other on his knees, and a box of bon-bons produced the desired effect of cementing their liking for him still more firmly.

"We must ask mother and auntie to have one, must we not?" he said, as they slipped down from their exalted positions to resume the interrupted castle building on the carpet. "Never mind, you shall keep those entirely for yourselves, I think I can find some for auntie," and he tapped his pocket and caused the children to roar with laughter at one of his droll grimaces as he spoke.

"Still keep your old *penchant* Ashley," laughed Miss Haldane as he handed her his little casket.

For reply he drew out one of the fantastic golden bars and held it before her. "When this has disappeared, I shall be a man of business! And now fair cousin," addressing Lady Laura, "I am here in response to your summons. What may I do for you?"

Lady Laura's voice trembled somewhat as she spoke. "It is so good of you to give up your time to me as you have done. You are our only friend, and I would not have you think me ungrateful for all your advice in the past. But, Ashley, I feel that this life is killing me. The worry and suspense are more than I can bear. Every knock upon the door, or footstep upon the gravel, makes my heart throb almost to choking. My sleep is haunted by terrible dreams, and every waking moment by the same terrible fear. Have I no redress? no chance of keeping my children save in this life of concealment? You told me when I first came here that I could only appeal to the law, and I have almost resolved to throw myself upon its mercy. They cannot in justice refuse my plea!"

As Ashley Dallas listened to her words, he slowly shook his head, and a look of pity stole into his merry blue eyes. His hearers little guessed the effort that it cost him to frame the answer he was compelled to give.

"My dear cousin, you spoke just now of pity and justice, but, alas, that I should have to say it, the cruelty and injustice of the law with regard to the custody and guardianship of the children of a married pair have long been acknowledged by all thoughtful men and women. The father alone has the absolute legal right to deal with his children; the mother has no legal status, no choice, no voice, lot or part in the matter. If you are rich enough to appeal to the Superior Courts, and you can prove such gross and scandalous misconduct on the part of the father towards the children as to disqualify him, and such misconduct on his part towards yourself as to legally entitle you to a separation, under these circumstances the Court might give you the custody of the children until they are sixteen. I know that as regards yourself, the plea of cruelty alone might entitle you to a separation, but could you bring forward such a charge regarding the children?"

Mr. Dallas awaited his cousin's reply, and Miss Haldane looked up inquiringly from her sewing, which she had resumed at the beginning of the conversation.

"No! I could not plead that against him, except in separating them from me," she answered despairingly.

Mr. Dallas shrugged his shoulders expressively. "Unfortunately, cousin Laura, the law gives him the privilege of doing so, for though the Act of 1857, which established the Court of Divorce, and Matrimonial Causes, gave a very large discretion to that

Court, in providing for the custody of children, still the construction which the courts place upon the Act of 1873 by failing to recognise the claims of mothers, and in constantly preferring the father, is still productive of injury to the children."

Lady Laura's head sank still lower upon her breast, and her hands, which had been lying loosely on her lap, suddenly locked themselves tightly together. "And is it possible, then, that a mother's rights are *nil* ?" Her voice had grown strained and husky as she put the question.

Mr. Dallas glanced across at her with a look of surprise, as he replied, "Well, you have at any rate quoted the exact words of one of our judges. But I am afraid that even as yet you have not comprehended the worst aspect of the subject."

Again Lady Laura's locked fingers nervously interlaced each other in restless agitation as she leaned slightly forward.

A shout of merriment burst from the children's lips as their castle suddenly fell to the ground, and both simultaneously rushed to climb upon cousin Ashley's knee.

"Go and play with Simmonds for a little while, will you ?" said Miss Haldane, rising and beckoning to them to follow her from the room.

Barbara's pretty red lips closed in an angry pout as she clung still closer to Ashley, and Archie, who invariably folllowed the example of his sister, began to rub his eyes with two chubby dimpled hands. But something whispered into their two little ears followed by another *bon-bon*, had the desired effect of sending them trotting off hand-in-hand in search of Simmonds or Jess Cameron to whom they had become sincerely attached. No sooner had the door closed upon their retreating forms than Lady Laura renewed the conversation at the point where it had broken off—

"You said—I had not—comprehended—the worst; then—let me hear it at once!"

She jerked out her words in broken gasps, It was evident to her sister and her cousin how frightfully she was suffering; so Ashley hastened his explanation to save her from further suspense.

" I was referring to the matter of guardians rather than the father," he commenced. " The law invests him with the power to appoint by will any guardian or guardians whom he pleases for his children, passing over the mother altogether, and against such guardians, the mother has no legal rights. And here, again, to prove that I am correct, I may also repeat to you a statement made by a certain Lord Justice, in reference to a particular case, he said: 'When this case was before me, in the autumn, I had considerable reason to believe that there was much misapprehension in the mind of the mother as to her rights as a mother; and I thought it necessary to explain that in point of view she has no right to control the power of the testamentary guardian. It is proper that mothers of children thus circumstanced should know that they have no right as such to interfere with testamentary guardians.'"

It was Miss Haldane who put the next question, and she, too, spoke in strangely agitated tones. "And supposing the father does not appoint a testamentary guardian, what then? Do our noble legislators permit the mother to assume the position?"

For an instant Mr. Dallas hesitated before replying, and both women looked at him with a curious interest in their gaze.

"Yes, the law then condescends to recognise the mother whom it interests with a limited share of parental power and authority. She is, *only then*, spoken of as guardian by *nature and nurture*. But she can make no provision for the guardianship of her children in the event of her own death, unless previously enabled by her husband to do so. And even when guardian by nature and nurture, if she does not bring up her children in the religious belief of her deceased husband, she is at the mercy of third persons, who may apply to the Courts for the appointment of a joint guardian with power to compel her to do so, or for the removal of the children altogether from her custody."

Both ladies remained thoughtful for a minute or two after the explanation, but Lady Laura was the first to break the silence. "I do not think for one moment that Hardress would avail himself of such a privilege as that," she said, without the slightest shadow of doubt in her tones.

"But there is still the possibility," suggested Mr. Dallas.

"I am afraid," broke in Miss Haldane, "that Ashley has clearly proved that your only chance lies in your remaining in exile, and I think for security's sake we had better leave England as soon as possible and settle in some remote part of France—what do you advise, Ashley?"

"I think it would be a good plan," he replied.

"Have you heard or seen anything of Hardress since you were last here?" timidly asked Lady Laura.

"I haven't seen him since the day that I hurled the steward's books at his head, and informed him that I felt myself disgraced at ever having served such a cowardly scoundrel. I suppose he gave it out at St. Kestor that you are remaining behind with the children on account of Archie's health. But the village folk have an idea that there's something wrong somewhere, and resent Miss Fairbairn's presence entirely. Some of them were positively uncivil to her when she tried to enact the Lady Bountiful amongst them."

Lady Laura started suddenly from her chair and stood erect before them, a bright pink flush lighting the pallor of her face. "Miss Fairbairn there! at St. Kestor!" she repeated in a half-dazed fashion. "Do you tell me that *she* is *there*?"

Mr. Dallas looked in bewilderment from one to the other. "Now I've gone and put my foot in it, haven't I?" he said, addressing Miss Haldane, with an appealing look.

His embarrassment was so evidently genuine that

she could not suppress a faint smile as she watched him. " I suppose there—there is—perhaps a reason for her being there," she suggested.

Ashley caught as the suggestion eagerly. " Of course, of course ! " and he flashed a relieved look of thankfulness at her as he spoke. " It's the election business. Sir Hardress nominated Sir Peter for Exeter; then off they bolted to the place where Sir Hardress's election was to come on, and they left Miss Fairbairn at St. Kestor."

" But the elections are over now. I saw from the papers they had both been successful," Lady Laura replied. "And *she* is at St. Kestor," the exiled wife repeated, as if to herself. " And I am the only obstacle which prevents her reigning there as mistress."

Miss Haldane involuntarily shuddered as she thought how very nearly that obstacle had been removed, and that the plans had actually been laid, but she kept her thoughts to herself, and turned from the subject by inviting Mr. Dallas to partake of high tea, then in course of preparation.

It was not much later than five o'clock, but the afternoon appeared unusually dull.

Ashley glanced at his watch, then strode to the window. " By Jove, we are in for a storm, I believe," he said.

The clouds were low and inky black; not a speck of blue sky was visible.

"Yes, there's a storm brewing," affirmed Miss Haldane, who had joined him at the window; but not one of them guessed that the omen portended the bursting of the terrific domestic storm which so shortly fell upon them.

CHAPTER XXVI.

THE STORM BURSTS.

IT was not until six o'clock had chimed that the storm broke with a terrible force, wrecking its pent up fury, in loud crashes of thunder, which pealed and reverberated, until even the most courageous were awed by its intensity. Again and again the blue forked flame darted from out the dark vapoury masses and played hide and seek amongst the trees in a weird fantastic fashion, and seemed to pierce every corner of the house with its leaping fiery tongue. The rain poured in torrents, intermingled with a shower of hailstones which pattered upon the windows in a sort of pebble chorus. It was not only unusual for such a storm to occur at that period of year, but it was also a storm of unusual, nay unparalleled severity—at any rate in the remembrance of any of the inmates of the cottage.

Tea was scarcely concluded, when the ominous sound first greeted their ears, but Miss Haldane, ever thoughtful for others, had left the table to seek Jess and Simmonds to bring them into the drawing-room while the storm continued. She found them both huddled in corners with their aprons thrown over their heads and faces, to shut out, as far as possible, both sight and sound.

The storm had continued with unabated fury for fully five minutes, when an exclamation from Miss Haldane suddenly diverted Mr. Dallas from his contemplation of the elementary disturbances. "Oh! My sister!"

Lady Laura lay back in an easy chair, but in an attitude of apparent rigidity, while her face was blanched almost to the hue of death, and her blue eyes were fixed with a terrible unseeing stare.

"What ails you, Laura? Oh speak to us," entreated Miss Haldane, as she knelt before her, chafing her limp cold hands within her own. There was no response, no sign that she even heard the words; but still the eyes were searching as if into far unseen space, with a glance that never failed or faltered.

"What can be the meaning of it!" Mary asked as she appealed again to Ashley in almost wild distress, while, he, too, leaned over and placed his hand upon the brow which was cold as marble.

"Send one of the women for some brandy, and let them get the children out of the way. It's only the effect of the storm; she'll be right again directly," and so Ashley administered comfort as best he could, though his grave looks very much belied his words.

Pouring the stimulant, which Jess had brought, into a small phial, he was about to place it to her lips when his action was arrested by Lady Laura waving him peremptorily back. Taking a firm hold of her sister's arm and slightly lowering her head, but still without removing her eyes from their fixed position, the two agitated watchers beside her, saw her lips move as if with difficulty, and then, in an unnatural and solemn voice, the one word " Wait ! " fell from her lips.

By this time the colour had receded from Miss Haldane's face until its pallor almost equalled that of her sister's.

A minute later Lady Laura rose from her chair, but still without heeding their presence, except to gently push them aside as they impeded her progress towards the window. In silence and suspense they watched her, the spell which held her under its magic influence seemed to have fallen over them also, and they waited for results.

As she stood before the uncurtained window, the lightning which appeared to grow more vivid with every recurring flash, played around her and enveloped her in its steely light until Mary shuddered, and covered her face with her hands.

As Mr. Dallas was again about to persuade her to leave her dangerous position, she voluntarily turned and faced them. The unnatural expression had faded from her eyes, but the appearance left behind was like that of some one who had been rudely awakened from profound slumber and had scarcely realised consciousness of external surroundings. Once or twice she passed her fingers slowly across her forehead as if trying to recall some forgotten incident or to collect her wandering thoughts.

When she at length spoke all the music and the hope seemed to have died out of her voice, without leaving even an echo of its old familiar tone. "It is no use to talk of escape now," she said; "the knell has sounded which is to tear my children away from me. I have seen something—I don't know what; I have heard something which I cannot remember; but it is coming—coming! Before the storm has passed, it will have arrived—the intangible something which I cannot name or describe."

Mr. Dallas and Miss Haldane looked at each other with the same unspoken fears in their hearts and gleaming in their eyes. Lady Laura was pointing with an upraised forefinger towards the window. Again a deafening peal of thunder, which seemed to shake the house to its foundations, boomed forth like a battery of artillery, The panes of the window were blurred by the rain, which dashed against them in great defiant drops. Again the heavy dark massed clouds were rent apart as if a yawning chasm loomed above the watery earth, and from its mouth issued forth the myriad-tongued fiery darts of living flame, with zig-zag lines and points that pierced the overhanging gloom. But the cry which rose from Lady Laura's lips was not the outcome of terror at the storm.

The lightning played upon and lighted up the face of a pallid and weird-looking figure, tall and slender, with large dark eyes, and long black hair. The figure was clad in a frock coat, and a soft felt hat, suggestive of clerical attire. As he passed the window, he was followed by a second figure, also the figure of a man, at sight of whom Lady Laura covered her eyes with both her hands, and with a moan of anguish fell back into the chair which she had so recently vacated.

The figure of the man who had risen as it were, a vision from the storm and stood before them in garments thoroughly saturated, and from which the rain was falling in glistening drops, was Hugh Penwood, while the person by whom he was followed was no other than Sir Hardress St. Kestor!

CHAPTER XXVII.

HUGH PENWOOD'S SECOND EXPERIMENT

LADY St. Kestor's prediction was certainly fulfilled in a most remarkable manner, when a minute later the unexpected visitors were ushered into their presence, or rather, when they made their entrance into the little room, for Sir Hardress did not wait any announcement of his arrival after gaining admittance.

It was certainly a most awkward predicament for all concerned. Sir Hardress and his wife could only meet as openly avowed enemies, and Miss Haldane had not seen him since her departure from St. Kestor some months previously, and was, of course, espousing her sister's cause against him, while his cousin, Ashley Dallas, had sought him out for the purpose of heaping upon him the most opprobious epithets which he deemed his conduct to deserve.

But Hugh Penwood's appearance upon the scene was not understood by anyone save Lady St. Kestor, who read in it the realisation of the fateful dread which she had experienced when she first sought to bar the doors of St. Kestor against him. It was upon him that she directed her attention, noting his dishevelled hair and haggard almost wild appearance.

Heeding no other presence, in spite of the restraining hand which Sir Hardress laid upon him, Penwood pursued his way until he halted before Lady Laura, and, with a deferential bow, laid upon her knee a soiled gray glove, which she instantly recognised as belonging to herself.

As Sir Hardress watched this bit of by-play, he gave vent to an ill-timed laugh. "Now, Penwood, it's time to cast that foolery aside," he broke in. "You have served my purpose, and now I've no further need of you."

The sudden manner in which Hugh Penwood staggered backwards, and fixed a wild inquiring gaze upon the speaker's face, was sufficient evidence that his share in the transaction was a blind and ignorant one.

"But the glove!" he gasped, pointing to the delicate little piece of soiled kid which still lay upon Lady Laura's lap where he had so reverently placed it. "What was it you said?" He clasped his hands upon his head with an almost frantic gesture. "Did you not say that she would—would—take my hand within her own, and thank me for restoring her lost property? Yes! that was it, but see!—she does not touch me, she does not thank me!"

Again Sir Hardress laughed a cruel sneering laugh. "Why don't you thank Mr. Penwood for the service rendered to you, eh Laura? He will think you have no gratitude."

Now that the crisis, which Lady Laura had foretold with such intense agitation so shortly before, had really arrived, she appeared to be fully equal to meet and cope with it. Not a trace of her previous terror remained, there was no shrinking or timidity perceptible as in response to her husband's words she rose and confronted Hugh Penwood. Pointing to the glove, which now lay at her feet between them, she said, in accents of mingled scorn and indignation, "Take back your ignoble trophy, Hugh Penwood, and cast it in the face of the man who has tricked you and used you as the tool by which he meant to secure his victim. Unwittingly, perhaps, you have been the means of placing me in the power of an anglicised Legree—of a thief who robs a helpless woman of her own flesh and blood. You have hunted me down, and brought him to the nest where my little ones are sheltered. You have ruined my life! Go!"

The eloquence, the despair, the contempt which she had thrown into the words held each one silent, and as her voice faltered and died almost to a whisper, a low agonised moan fell from the lips of Hugh Penwood. Perhaps it was the sound of it which roused the new energy within her, for her voice again rose high and clear, "From the first moment that I saw your face I shrank from you."

Hugh Penwood winced at this open declaration, but if Lady Laura saw it, she never heeded it, but continued as before. "Even then I felt the shadow of the influence fall across me, which you were to exert so fatally upon me. I tried to shun you, but

Fate would have you do your work. Now go, lest I should be tempted to curse you—go, and never let me look upon your face again!"

Sir Hardress had not sought to interrupt his wife, for the simple reason that so long as her reproaches were not directed against himself, he rather enjoyed the discomfiture than otherwise, and allowed Hugh Penwood to pass from the room with a nonchalant, "I'll join you directly. Ask the servants to give you some brandy, that is if they possess such commodities in this benighted hole," looking around contemptuously.

But Hugh Penwood was like a man walking in a dream, and it was questionable whether he was actually conscious of the fact that Sir Hardress was addressing him. As he reached the door, Mr. Dallas rose, and linking his arm within his own led him from the room.

"And now, madame," commenced Sir Hardress, scarcely waiting for the closing of the door, "I will proceed to business. You have enacted the *rôle* of leading lady quite long enough in this little comedy-drama, for, upon my word, your mock heroics are just about the richest I have ever witnessed. But I think you have occupied the boards long enough, so you had better come down from your pedestal of ranting sentiment."

Lady Laura, so far, listened in silence, and though Miss Haldane had to bite her lips to keep the words from rushing out, she felt that the time had not yet arrived for her to speak.

"I'll teach you and your sister, too, who I suspect has led you into this fool's mess, what are the consequences of trying to thwart or defy me! I warned her once what the result would be; now she shall keep you, provide for you, and be branded with conniving at your shame and disgrace. Never shall you darken my doors again; from this moment I cast you off for ever!"

In her indignation Mary Haldane rose to defend her sister from his wrath, but Lady Laura silenced her, and faced her husband as fearlessly as she had previously faced Hugh Penwood.

"Shame upon you for the coward that you are, Sir Hardress St. Kestor," she answered him. The delicate pink which had risen to her cheeks had turned to richest crimson, and the gentle blue eyes flamed and sparkled with a light such as had never kindled there before. "Your threats are idle ones, and I defy you to carry them out. You may do your best, or rather your worst, to separate my children from me, but where they go I will go, even to returning to St. Kestor. I am your lawful wife, and until I have forfeited my right to that title my place is in your home, and you cannot thrust me from it. I have feared you too long, but that is over now! I will fight for my children to the bitter end, bearing your insults and brutality as best I can, if by so doing I can remain beside them. You may kill me at last, but then only will you succeed in separating us."

Sir Hardress's face had gradually been growing whiter with suppressed rage; if hatred could have killed at that moment, she would have fallen a corpse before him.

Lady Laura thought he would attempt to strike her, as he had done before, when she had dared to refute his statements, but the blow which he had prepared fell with far greater weight and force upon her than any physical blow could have done. "I will drag you through the mire of the divorce court," he said, fixing her with a menacing look; "I will swear that I followed one of your guilty lovers to the house in which you had hidden yourself for the purpose of receiving his secret visits, and I will also swear that I found my own cousin, Ashley Dallas, with you, after I had discharged him from my house in consequence of a quarrel concerning you."

Lady Laura's eyes opened wider and wider with amazement and horror. "You would never dare do such a thing! You could not prove your vile accusations." Her voice had suddenly grown hoarse and strained; her imagination had never conjured any thing half so terrible as this. She trembled from head to foot, and grasped the back of a slender chair for support.

Miss Haldane rose and placed her arm around the agitated woman.

"You would have to explain his presence here," Sir Hardress explained, without an atom of pity.

"My sister could easily explain that he was simply here in his professional capacity," Mary replied.

"Pshaw! what would that go for? No, she'll have to invent a better explanation than that to satisfy common sense practical men, or a British jury."

"I think I could give them a thoroughly satisfactorp explanation of my presence beneath this roof if it were required, and to you, too, if Miss Haldane will allow me." It was Mr. Dallas who spoke, having returned to the room in time to hear the remarks concerning himself.

A contemptuous smile curved Sir Hardress's lips as Ashley advanced. "I don't discuss my domestic affairs with an eavesdropper," he drawled out, coolly turning his back upon him, and helping himself to one of his favourite cigarettes, "and I decline to listen to any explanations from you."

"But you shall listen to my explanation," thundered Ashley, crossing over to where he stood, "whether you like it or not!"

"Really, I should advise you to refresh yourself with a little of your barley sugar, for you are anything but *sweet* in your present mood. I daresay you have been playing the part of mentor to the lady who calls herself my wife, but platonic cousinship never goes down in a court of law, you know!"

Ashley cast a quick look of assurance at the two ladies before replying to his cousin's repellant sarcasm. "I should be ashamed to retaliate with pleasantries such as you adopt," he said, "before the lady whom I hope soon to make my wife, the lady to whom my visits here are addressed. Under more favourable circumstances I should have acquainted you with my desire to wed your sister-in-law, Miss Haldane."

As he concluded he raised Miss Haldane's hand to his lips with a reassuring pressure and a murmured " Forgive me," in an impassioned undertone, and Miss Haldane, acting with her usual ready wit, took her cue from Mr. Dallas.

"Will not Sir Hardress congratulate me?" she asked; and neither her impromptu lover nor her sister could detect, from her tone or manner, whether she intended to propitiate him or goad him still further by sarcasm.

When Sir Hardress raised his head to reply, they all noticed that his face had grown strangely livid and distorted, and the contemptuous smile, which he flashed at his cousin was wan and sickly, as though robbed of the meaning which he had intended it to convey.

"I wish you as good luck with your wife as I've had with mine, old fellow!" he murmured. But his voice was unsteady, and the mirthless laugh which accompanied the words died at its very birth.

"Let the children be prepared for departing with me at once," he commanded, with an assumption of his old tyranny.

"Oh, no, Hardress, not to night," interposed Lady Laura, rushing to arrest his hand, as he laid it upon the bell.

"Yes, this very night, without delay," he repeated, endeavouring to push her aside.

Simmonds replied to the summons, her face disfigured by weeping, and afterwards backed out of the room with her apron raised to her streaming eyes.

"Then I depart with you also," Lady St. Kestor asserted in decisive tones.

She had almost reached the door when her husband, by a rapid movement, placed himself in front of her, and flung out his arm to bar her progress. But the impulsive action, with the intense excitement, by which it was accompanied, fulfilled a far different object from the one intended. With a low moan, Sir Hardress slid to the ground.

In an instant Lady Laura was beside him with his head pillowed upon her knee. An ashen gray tint had over spread his face, and a faint blue line had crept around his lips. Ashley laid his hand upon his heart, but if it had not ceased to beat it beat so faintly that he could not discern it.

In hot haste Jess was despatched for a physician who resided but a short distance beyond the cottage, and who fortunately arrived a few minutes later. Between them they carried Sir Hardress to the couch, and forced a spoon containing brandy between the colourless lips and close set teeth. "Better not trouble him further," said the physician gravely. "It's nearly over!"

The ill-used, sorely tried wife forgot her wrongs and kneeling beside him, with gentle touch laid a caressing hand upon his brow, where already the death dews were gathering thick and fast.

The dying man unclosed his eyes and let them rest upon her for a moment with a world of love shining in their depths.

The wife conveyed her forgiveness by a kiss of peace.

One word fell from his lips, ere they were sealed for ever. That word was the name of a woman. The name of the woman was MATHILDE!

The physician placed his hand over the eyes of his quondam patient. "Syncope," was the word he uttered to Ashley Dallas, when they were left alone together. "To a man of his temperament any shock meant sudden death; he must have suffered from heart disease for some years."

And in a darkened chamber, alone, lay the wife who was now a widow, and the name which she would hear ringing in her ears for many long days to come was "Mathilde."

CHAPTER XXVIII.

MASTER DICK.

IN spite of pain or death, or broken hearts, the wheel of life still revolves in even measure, the day dawns and the night falls, the sun shines as brightly and the moon sheds her radiance with serene indifference upon all mundane affairs. Once again Mary Haldane wended her way towards Melville Street and halted before the door of the perruquier's at 203. If anything the shop appeared gloomier and dingier than before, for the sun was streaming brightly upon the dusty panes, and glinting across the dusky switches of hair which had once been golden or raven, as the case might be before the long exposure and neglect had dulled and destroyed their luxuriance. As Miss Haldane opened the door, the clanging bell rang with a muffled sound, a sound which caused a chill presentiment to fall upon her. In response to the muffled summons, the door of the little office at the end of the shop was opened, and from the shelter of the dingy green blind Jacques emerged—Jacques with a face blotched and puffed and eyes red and swollen from copious weeping.

Miss Haldane advanced towards him—"Why Jacques, what is the matter? don't you remember me?"

For a second Jacques showed no sigh of recognition, then the remembrance suddenly flashed across him—"Oh, Miss, is it you?" he said, "the young lady that saw Master Dick. Well only to think that you should come again just now. Why the Master was only talking about you the other day," and he lifted a corner of his white slip to wipe away the great tears, which at the mention of his master's name had commenced to chase each other down his pallid cheeks.

"Won't you tell me what is wrong Jacques?" Mary asked.

"The shop'll never see the poor master any more Miss," Jacques managed to gasp between his sobs, "never till he's carried out of it in his coffin, and they may as well bury the models along with him for what use they'll ever be again."

"He is ill then," Mary said, as he paused for breath, "how long has it been Jacques?"

"Its near upon a month since he was first taken," he answered, "but he's only kept his bed a fortnight. I knew there was something going to happen by the way he kept on talking to Master Dick—oh it was cruel—it was cruel!"

Jacques seemed to take a morbid pleasure in thus soliloquising, and to have almost forgotten Mary's presence until by speaking she recalled him to himself.

"I had hoped the news that I was bringing to Mons. Pierre would have been very welcome to him, but I am afraid that I am too late."

For the first time the boy evinced a show of interest, he almost ceased sobbing, and fixed his lustreless eyes upon the speaker in mute enquiry.

"I came to tell him," Mary said, as if in answer to the mute but enquiring gaze fixed upon her, "that by his art and skill and advice, he enabled me to overcome a great wrong and avert a crime; that he was indirectly the means of restoring to a suffering mother the little children of whom she had been robbed."

Jacques eyes seemed to gradually regain their lustre, they opened to their fullest extent in wonderment and surprise as he listened. "You don't say so, Miss," he exclamed at length, "what wonderful news for the master after all these years, and so often as he's talked about his wasted life too!" and the tears again rolled down his face, but they seemed less bitter as if some of the sting had been taken out of them.

"Then you think he will be able to understand Jacques? dare I ask to be permitted to tell him myself?" and there was an expression of soft entreaty in Mary's eyes as she spoke.

"Oh, Miss, how can you ask?" Jacques answered, speaking with more animation than had perhaps ever been manifest in his voice before, "why he'd be only too delighted! Come this way," and he started at once to leave the shop.

"Wait a moment!" and Miss Haldane laid her hand upon his arm. "The surprise may be too sudden, had you not better prepare him for my visit?"

Jacques looked upon her in surprise, then shook his head with his usual slow and apparent indifference, "oh no!" he said "he would like you to go now, it will be alright!"

Mary followed somewhat reluctantly keeping at a safe distance until Jacques should have given some intimation of her presence.

The little bedroom was scrupulously clean and tidy, not an article of furniture was out of place, and the bed with its spotless white coverlet was not disarranged by a single fold or crease.

"She's come, sir," was Dick's introduction, "there's master. Dick s young lady brought you good news; can you listen to her, master?"

"I thought she'd come, my lad!"

It was the thin quavering voice of Mons. Pierre, and as he spoke one small shrivelled hand was withdrawn from its resting place and extended towards Miss Haldane.

In another instant it rested within her own in a long warm hand clasp, as with a start of surprise she once more gazed upon the perruquier. By some sudden transformation the little parchment-like face seemed to have become rejuvenated, the skin appeared so smooth and fair, and there was even a delicate tinge of pink in the cheeks which seemed to have lost their hollows in so wonderful a fashion.

The grey locks had changed to silver white, which lent a still more softened expression to the face, and the blue eyes shone with a brilliancy which could not have been excelled in the first flush of youth.

"Ay, I don't look much like a dying man," and Mons Pierre smiled as he read Mary's unspoken thoughts, and pointed to Jacques to place a chair for her by his side.

"But it is true, nevertheless," he continued, as Mary seated herself in the chair placed by Jacques.

"What is it?" she asked, in so low a tone that she scarcely heard the words herself.

"Paralysis, my dear!" Mons. Pierre answered, "it has me in a pretty tight grip already, save for my arms and a small portion of the upper part of my body I am a useless log. Thank God it has still left me consciousness and speech, indeed, I think my faculties have sharpened, as my limbs have lost their life, and I live over and over again the different scenes and events of my four score years and ten. I'm like the rest of the world, Miss, I can see now what I ought to have done and left undone—the errors and mistakes —now that it is too late!"

"Don't talk like that, Mons. Pierre," said Mary, giving the bony hand, which was still held within her own, a sympathetic pressure. "After all, this life is but the school of experience, we each learn our lessons and take our punishment, with now and then a prize thrown in. I came here to-day to tell you that the cause in which you so materially assisted me, which in fact might never have been won but for your art and skill, has not only brought happiness to a suffering woman's almost broken heart, but saved her from death, a death which would have rendered two tender little children, orphans."

There was a suspicious moisture in Mary's eyes, and a tremor in her voice as she spoke, for the look of joy which shone in the old man's eyes seemed to illumine his whole countenance, and their gaze seemed to have travelled beyond the confines of earth. He appeared to have forgotten Miss Haldane's presence, for with that far-off look in his eyes he repeated to himself several times in succession, " It's all right, Nita, my love. I've lived and waited a long time for it ; it has come at last. It has come at last." Then suddenly he turned his gaze upon Mary, and outstretched both feeble hands towards her. " May the old man's blessing be with you and yours, and rest with you for ever," he said, " that the great God will watch over and protect you both here and hereafter."

As his voice ceased, Mary bowed her head and pressed her lips upon the hands which still clasped hers. " God grant it may be so," she said, " and that when the toil of life is ended we may meet again."

" Amen," came in quick response from the old man's lips, but it was in a half whisper, as though life was already fast deserting him.

Mary looked up quickly into his face, and was startled at the sudden pallor which had come across it, but even as she looked the faint delicate tinge of colour stole back again into his cheeks, and his voice had regained its former strength when he next spoke.

"He's here, Miss, close beside me," he said, "poor little Dick, we are never parted now," and he indicated by a gesture that the waxen substitute of his lost child was indeed beside him. Yes, there was the outline of the little form beneath the bed-clothes. Turning down the white coverlet, Mary gazed once more upon the waxen features of Master Dick. Lying as it did upon the pillow with its long golden curls streaming carelessly around, the little model looked more real than ever. The large blue eyes with their somewhat heavily-fringed lashes might have been seeking their reflection in Mary's own as she leant over it; the lips, slightly parted, just showed the childish teeth. There was a pathetic expression about the face undefinable, yet perceptible. In life, one might have said that the constant companionship with none but the solitary old man had brought it there. The figure was clad in a boy's suit of somewhat rusty-looking blue velveteen with a holland pinaforte, and there were even creases in the velvet, and one little elbow had been patched as if worn with the wear and tear of every-day life; the pinafore had numerous creases also, and one fat dimpled hand was holding a leaden toy soldier. Mary almost shuddered as she turned away from its contemplation, it was such a mockery, this semblance of life; it seemed to her such an empty substitute for the reality of existence—a form which was the counterpart of life, yet which had never been inhabited for so much as a single moment with the spirit of life giving force: an empty soulless casket with nothing to gain and nothing to lose, no link to bind either to earth or to Heaven, even by so much as the common tie of a human affection.

"It's a shame to bury the little lad out of sight." Thus the old man broke in upon her reflections. "I always intended that we should be laid side by side at the last, but perhaps Nita would not like it, and he would have a friend in you."

Again the words jarred upon Mary Haldane's sensitiveness, but after all it was his mania, she told herself and she would humour him whatever he might ask of her.

"Yes!" he continued, "I leave my little Dick to you, Miss, if you will accept him. I would rather have seen him melt before my eyes than give him into anyone else's keeping, and I took such pains to have him perfect," and once more he fondled the dimpled hands and pressed his lips to the waxen cheeks; "and he's fully repaid me, Miss, for all the time and labour I spent over him. You talked about the children, little children; perhaps they won't object to my little Dick for a playmate—there's no vice about him," and he smiled a sad, weary smile, "and if you tell them that the old father fashioned him to fill up the gap left in his heart when his little son was taken away from him, they'll understand, for children have more sense and comprehension than many people will give them credit for."

"And you really wish me to have Master Dick?" Mary answered, wiping away the tears which there was no disguising or repressing. "It does seem strange how events come about, but I promise you, your treasure shall also be my treasure, I will guard him with the most precious care, but I trust that the time may be far distant when he must leave your keeping."

"Nay, nay, Miss, don't say that," Mons. Pierre exclaimed, "this helplessness is but like a living death. I pray and trust that my release may be soon at hand, I only crave for patience unto the end. There is one thing more I would like to ask of you, and yet I fear lest I ask too much." His voice sank lower, and a sadness crept into his eyes, but Mary was quick to re-assure him.

"Speak," she said; "don't pain me by any lack of trust. Only give me the opportunity of repaying you, if ever so slightly, for what you have done for me and mine."

He closed his eyes contentedly, and murmured so low that she could scarcely distinguish the words, "Poor Jacques! Will you give him a helping hand, and take a kindly interest in him? He's a good lad, a faithful lad, but he can't keep awake, and many masters would be less lenient with him than I have been. I don't think his span of life will be a very long one, Miss, but you'll find him faithful unto the end."

"Have no fear on Jacques's account, Mons. Pierre," Mary answered. "I had already thought of him, and his future welfare shall always be my consideration,"

T

"God bless you, Miss! If only he could have taken to the shop he might have done well, but it's no use, he hasn't the wits for it, he never could manage the models or the pigments, though I've tried to teach him the last few years."

"But something might be realized for him by the sale of the business, could it not?" Miss Haldane suggested.

"You see, Miss, it's the models," he explained. "We do very little else, all the rest is a mere blind, and we are out of date, behind the times, Jacques and I. No! The models must go—I've got some queer fancies, and I can't think of them falling into the hands of strangers."

Mary hesitated for a moment, and a warm flush suffused her face as she spoke. "It may seem presumptuous of me, Mons. Pierre, to set a value upon such works of art and ingenuity as your models, but I, like you, have queer fancies sometimes, and I can't bear to think of their destruction. Let me purchase them, the purchase money to be Jacques's patrimony. You won't refuse me, Monsieur?" she urged, as the old man made a dissentient gesture. "It is so little to ask, and yet so much."

"You are good, indeed," he said, once more detaining her hand within his own. "After all, my dear, I'm not a poor man, for I've earned the money fairly and spent but little, so poor Jacques will never come to want. I daren't have hinted that you should have my models, they would be a queer museum for you; but there, my dear young lady, if you will but honour me so far, why—they shall come along with little Dick. There is Nita, my pretty little Nita, Dick's mother, you know. Even Jacques has never set eyes upon her face. When the end comes, I'd like to have her laid against my breast, close to my heart; you'll tell them, won't you?"

Mary bowed her head in assent.

"Pass me the helmet from the mantel-piece, and you shall see my beautiful little Nita."

Mary rose and took from the mantel-shelf the helmet which he had spoken of. It appeared to be simply an ornament composed of some sort of plaster and fashioned in the shape of a helmet, but by pressing it upon a certain spot, the crown divided from the lower portion, and as Mons. Pierre drew forth a bust from its hiding place, a low cry of admiration fell from Mary's lips. It was only a small bust, almost a miniature, but fashioned so exquisitely, so perfect in every detail, and of such wondrous beauty that her exclamation was not to be wondered at. It represented a young girl, apparently not more than nineteen or twenty years of age, with every feature clearly and regularly cut. The eyes were of a deep violet hue, shaded by heavy drooping lashes; the eyebrows were classically arched, and the forehead, though somewhat low, was broad and well shaped, while a mass of soft golden curls fell over the temples in graceful profusion. The luxuriant golden hair was carelessly brushed from the nape of the neck and coiled Greek fashion at the back of the small head, which was poised so gracefully upon the swan-like throat and sloping shoulders. Everything about her seemed dainty, the tiny shell-like ears, the pouting rosy lips, even to the arch dimple in her chin. It scarcely seemed possible to Mary that a woman could have been so beautiful.

The old man watched her surprise and admiration with a gratified smile.

"It is almost too beautiful," she said, as their eyes met.

"And yet my poor skill could not do her justice,' he said, his eyes fixed upon the waxen beauty, as if feasting anew upon her loveliness. "She was a perfect woman—a perfect woman yes, as you say, too beautiful" and to Mary Haldane's horror the gentle tones had grown fierce with anger, and a furious light blazed in the eyes which had before been softened with love.

"Ay, ay, Miss," he continued as he noted her expression of dismay. "Fair faces and black hearts, they say will be found together. A woman's beauty—a man's curse. A few hours' pleasure for her, a lifetime of ruin for the man. And yet, oh God how I loved her—my poor little Nita! I wonder how soon we two are destined to meet again," and once more he was all tenderness, pressing his lips upon the golden hair as if in remorse for his previous bitterness. "Yes, you shall lie against my heart once more," he said, "your dainty golden head shall be pillowed on my breast—our resting place will be cold and dark and silent, my poor beautiful little wife!"

There was a noise outside as if someone was ascending the stairs. A startled nervous look flashed into his eyes, "take her away, put her out of sight," he said holding the bust towards Mary with nervous trembling hands. As she advanced to receive it from him, he was seized with a sudden tremor, his hands lost their grasp and the waxen bust of the beautiful Nita fell to the ground shivered into a thousand atoms, all that remained to tell the tale of what it had once been was the golden hair with its glimmering sheen lying amongst the scattered morsels of her fair falsity.

Neither spoke a word, Mary stood as if rooted to the spot, gazing upon the destruction. But over the old man's face crept the grey pallor of death. As the door opened and Jacques entered with a tray containing food, he essayed to speak, but the jaw dropped heavily, and his eyes glanced from one face to the other with a wistful yearning in their depths. Speech was gone and ere Jacques and Mary could render any assistance the grim visitor had despatched his errand, and Mons. Pierre had passed from mortality to eternity. His prayer had been granted and death the angel of release had set his spirit free from the bondage of the helpless body which had but fettered him to earth.

With a great cry of despair Jacques had flung himself on his knees by the side of the bed, " Oh master, master," he sobbed, " don't leave poor Jacques and Master Dick—don't leave us ! "

" Hush, Jacques," said Mary, laying a kindly but

restraining hand upon his shoulder. "His troubles are over, don't chain him to earth by your lamentations, come away, and trust to me for the future," and thus she led him from the room, and with fresh food for thought, an hour later started on her homeward journey, with a promise to return before the time appointed for the funeral.

CHAPTER XXIX.

MONS. PIERRE'S ROMANCE.

How little it is given us to know or read of the inner thoughts and lives of those by whom we are surrounded, and how very far short of the reality falls the elaborate guess-work of our imagination. Who among us would think of seeking for romance and tragedy in the career of a humble little wig and model maker?

And yet the contradictions of the world and the contrariness of human nature in general, is one of its prevailing features and we may jostle elbows with a hero or a villain in sublime unconsciousness of the fact, as we walk along the street, or pursue the most commonplace occupations.

When Mary paid her next visit to 302, Melville Street, she was admitted by a tall elderly woman whose age might be put down at almost any figure between fifty and sixty. She was remarkably thin, and yet there was a roundness about her figure which robbed it of even a suspicion of angularity, her carriage was graceful and her deportment dignified, she appeared what she was, every inch a lady.

"Miss Haldane?" she said, as she held the door open for her to enter.

"Yes," Mary answered, following her through the passage, past the office where the green blind was lowered and into a small room, at the extreme end which was the ordinary living room, half kitchen, half parlour.

It was substantially and comfortably furnished, and bore every sign of scrupulous cleanliness, and Mary's observant eyes could not fail to note various indications of a woman's presence and care. As the woman placed a chair for the visitor's acceptance, Mary glanced up into her face and thought she had never looked upon a sadder or a kinder one. The complexion was exquisitely fair, and though the features were wonderfully regular and well defined, she was not a handsome woman, not even pretty. Her hair of silvery grey was still plentiful and was arranged around her face in a sort of framework of natural curls, and surmounted by a neat muslin cap. Over her plainly made, closely fitting black gown, she wore a large muslin apron, and a white handkerchief was pinned across her breast, something after the fashion of the quaker garb.

"Would you like to take it up stairs at once, Miss Haldane?" referring to a large white wreath which Mary had placed upon the table. "How lovely the flowers are!" she said, "poor Pierre, poor Pierre! thank God he is at rest at last! I am his wife's aunt," she explained, as they turned to leave the parlour, "Judith Lepré, and I, who know what his existence has been all these years, can rejoice at his release."

They had reached the door of the bedroom, Miss Lepré noislessly turned the handle and the two women entered the chamber in silence. The simple coffin stood upon trestles, and a large cross of white arum lilies was laid across his feet. The face had resumed its old placid expression, it was as if peace and rest was stamped upon the closed eyes and rigid marble brow.

When Mary placed the wreath of flowers at his head, she also slipped within the cold dead fingers a curling golden tress which she had saved from the fragments of Nita's ruin. " He wished it," she said, looking up at Miss Lepré.

The elder woman slowly bowed her head as if in assent, but the sad expression deepened in her eyes and seemed to settle over her face, as she turned away with a deep sigh without having spoken a word. In silence they descended the stairs and re-entered the parlour. With the same stolid expression upon her face Miss Lepré set about her preparations for tea. The simple meal was soon prepared, Mary noting the while, with admiration, the elegance and grace of her every moment. It was not until they were seated at the table, each making but a poor pretence at partaking of the fare provided, that Miss Lepré's face lost its stony expression, and even then it seemed to be with an effort that she cast off the reserve which had so enshrouded her.

" How much did Pierre tell you of his story and

Nita's, Miss Haldane?" she asked, fixing an anxious enquiring gaze upon her as she spoke.

"Oh, nothing!" Mary answered with relief. "He begged of me to place a lovely cast of her beside him in his coffin, and as he passed it over to me," her voice trembled with emotion, and the tears welled into her eyes at the recollection, "before I had time to take it from him, it fell from his hands and lay at my feet shattered to atoms.

"How strange!" Miss Lepré ejaculated, "to have kept it all these years and for it to be destroyed like that, at the very last too. My dear it was a strange coincidence, it seemed as if she was'nt to be beside him—she wasn't worthy to be—no not even her waxen image!" and the same angry light that had shone so transiently in Mons. Pierre's eyes once before at the thought of her sin, whatever it might be, gleamed in Judith Lepré's eyes with a still fiercer light, while indignation trembled in every tone.

Mary leaned slightly forward over the table, and her voice was lowered involuntarily. "Miss Lepré," she said, "I believe it was the sudden shock of seeing his beautiful handiwork destroyed that killed him. It brought on a second attack of paralysis; I shall never forget the look in his eyes when he found that his power of speech was gone, and it was all so sudden, now that I try to think of it it seems impossible to realize that it is so."

"Would you care to hear Nita Lepré's story, Miss Haldane? You have heard so much it is best you should know what there is to tell, and had he lived, Pierre would have told you, I am sure."

"Yes, I would like to hear it," Mary answered, "but not if it pains you to speak of it, as I am afraid it will."

Miss Lepré shook her head, and smiled one of those sad smiles which seems to speak of the heartache heartache that forces them upon the lips.

"No, my dear, it is so long ago that I can speak of it now," she said, "the wound has had time to heal, although the scar remains."

"She was my brother's child," Miss Lepré commenced, "and although her father was only a poor man, still he was a gentleman, for we Lepré's come of a good old stock, though perhaps I should not be the one to say it. Although of French origin our family had been settled in England for many years, and most of my family had married either English husbands or wives. But my brother, Nita's father had met a beautiful Italian girl during one of his wanderings abroad, married her, and brought her to England without ever making enquiries as to her family or connections. All that we ever knew concerning her was that she was teaching in a pension at Bruges, from whence she eloped with him, but more than that we never knew. She was, as I said, very beautiful, and equally vain and shallow. Her education was above the average, and she sang like a nightingale. To have heard her sing one would have credited her with the soul of a saint. After nearly two years had elapsed, Nita was born, but she seemed to have no love even for her child. Day by day she grew more discontented, heaping bitter reproaches upon her husband for not being able to let her live in luxury and affluence. When Nita was a year old, she left him, and deserted her child, not leaving so much as a scrap of paper to give a clue as to her whereabouts or intentions. And from that day to this not a word has been heard of her; she disappeared as completely as if the grave had closed over her."

"And—do you think she destroyed herself?" Mary asked hesitatingly.

"Oh, no! She wasn't the woman to do that sort of thing," Miss Lepré answered decidedly, "she was too selfish and too cowardly. For a long time my brother made every effort to obtain tidings of her," she continued, "then when all efforts proved futile, he devoted himself body and soul as it were, to the care and welfare of his little daughter Nita. Every day that dawned the child seemed to grow more like her mother till the resemblance became almost painful, only that whatever perfections the one had lacked, seemed to be atoned for in Nita. At seventeen years of age she was the most beautiful girl I had ever seen. To what extent she might have inherited her mother's qualities and disposition we none of us managed to ascertain. Her moods were so variable, one moment all tears, the next all smiles, which like the sunshine dries the raindrops while they still sparkle on the rose leaf, her petulance and her waywardness like a passing cloud, would be atoned for by an outburst of petulance, penitence, and affection, and above all she seemed such a child for her years.

Then came Peter Rossiter upon the scene. He was travelling through Belgium with some friends and happened to see Nita at service in one of the churches. Struck by her beauty, he made enquiries concerning her and managed to obtain an introduction to my brother. From the first he was frank and outspoken as to his family, position, and anticipations, and also as to his admiration for Nita. His father was a substantial city man with a capital business, which he was waiting to hand over jointly to the two sons who comprised his family. The only bar to the union was Nita's extreme youth, my brother strenuously insisting that two years should elapse before any engagement being entered upon. Peter, or Pierre, as Nita called him, telling him one day that it was a shame to call him by so ugly a name as Peter, when Pierre was so much prettier, and answered the same purpose, and so we all fell into the habit of thus addressing him. That he would have faithfully kept to the compact I firmly believe to this day, had not Nita resolved that it should be otherwise, and what man is proof against the battery of a woman's armour? All her wiles and fascinations she brought to bear upon him, maddening him by her coquetry, and yet tempting him by her only half veiled admiration and preference for himself. At last she worked upon his feelings to such an extent, that a secret marriage was the result, and her excuse was, when her father taxed her with her disobedience and undutifulness, 'I was so tired of this dull life the same from day to day. I wanted to go to England—to London, and have plenty of money, and see what there was to be seen!'

"Alas! that tells the whole story! There was no mention of love for her husband, the advantages which were to be gained, constituted her sole idea of marriage. When Pierre's father heard of his son's marriage with a penniless foreigner, in his rage, he passed over the whole of the business property, and plant, to the younger brother and cut Pierre out of his will, and before he had time to repent of his severity, or at any rate to make restitution, the summons came for him which brooks of no delay and never halts to ask whether it pauperises or enriches. And so Nita Lepré paid for her disobedience. Two months after her marriage she found herself the wife of a poor man, who had to fight his way in the battle of life, and carve his fortune with only the tools of his own industry. It was a cruel awakening from the beautiful dreams tinged by the rosy dawn of hope to the black night of reality—of toil and even poverty. So soon as the news came of the old man's death, for she and Pierre had remained with us—he exerting himself by every means in his power to obtain some sort of employment—Nita was more like someone insane than a rational being. She taunted her husband with having entrapped her into a marriage by false pretences, begging and praying of us to find some means of undoing the tie. All our threats, entreaties, and expostulations were useless to stem the torrent of her rage—it seemed as if all the pent-up passion of her lifetime was let loose. Bitter as had been the blow to Pierre of the shattering of all his hopes, and the subsequent death of his father, without even the satisfaction of a reconciliation having taken place between them, it was as nothing to what he suffered as he listened to his wife's reproaches, and he realized that her love for him had been a sham and a lie, in order to gratify her selfish desires for freedom and luxury. He lost all ambition, all desire to earn a future for himself, and startled us one day by the intelligence that he intended to work his passage out to Australia—that he would leave Nita as free as if their marriage had never taken place, stating that he never again intended returning to Europe. Well, my dear, I don't know what she said to him, but that same night he told us that Nita had persuaded him to give up the idea of going abroad, at any rate for a time, as they had patched up their little grievance, and he hoped neither her father or myself would ever refer to it, or cast the slightest blame on her again.

"And so she lulled him into a fool's paradise, casting off her sulkiness and depression and being her old winning affectionate self as of old. Pierre had always excelled in the art of modelling, practising it merely as a pastime. It was Nita's own suggestion that he should turn his skill in that direction to practical account, and it was really wonderful in what a short time he succeeded in gaining a connection with several of the leading toy merchants for the heads and limbs of wax dolls. And so again she persuaded him to leave for Paris, and at last he consented, though much against the wish of my brother. But Pierre could deny her nothing. So to Paris they went, renting a small flat, and for a time all seemed prosperous and well. We should never have heard the rights of the story from Pierre, but my brother had insisted upon Lisette, an old servant who had been in the family for years, accompanying them to Paris, and this is what she afterwards told us. For the first three months Nita seemed fairly contented, though there were occasions when she lamented bitterly the cruelty of the misfortunes of which she had been the victim. She next fell into the habit of accompanying her husband as far as his place of business daily, returning home by the omnibus, he being more than delighted at the little wifely attention thus bestowed upon him. But Lisette began to notice that upon her return, she invariably evinced some sign of discomfiture, sometimes it would be by one of her petulant outbursts of discontent, and sometimes by a strange excitement which she made no effort to repress. And in a short time it began to be the usual thing for her to go to the Boulevard or the Park after the mid-day meal 'just to watch the people,' she said, occasionally barely reaching home before the hour at which her husband returned. One day she would bring back with her a piece of lace or a flower for her hat which she would say she had managed to pick up very cheaply, and once, in a gay mischievous mood, she flashed before Lisette's astonished eyes a gleaming jewel.

"'There, Lisette! What do you think of that?' she asked her, 'isn't it enough to almost blind you and take away your breath at the same moment?'

"'Oh, Miss Nita!' Lisette fairly gasped. 'A diamond! How did you come by it?'"

"But Nita only laughed again, a long rippling musical laugh, and held the diamond, which was set in a little heart-shaped brooch, before her eyes, just where the light could fall and scintillate upon it. Then she suddenly flung it upon the table as if it were worthless. 'Why, you foolish Lisette,' she said, 'how ignorant you are. Can't you see that it is only paste—a brilliant—and not worth a couple of francs? Where am I to get diamonds from, I should like to know?' and she picked up the brilliant from the table and pinned it so that it was hidden among the laces at her breast.

Six months after their settlement in Paris, the baby, little Dick, was born, and with the advent of the child Pierre's cup of happiness was filled to the brim. He believed that Nita's life would no longer lack any element of content. But, alas! for poor Pierre, how soon was that cup of happiness to be dashed from his lips—how much better for him if he had taken that voyage to Australia when he first discovered her falsity; it would have saved the second blow which ruined both their lives. When Dick was but six weeks old, she disappeared, and even as her mother had done before her, left not a trace behind. She deserted her husband and her child, a helpless little babe, without leaving a word of regret or farewell. That her flight was planned was easily discovered, by the fact that she had taken a portion of her clothing, as much as she could conveniently carry. But Pierre did not act as her father had done under similar circumstances—he made no attempt to find her, but in the letter that he wrote to my brother he said, " I could never have contented her, and now that the sin is accomplished I shan't interfere with her happiness. After all, she is but a child, and whatever punishment the future may hold for her, it shall never strike through me ; the hand that has loved cannot be the one to slay! Our child shall be taught to think of his mother as dead, for indeed she is dead to us.

"So soon as he could complete arrangements, he sold up the home, gave up his situation, and started for England with his child. The next blow that fell upon him, was the loss of little Dick, whom he almost idolized. For some years afterwards we never heard from him, and how they were spent we never enquired, but when at last he made his appearance, suddenly and unexpectedly, he was a changed man in every sense of the word—a mere wreck of his former self. And so he has lived until now. Can you wonder that death is a happy release for him?" and Miss Lepré leant back in her chair and silently wiped away the tears which had gathered in her eyes during the recital of the story.

For a minute Mary Haldane was silent. " It seems almost incredible," she said at last, " but what a punishment must await such perfidy as hers. I do not envy Nita Lepré either in this world or the next."

" Wait a moment, the story has a sequel." Miss

Lepré slightly raised her hand and dropped her voice still lower. " Perhaps it is the saddest part of the story. She deserved her fate as far as the world's judgment goes, but the question arises, ' Are we all to be judged from the same standpoint ? To what extent was heredity responsible for her shortcomings ? ' ' It was the bad blood in her veins,' my brother exclaimed when he first heard of her flight. God knows I would not wish to condone sin, and, of course, natures such as hers are those which should, and must, fight the hardest battles against self, by sheer moral courage. How many there are who never stray, perhaps because they are never tempted. To the one palate even so much as the taste of the wine cup mean desire, which, if once satiated, leads to ruin, while to another the effect produced may be nausea ; true, indeed, it is, that one man's meat may be another man's poison. But, dear me, how I am wandering on. Let me see, what was I telling you ? The sequel ! Yes, of course. Nita had not a very long spell of happiness after all. Not much more than five years after her flight there came a letter from her to my brother. Neither of us recognised the handwriting, or I don't suppose he would ever have opened it, but having done so, a word or two which caught his eye in glancing at it impelled him to read it through. There was no name mentioned in it. She simply said that the man who had persuaded her to fly with him was passionately jealous and suspicious, fearful scenes constantly taking place between them. ' It has been my punishment,' she said, 'for my sin. I loved this man and sacrificed all for him, if even it was the faithfulness of guilt. I can bear it no longer—I am mad, desperate, and to-night ends all! When you read these words, the river will have claimed its prey, and Pierre will be avenged. Even in death I dare not ask for your forgiveness, but think sometimes, with pity, of your lost, broken-hearted child—Nita.'" Miss Lepré's voice trembled, and she raised her handkerchief to her eyes, and for a minute or two longer both women remained silent.

"Then you really think she committed suicide?" Mary asked.

"There is no doubt of it," and Miss Lepré removed the handkerchief from her face. "A week later we received a newspaper containing the account of the body having been discovered in the Seine, besides other confirmatory information."

"Poor misguided girl," said Mary. "One cannot help pitying her after all. She sinned, and she suffered, how deeply perhaps none of us may guess. I thank you, Miss Lepré, for your confidence in me. I think Nita's story has softened my heart, and will cause me to look upon those around me with far different feelings and ideas than I have before experienced."

Further conversation was interrupted by the entrance of Jacques, who looked more pallid and stolid than ever—all tears and excitement had left him, his indifference had merged into apathy, or so it appeared. Once again Mary rose to take a last look at the little wig-maker, and it seemed impossible to realise that the peaceful unconscious clay had once been racked by the wear and tear of human emotions, of romance and tragedy, a tragedy which was yet to score one more point. The following morning, which was the day fixed for the funeral, upon entering the room, Miss Lepré found Jacques stretched upon the floor by the side of the coffin. She tried to rouse him, thinking it was simply one of his somnolent fits, but to her horror, the truth dawned upon her—that he was lifeless. His old master's words had proved strangely and fatally true—" He will be faithful unto death!" By the side of the master whom he had loved so well he passed into the world of shadows. Poor Jacques was provided for—he would never stand in need of human aid. Perhaps the strangest bequest was when, a day or two after the funeral, Miss Haldane received the peculiarly constructed cases containing the models and little Master Dick. They were, indeed, realistic mementoes of the fateful never-to-be-forgotten experiences of that portion of her life.

CHAPTER XXX.

ASHLEY DALLAS PLEADS HIS SUIT.

"DEAR Mr. Penwood,—I am inexpressibly grieved to learn from Ashley of your serious indisposition, especially as I am aware that it dates from that fatal night a month ago, from your exposure to that dreadful storm, and the exciting events which afterwards occurred, and which I shudder to recall. Your condition has been kept a secret from my sister, as we have not dared to add to her already distressed state of mind. I should, however, have devised some means of visiting you at the Inn, had I not been forbidden by the doctors from doing so, but I need hardly say how anxiously I have waited each day for news concerning you, and now I am impatiently awaiting the withdrawal of the medical fiat. You must not be so despondent, but look on the bright side. Truly it was an unlucky day for you when you first set foot in St. Kestor, or rather when Sir Hardress first shook your hand in friendship; but there, 'speak no ill of the dead, peace be to his ashes.' But the shadows are nearly gone, and soon you will be stepping out into the broad light of day.

"Ashley has told you already of my masquerade at Craig-Feldie, under the guise of a sewing-maid, and how we subsequently escaped by the aid of Jess Cameron. A letter purporting to be from Mathilde, whose handwriting I easily feigned, procured the custody of the children without the slightest difficulty from the Matron of the Orphanage. My good friend, Mrs. de Grey, then placed the cottage at our disposal, it having very fortunately been unoccupied for some little time. It seemed rather singular that, on the day you unearthed us in our retreat, we had decided upon deserting it and leaving England for the Continent.

"But we all have to learn that '*L'homme propose mais Dieu dispose.*' Who among us could have foretold that ere the night had passed away, Sir Hardress St. Kestor would have gone over to the great majority? But what an awful thing it seems, that the law, not content with making a father supreme during his life, sanctions the exercise of the most brutal tyranny after his death, by allowing third persons to step in between the widowed mother and her children, to continue the tyranny in his name and in pursuance of his legal rights. And yet such is the cruelty and injustice under which my sister is suffering even at the present moment. Never shall I forget her terrible anguish and our own dismay, when, at the reading of the will, it was discovered that Sir Hardress had appointed Sir Peter Fairbairn and his niece the guardians of the children. To think that the wife should be legally compelled to hand over her children to the custody and care of the woman who had been little else than her husband's mistress, who had usurped her place in her husband's affection, and been at the root of all the domestic misery that followed.

"When Laura heard it, she fell insensible from her chair, and when Dr. Raynell first raised her he thought the shock had killed her. For three days she remained unconscious, and narrowly escaped an attack of brain fever. Then came a letter from Miss Fairbairn, offering to make terms with her on these conditions: That Laura should be allowed the custody of her children, provided she undertook to chaperone Mathilde during the forthcoming London season, and to obtain her presentation at court. St. Kestor, moreover, was to be open to herself and Sir Peter, as well as her town residence; in, fact, they were to be introduced everywhere, and treated as her most honoured and intimate friends.

"A frightful price, I can hear you say, for a mother to be called upon to pay for her children's society. But such is the yoke to which my sister has bound herself; it is only a new form of penal servitude. And to think that as she lay with her arms clasped about her husband's neck, in the solemn embrace of forgiveness, the last word which she heard from his dying lips was the name of this woman, the woman who is in the house while I am writing these words, and whose sombre garments appear to me but a mocking desecration of the weeds donned by his widow, not out of respect for his memory, but for the sake of appearances. There is only one loophole of escape for us, one ray of hope, and that is that this woman may gain a titled husband—for that is the great aim and object of her life; then we may get rid of her baneful influence, and please Heaven that it may be speedily!

"In conclusion, let me assure you not only of our united good-will towards you, but also of our deep sympathy for you, both in the matter of your sickness and the shameful fraud practised upon you, and which Ashley related to us after your explanation. You may expect a visit from Lady Laura, along with myself, so soon as we may be permitted to see you, And in bidding you adieu, believe me to be sincere in subscribing myself, your true and earnest friend.   MARY HALDANE."

Miss Haldane had just reached as far as the signature of the above somewhat lengthy epistle, when a shadow darkened the window of the library, where she sat beside an old-fashioned oaken escritoire. The next instant, Mr. Dallas entered by the partially opened window, and halted in front of the escritoire.

"Is it really true that I have been fortunate enough

to find you alone at last?" he said, looking down upon her blushing face with a lover-like glance. "Do you know I sometimes think that there is more of design than accident in those children always hanging around you? But now that the opportunity is at last within my grasp, I should be more than mad to let it slip."

Miss Haldane had lowered her head and kept her eyes resolutely fixed upon the letter lying before her, but she did not resist Ashley's embrace, when kneeling beside her, he placed his arm around her, and drew her head upon his shoulder.

"My darling," he said, "when for the purpose of defending your sister's honour, I hazarded that bold venture to Sir Hardress by declaring you to be my promised wife, you little guessed that I was but expressing what had come to be the one passionate desire of my life, a desire which had been growing upon me longer than I can fix a date for its commencement. At first I thought it was admiration of your courage and untiring devotion and unselfishness which I was experiencing, but I have long since found out that it was love. And yet I dared not speak to you of its existence under the circumstances, while I knew that my services were so necessary to you, lest it might appear that I was taking advantage of the obligation which Laura would persist she was under towards me. Then came the moment when the rash avowal of my love rushed to my lips before I had time to consider what would be the result, and I was ready to curse myself for the folly which I told myself over and over again you would never forgive Then when I saw you still kind and friendly, I ventured to think that you would not resent it for your sister's sake, and during the last few days a wild hope has again taken possession of me that you will perhaps listen to my suit. Mary, my darling, will you be my wife?"

Mary withdrew her hands from his close grasp and with nervous fingers toyed amongst the loose papers upon the escritoire. But the coyness and hesitation were but momentary. The next instant she turned and looked into his handsome blue eyes with a winning, trustful smile, at the same time running her fingers through his sunny locks, and stroking his bronzed cheeks with playful caresses.

"I am but a plain, homely little woman, Ashley."

But Ashley was answered, and pressing his first lover's kiss upon her lips, bade her desist from depreciating his property.

Releasing herself from his embrace, in beautiful confusion, Mary pushed him away from her. "Before I resign myself and my freedom into your keeping, my liege lord, I must impose one condition upon you," she said, with an arch imperiousness; "will you promise to exert all your power and influence, either directly or indirectly, to obtain an entire abrogation or amendment of the law which has caused us all so much suffering—not on our own account alone, but for the sake of every woman, wife, and mother in the land?"

"That I will," asserted Ashley, again taking both

her hands in his own. "It shall be the one great object of my life, and more than that, only give me the power, and I think I may be able to rid your sister of the tyrants that are oppressing her."

Once more Mary flashed one of her merry roguish glances from her soft brown eyes, and in a half-solemn half-mocking tone, resigned herself to his arms, saying, "Then you may kiss me!"

CHAPTER XXXI.

SIR PETER'S FAMILY SKELETON.

"NOW, Laura, dear, you have only to be your own dignified self, and maintain a freezing silence, and all will be well."

It was Miss Haldane who spoke. She and her sister were standing together in the library, and the faces of each of the ladies bore decided signs of excitement, not to say agitation. "Ashley will be more than a match for them, my dear," continued Mary. "Oh! shan't I enjoy seeing my lady tackled at last."

Lady Laura could not repress a faint smile at her sister's somewhat slangy expression.

"No! Ashley has not been called to the bar for nothing."

"No, and Ashley will call somebody else to the bar in a very short time, and it will be the bar of justice, fair cousin, I promise you," said Mr. Dallas, as he joined them at the oriel window. "I have requested Sir Peter and Miss Fairbairn to grant me the honour of an interview before we dine, and I shall not be overwhelmed with surprise if your dinner-table this evening lacks two of its accustomed guests.

The sound of rustling silken robes sounded without, even as he spoke, and the next moment Mathilde Fairbairn entered the room, clad in the most obnoxious trappings of woe, her portly form weighted beneath a mass of heavy jet which glittered with every movement.

She gave a slight start upon seeing the two ladies already in possession of the library, and glanced hastily at Mr. Dallas as if seeking from him an explanation of their presence. But Ashley's expression told her nothing. He merely offered her a chair and remarked that he "hoped her uncle would soon favour him with his presence."

"If you requested it, I suppose he will obey," she answered with a slight shrug of the shoulders; "that is if he should happen to keep awake. I was not aware that your interview implied a family gathering, though," and she lounged back in her easy chair, indolently fanning herself with a huge black fan.

"Yes, purely a family gathering," assented Ashley, "for the transaction of a little family matter. Ah, here comes Sir Peter," as the door was opened to admit Sir Peter Fairbairn, Knight (to give him his favourite form of introduction).

"Ah! quite a select and social party," he said, bowing as he entered, and his gaze wandered over the room, a trifle uncomfortably. "My dear Dallas, what can I do for you?"

He drew one of the tall-backed oaken chairs close to the table and leisurely seated himself as he spoke.

"A great deal, Sir Peter," answered Mr. Dallas,

"and with your permission I will proceed to business at once. I think, Laura," he continued, "you have a letter in your possession which I shall require for reference."

Without a word, Lady Laura rose and took a document from a locked drawer in the writing table. Sir Peter leaned forward, his keen searching glance fixed upon the letter, and even Mathilde's face lost its usual languid expression as she watched and listened.

As Ashley deliberately withdrew the contents from the envelope, he said, "Miss Fairbairn, you will doubtless recognise the letter in my hand as being the one written by you to Lady St. Kestor, the day before your arrival from town."

Miss Fairbairn merely bowed haughtily in assent.

"It is to certain matters contained in it that I wish to draw your attention," continued Ashley, unfolding it before him, and laying his finger upon a particular paragraph. "You herein refer to the mysterious clause inserted in the will of the late Sir Hardress St. Kestor, leaving the children under the joint guardianship of yourself and Sir Peter, and you offer to make terms with her ladyship under these conditions: 'I will give up the custody of the children if you are willing to pay me the price that I stipulate. You must act the rôle of chaperone to me during the forthcoming London season, and obtain my presentation at Court, and St. Kestor shall be open at any and all times to receive Sir Peter and myself; and also your town residence. In short, I wish to be introduced everywhere, and on all occasions to be treated as your honoured and intimate friend.' How such a proviso ever came to be inserted, and under what influence you are doubtless better acquainted than we are. But in spite of all the domestic misery that has arisen in the past I cannot believe that my late cousin ever intended that cruel and barbarous condition should ever be carried out. Unhappily, his painfully sudden end prevented his justifying so rash an act."

"Excuse me, Mr. Dallas," interrupted Sir Peter at this point, "I don't see what all this rigmarole is to lead to. His wishes are down in black and white, and all the talk in the world won't alter that fact."

"I must trouble you to exercise your patience yet a little longer," replied Mr. Dallas, "when I think you will admit that I have led up to something. I quote once more from your niece's letter, 'After all, what I have asked is but a meagre price for a mother to pay for her children. Consider well, how much you have at stake, for I shall not place before you a second opportunity.'"

Ashley refolded the letter, and returned it to the envelope. "That Miss Fairbairn and Sir Peter, is the matter which I have invited you here to discuss."

"Does Lady Laura agree to my conditions?" broke in Mathilde in a hard cold voice, flashing a defiant look at the two sisters who still remained in the oriel window.

"On the contrary, Lady St. Kestor not only refuses

to negociate with you for the barter of her children, but she defies you at your peril to come between her and them."

"Uncle Peter, do you hear that?" Mathilde rose from her chair and crossed to her uncle's side. "Her ladyship dosen't want the brats after all. You'll be a good, kind father to them, won't you?" and her vulgar, mocking laugh rang through the apartment, though it was but a forced laugh, after all.

When Mathilde's burst of ill-timed merriment had somewhat subsided, Ashley again spoke, "As a matter of formality I musk ask you, Miss Fairbairn, if you refuse to give up the custody of the children to their mother?"

"Answer him, Uncle," she replied, giving Sir Peter a sharp rap upon the shoulder with her fan.

With a ferocious gesture Sir Peter brought his hand down upon the table as he exclaimed, "Refuse—yes, of course we do. If my lady wants the brats it will have to be on my terms now, and she shall beg for them on her bended knees, as she once begged to me before."

Involuntarily Lady Laura shuddered at the recollection, and for the first time she turned and faced her enemies. But there was very little of her old fear expressed in face or manner.

Ashley Dallas suddenly assumed a most professional air; placed one foot upon a chair, and leant slightly forward. "Miss Fairbairn," he asked, "do you remember your aunt Jessie Cameron appearing at Craig Feldie, one day about Christmas time, when

Sir Hardress and Lady St. Kestor were your uncle's guests?"

Mathilde winced perceptibly at the mention of Jess Cameron's name, and Sir Peter hurriedly changed his position.

"Really, I have no recollection of such a person," Mathilde answered, thoroughly on her guard.

"Then of course you don't remember a conversation which occurred between you, during which was revealed the secret of Sir Peter's life!"

"The secret of my life!" ejaculated Sir Peter, white to the very lips.

"Yes! Family skeletons have a trick of rattling their musty old bones at the most inopportune times," said Ashley, following up his advantage; "and there is still another incident connected with that interview, Miss Fairbairn," he went on to say, "the mere mention of which will probably be the means of refreshing your memory. You cannot have forgotten that Mrs. Cameron drew your attention to the fact that you and she were not the only occupants of the library."

The colour gradually heightened on Mathilde's face, and a strange, restless expression flashed into her bold black eyes, as Dallas continued—"You drew aside the screen which shut off that portion of the room from view and discovered a lady whom you believed to be sleeping."

"You deceitful wretch!" half gasped, half shouted Mathilde, turning upon Lady Laura in her frenzy.

"Then you admit your recollection of the circum-

X

stance?" asked Ashley, apparently unheeding her anger.

In an instant Mathilde realised how she had betrayed herself, and mortification held her dumb, while Ashley proceeded, "Fortunately for Lady St. Kestor, upon the occasion referred to, she was enabled to obtain a weapon with which to defend herself from your attacks, and that weapon, Sir Peter, is your family skeleton. Shall we blazon it before the world that you and Miss Fairbairn—"

"Silence! For Heaven's sake don't—don't give it a name," gasped Sir Peter, rising and stretching forth his hands, as if in appeal, towards Ashley, who immediately hesitated.

"You coward," sneered Mathilde, venting her wrath upon her uncle. "Do you think I shall give up the advantages in a moment which I've worked so long to obtain. Pshaw! who would believe their story—who's to prove it?"

"Mrs. Cameron herself will prove it if necessary," replied Ashley.

"But my uncle can deny it, and he shall," answered Mathilde, her courage apparently undaunted.

"So far, so good, Miss Fairbairn," remarked Ashley complacently. "The next point upon which I must engage your attention is by far the most serious upon which I have yet touched. It is a weapon held by another lady of the family to be used in case of need, and I am sure she will regret as much as I do that you force us to unsheath it. Miss Haldane overheard a conversation (also at Craig-

Feldie), the purport of which was to arrange—I will put it plainly—to arrange the murder of Lady St. Kestor, whom for various reasons you wished to be rid of. As you are aware Lady Laura escaped by the aid of Miss Haldane from Craig-Feldie. The potion prepared by you she brought away with her and placed in the possession of an analyst. And now, Miss Fairbairn, if it pleases you, we will discuss the matter of terms again."

An awkward silence ensued until Sir Peter, whose features were almost livid, whispered something to Mathilde, who stood erect, with a sullen look of hatred and defeat stamped upon every line of her face. She fixed her eyes upon Mary Haldane, then upon Lady Laura, and appeared as if she was about to speak, but again maintained a stolid silence.

Lady St. Kestor, generous to the last, suddenly left her sister's side, and advanced towards the table in the centre of the room.

"Now things have gone so far I'm sure Mr. Dallas will excuse me for speaking on my own behalf," she said in her sad but gentle tones. "I am sorry, Miss Fairbairn, that it has been necessary to reap up so much that has been unpleasant. All that I ask from you, is your written promise that you will never molest either myself or my little ones again. And for all else you have my full and free forgiveness. The knowledge that I accidentally obtained concerning you will henceforth be sunk in oblivion."

"Well, Uncle, the game's up, so the sooner we get our traps together and migrate from this miserable hole the better," and Mathilde hustled the old man from his chair with but scant ceremony, and would have hurried him from the room without even deigning to reply to Lady Laura, or speak to any of those present.

"Perhaps you will be good enough to place your signature to this document," interrupted Ashley, producing a legal-looking paper, and spreading it open upon the table.

With a bounce and a flourish Mathilde scrawled her name and flung down the pen, while Sir Peter followed suit, but in a much milder fashion. As they passed from the room Sir Peter held out his hand to Miss Haldane.

"You're a brick, Miss Mary, and I always admired you," he said.

"And you are a bad man, and I always destested you," answered Miss Haldane, contemptuously disdaining his proffered hand.

As they reached the door Mathilde flashed a look of hatred at the three whom she had been compelled to leave to peace and happiness. "I suppose I may kiss the dear little children, my quondam charges, before I go," she called back to Lady Laura as a parting shot, but Lady Laura could afford to smile at a remark which had lost its power to sting.

Half-an-hour later a carriage bowled along the drive, and, with its departing wheels, rolled the last load and the last fear from Lady St. Kestor's heart.

And Ashley Dallas proved a true prophet. The dinner table that evening lacked two of its accustomed **guests.**

CHAPTER XXXII.

HUGH PENWOOD'S NARRATIVE CONCLUDED.

"JUNE 1st.—The closing time of my life is at hand, and, as a dying man, I dare to write to the woman whom I love, the words which in life I could never have uttered. To this dumb and trusty friend (my diary), who has been my sole confidant for years, I have alone poured forth a confession of my mysterious attraction towards the woman to whom I dedicate it in my dying moments. But it is the first time that even to myself I have dared to designate my mad infatuation by its true name—the name of love. But I am on the brink of the grave, and Death is a true leveller of all distinctions. If she reads these words (and I have left instructions for the sealed packet which will contain my life's record to be forwarded to her as my last gift) she will learn what a strange battle I have fought with self, since that first evening at St. Kestor, when I held her hand within my own, and looked into the eyes which were destined to exert so tragic an influence upon my life. She will learn how I wavered at deciding my own destiny, and how fate

decided for me that moonlight night when I staked
my chance under the roof of the humble school-house.
My goddess! my queen! how I blessed the reluctant
moon and the dallying clouds for favouring the passionate longing of my heart. Then—she was a wife,
and even to thee, my dear old friend, I dare not
express my delight and gratitude; and besides, I was
only the village schoolmaster. Now—she is a widow,
and I am almost beyond the ken of social or earthly
distinctions, and it pleases and unburdens my mind
to confess my love, though that love has brought me
to an early grave. From the day that I set foot in
St. Kestor my life was changed for me. I felt like a
new being under new conditions. When I fancied
that Sir Hardress treated my darling (yes, even then
I styled her so in my own heart) with aught save
kindness, I seemed to be possessed with all the
instincts of the savage, ready to spring upon him. I
thank God that during the last sad events which
occurred I remained in ignorance, or I might now be
preparing to appear before the Great Judge with the
crime of that man's murder upon my soul, and my
hands smeared with his blood. As it is, I can pass
away in peace, looking forward to a joyful awakening
in the 'Land of Promise,' for I know that there is no
hope for me here. That fatal disease which seized
my young mother for its prey has also set its seal
upon me, and is already hungry to claim its victim.
The long exposure to the bitter cold and soaking rain
settled upon lungs, which were constitutionally weak,
and rapid consumption is the result which will end

all. But I would not have the gentle and outraged lady reproach herself for having any share in bringing it about. I can die at rest, knowing that when she reads these words she will understand that by my blind ignorance I suffered more than she did in her outraged dignity. But one tear from her gentle eyes, shed for my memory, will suffice to wipe out all my suffering and agony a thousand-fold.

"They tell me that she is coming—my queen—my darling—my love—to say good-bye to me, to clasp my hand, while I cross the river, the river which even now laps close to the shore at my feet. It is more like an ocean than a river, for I can see great silver-crested waves towering one above another until the creamy foam gradually comes nearer and nearer, closer and closer, until—Ah! I cannot trace the letters any further, my fingers grow stiff and sight fails me, but Lady Laura will hold my hand ——"

The narative broke off abruptly. These were the last words that Hugh Penwood wrote though consciousness never failed him. Lady Laura let the book sink upon her lap, and not one, but numberless tears fell thick and fast upon it in pity for the writer's suffering. His last wish had been fulfilled, for Lady Laura had watched untiringly beside him during the two days and nights which intervened before his death, and as his eyes unclosed for a last look while on earth, upon the face which he loved so well, she stooped and pressed a kiss upon his brow; and so, with his hand held fast in hers, his spirit passed out from the world of toil and suffering, to enter into "the Perfect Peace which passeth all understanding."

Lady Laura turned back to the earlier pages of the book where he referred to his childhood:—

"At the early age of six I was taken away from my mother and sent to a cousin of my father's to be brought up with his children, or to rough it, as the stern uncouth man termed it, on the Highland mountains. My mother was a gentlewoman, and in marrying my father made quite a *mesalliance*. He inveigled her into the marriage for the purpose of obtaining her fortune, but upon the death of her father, it was discovered that he had willed it away from her. Her husband's anger was unbounded. I, her only son, was dragged by sheer physical force from her arms. I believe my father had always hated me even more than the gentle woman who had sacrificed her kindred and her home to follow his fortunes, believing that he loved her. Soon after that I heard that my mother was dead, and I thought that my young heart must have broken with the wild intensity of my grief. I must have inherited many of her qualities and instincts, for I was never so happy as when engaged in studying, seizing all books that came into my way. When about twelve years of age I ran away from my uncle and cousins to seek my own fortune, and after knocking about the country for several months fell in with an old gentleman, who took me into his service, and aided me considerably with my studies, and at whose house I was enabled to cultivate my passionate love for music. The death of my benefactor again threw me upon the world, when I underwent the various experiences described in another part of the volume. I was born under an unlucky star, and, so far, it has shadowed my existence. What the end will be I know not, whether it be near or afar."

Again Lady Laura closed the book with a sharp sudden movement. That reference to the end which had been accomplished so tragically was more than she could bear.

At the same moment Jess appeared, leading by the hand her little boy, who presented a perfect picture of health. "May I trouble you, my Lady," she asked, "to let me take Donald to the Lodge to spend the day there?"

"Oh, by all means go," her mistress answered; but as the woman was turning away to leave she called her back again, and beckoning the boy to her side patted him affectionately on the head.

"Are you learning to be happy, Jess?" she asked her.

"Yes, my Lady, as happy as I ever can be, thanks to all your goodness and kindness; but I can't help my heart going out to the bonnie lads I've left behind!" and she raised her apron to her eyes to dry the falling tears.

"Ah Jess, it's a cruel love which causes a mother to have to hide, like a hunted criminal, to keep her own," Lady Laura replied, "and I fear there are many mothers in exile from the same cause. But take courage and wait with patience till you can look forward to seeing your boys again. And I don't think you need fear Sir Peter discovering you here."

When Jess left the room she pressed the little one to her bosom, as though she feared that he too might be snatched away from her.

CHAPTER XXXIII.

SO SOON?

"SO soon, Ashley?" It was Mary Haldane who spoke. She and her lover were standing in the embrasure of that oriel window where he had wooed and won her, and once again he was earnestly pleading his suit, urging her with all the eloquence at his command to consent to a speedy marriage. "It is scarcely two weeks since poor Hugh was buried," she continued, looking right out on to the lawn beyond.

"Do you think Hugh would wish us to postpone our happiness on his account?" Ashley answered, "and if we waited for a year, it could not possibly benefit him in any way."

But Mary still remained unconvinced. "It will appear as if we are in such a hurry," was the next excuse offered.

"Well, and so we are," interrupted Ashley, with a laugh.

"Speak for yourself, sir!" and Miss Haldane drew herself up with one of her old imperious gestures, "how dare you make such an assertion?" and she flashed one of her piquant glances at him as she spoke.

"Most gracious queen, I humbly apologise!" and Mr. Dallas dropped gallantly upon one knee before her, and reverently raised her hand to his lips. "But Mary, darling, you won't raise any more objections, will you?" he said, placing his arm around her. "Why should we delay our happiness a moment longer than is absolutely necessary? I want you for my wife, and I'm not inclined to wait! Think how much better we can work together over our mutual hobby—the task that we have set ourselves to accomplish as far as lies in our power. I am to work in Parliament, and you shall have your drawing room meetings and your private assemblies for the furtherance of our great cause. Even now I can hear the blessings of the wives and mothers showered upon you for your efforts on behalf of them and their little ones!"

"Oh, Ashley, you know where to find the weak points in my armour, do you not?" Mary replied. "There is but little doubt who will have it all their own way in the future! But there, you are a dear good fellow, and Laura would say I have teased you unmercifully. Have your own way—when do you propose to carry me off bodily?"

"The fourth of July," he answered promptly, without so much as a moment's hesitation. "That was my mother's wedding day," he explained, as Mary looked at him in somewhat of surprise.

"Oh my, was ever such a sacrifice demanded of a

woman before, I wonder? June the nineteenth," and Miss Haldane proceeded to count the number of days upon her fingers to the fourth of July "Just sixteen days, counting from to-day, in which to procure my wedding trousseau. Oh, it's positively barbarous. Why, one of the chief delights of getting married is choosing all your finery. You must have morning gowns, and tea gowns, and visiting dresses, and tailor-made dresses, and evening dresses, and hats and bonnets, and laces and flowers, and boots and shoes of every shade and description, and umbrellas and sunshades for every different costume that you wear, and heaps of other things."

"But you can't possibly wear them all at once," Ashley interrupted in dismay, "why can't you have just ——"

"Whatever has that to do with it?" Mary broke in, before he could finish what he was about to say. "Whoever said we wanted them? Its the custom, and so we follow it. Of course, everybody knows it would be much better to buy things as the seasons come round, or when you want them, but it isn't the fashion to do it in that way, so we shall go on spending the money and enriching the milliners and the costumiers and wearing ourselves out by long wearisome visits, fitting on this thing and the other, as if we were so many lay figures, for the artistes to experiment upon."

"Then I am sure you ought to be eternally grateful to me for saving you from such a fate," said Ashley, his courage restored, for he knew that such was not the style of programme to recommend itself to Miss Haldane's liking, " so kiss me and say ' Ashley, you are always right ! ' "

"Ashley! you are simply incorrigible!" and Mary laughed heartily as she gave him the asked-for kiss ' but I am grateful ! "

"And it is finally settled that the important event takes place on the fourth of July ? "

" I suppose so ! " Mary replied with an air of mock resignation.

"Then I am off to make preliminary arrangements, so adieu my love, and remember the fourth of July ! " and with a happy careless laugh, he left the room by the open window, which was his favourite mode of exit.

CHAPTER XXXIV

WEDDING BELLS.

THE fourth of July—a date to be celebrated by the nuptials of Mr. Dallas with Miss Haldane. One of those perfect summer days, when the sky is a broad expanse of shimmering blue, and the air is resonant with the drowsy hum of insect life. A day when nature seems to have donned her holiday attire and the flowers jauntily raise their heads to greet the bride in passing. Long before the hour appointed for the ceremony, the old grey stone church is filled by an eager and enthusiastic crowd, and the churchyard path is lined with rosy-cheeked children laden with flowers to strew before the bride as she comes.

It is a simple, quiet wedding; but the good wishes and the blessings which are showered upon the happy pair, proceed from genuine and honest hearts, and are laden with sterling sincerity.

At the conclusion of the honeymoon, which will be, by necessity, a short one, for Ashley has received an invitation to stand for one of the divisions for the County of Devonshire, it had been agreed that the newly-made bride and bridegroom should spend the first portion of their married life at St. Kestor with Lady Laura, who shrank from remaining amongst the depressing associations when deprived of the society of her sister, yet at the same time deeming it advisable to continue to reside in her husband's late home for some little time, though it was her intention to take up her residence in town, when Mr. Dallas's Parliamentary duties should necessitate his presence there, for there was not so much as the shadow of a doubt in any of their minds that his candidature would be other than successful, for his family was an old one and exceedingly popular in the county. having regularly sent its representatives for the last fifty years to legislate for their country's welfare. And perhaps, of all the scions of his race, Ashley was one of the most popular and sought after. His easy good nature and thoroughly genial temperament, combined with a certain quaint originality, made him a favourite wherever he went, and as he used to express it himself, " if he had a dry speech to make, he always oiled it with a bit of humour!"

The wedding breakfast was over. Mary had changed her bridal robes for the quieter travelling dress of silvery grey and the maid having been dismissed, the two sisters were once more alone.

Lady Laura had dreaded the parting more than even she had admitted to herself, and now that the crucial moment had arrived, keenly though she felt it, she was still anxious to hide it as much as possible from her sister's observant eyes.

"What a busy time we shall have when we return," said Mary, raising her eyes from the long glove which she was engaged in buttoning, "and we shall be away so short a time that you will hardly miss me a little bit!"

Lady Laura smiled faintly, and struggled bravely against displaying any emotion; she had determined that there should be no tears shed upon her sister's wedding day.

"Why, I don't believe I have congratulated you, Mary," she said, kissing her affectionately, "I won't say that I hope you will be very happy, dear, because I am sure you will, and I quite expect you will worry and tease Ashley's very life out of him!" and she laughed and pinned the bride's little veil around her softly plumed hat and fixed her draperies in the most becoming folds. "There comes the carriage," as wheels were heard along the drive and the sound of horses' hoofs crunching the gravel. "Good-bye, dear, and God bless you, and send you safely back to me," and the next instant the sisters had their arms around each other, to the utter disregard of Mary's elaborately-arranged toilet.

"Auntie Mary! Auntie Mary! Are you ready? Uncle Ashley wants to know." Archie's and Barbara's voices sounded in chorus as they pommelled lustily upon the outside of the door.

"You can come in, darlings," said their mother, and immediately the door was flung open to admit the two youngsters who stood almost breathless with excitement and the rush they had made, each trying to be first to deliver the message.

"Gently—gently!" said Lady Laura, in quiet remonstrance.

"Well, mother, Barbara always pushes so and tries to get in front of me," said Archie who looked much more sturdy and healthy than previously.

"Uncle Ashley told me to tell Auntie Mary and then Archie wanted to," said Barbara in self-defence.

"Cook's got such a lot of rice to throw over you Auntie Mary!" Archie continued heedless of Barbaras explanations, "I told her I should tell you to shut your eyes, and she said I must'nt say a word to you about it, but I said I should and I have done," and master Archie crossed the room to the window with his hands in the pockets of his velvet knickers wherein reposed a silver coin just bestowed upon him by his newly made uncle.

"Yes, and cook's going to throw a shoe at you too, I heard her telling Grames," said little Barbara throwing her arms round her Auntie's neck, "I hope it won't hurt you very much," and the tears rolled down her little face as she spoke.

"Girls are silly!" said Archie, who was still standing by the window watching the prancing horses on the drive below—"old shoes are for luck!"

"No, I'm not silly!" answered Miss Barbara indignantly, "and I don't like luck—if it hurts!"

"I think you are a very sensible little girl," said Mary, "and I want both you and Archie to promise to take care of mother until Auntie comes back again, will you?"

"Oh yes!" they both answered, "we are going to

have a quiet little dinner party all to ourselves this evening," said Archie, "mother, Barbara and I!"

"And me too!" chimed in Barbara.

"Well, and did'nt I say you? what a little stupid you are!"

"Now, children, no quarrelling. One more kiss each, and then you must tell me what you would like me to bring home for you—a nice present each!"

Barbara's eyes opened to their fullest extent, and a rosy flush suffused her face. "I should like a big doll," she said, extending her arms, "with long baby clothes, and eyes that will open and shut, and wax arms and legs, and one that can talk, and say Mamma and Papa!"

"But babies can't say Papa and Mamma," interrupted Archie, "can they Auntie?"

Barbara could not repute so logical an argument, and waited in breathless anxiety for her Auntie's reply. Miss Haldane, or rather Mrs. Dallas was fully equal to the occasion, "I don't know what Paris dolls and babies can do," she said, "because I have never been to Paris before, but I will try and find a baby doll who can say Papa and Mamma! And what would you like Archie?"

Archie stood still with his hands in his pockets, and was just executing a series of peculiar sounds purporting to be whistling; he was fully enjoying the importance which the possession of that silver coin endowed him with. "Oh, I should like a horse!" he answered, "a brown one made of real skin, with a saddle and reins and real stirrups—one that I can ride on you know, and I would like a stable to keep him in, a stable with a door that will shut, and I shall name him 'Lion,' Auntie Mary!"

Mary laughed, but his mother smiled half sadly, "Oh Archie, how impetuous you are!" she said, "and it is very wrong of you to be so extravagant. What you have asked Auntie for, would cost ever so much money, a great deal more than you think!"

"But can't she ask Uncle Ashley for the money if she hasn't got enough?" persisted the son and heir.

"Run down and tell them that we are coming," said Lady Laura, in order to get rid of them.

Then all was bustle and confusion; there were hand shakings and congratulations mingled with the leave takings. At last amidst the showers of rice which completely enveloped them, the happy pair were seated in the carriage, and as it moved away cook flung an old white satin shoe with such an accurate aim that it alighted on the top of the carriage, and the old coachman, with a sly smile, transferred it to his pocket as a lucky omen for his own daughter's wedding which was to take place a week later.

Lady St. Kestor, with her two children, stood upon the steps so long as even the cloud of dust was visible, which had been raised by the carriage wheels, and the few guests watched from the windows until their hostess re-entered the dining room.

An hour later the last of the guests had driven away and Lady St. Kestor had already begun to hope and look forward to the time of her sister's return.

CHAPTER XXXV

NIL DESPERANDUM.

THREE years have passed away since the events which were last related; to a certain extent uneventful years, and yet, by steady and persistent efforts, to be productive of much in the future. Lady Laura still remained a widow, but with the lapse of time, she had regained much of her old content and sunniness of disposition. Archie had developed into a fine manly boy, a year's absence at school having had a most salutary effect upon him, while Barbara had also benefited by the instruction and supervision of a governess.

With Mr. and Mrs. Dallas the march of time had been specially marked by the advent of a little son and daughter, who were patronised to an unlimited extent by their most juvenile Uncle and Aunt, in the persons of Archie and Barbara St. Kestor. Nor had their prophecies in the past been without foundation, for Ashley had come off victoriously, and for nearly three years had M.P tacked on to his name. And those plans which they had discussed with so much earnestness and enthusiasm had not been allowed to float away into mere air castles. Bravely and persistently had the husband and wife struggled to bring about amendments and alterations in the law for the furtherance of the cause which they had so much at heart. And, by degrees, they had gathered round them a zealous and faithful band of co-operators who devoted alike time and energies to bring about the desired results. And there had been times when those anxious hearts had beat high with hope, when their efforts were almost crowned with success, but to be dashed away at the last moment by an opposing force or a few obstructionists. But *nil desperandum* was the motto which they had adopted, and the brave hearts were not to be daunted by failure—it was merely a question of time, and the might of right must conquer in the end.

In a picturesque two-storied house, with its gabled roofs and Elizebethan front, Mr. and Mrs. Dallas had, figuratively speaking, pitched their tent. The house stood in an old fashioned well-kept garden, comprising about half-an-acre of ground and was situated on the banks of the Thames, just below Richmond. It was not a pretentious residence by any means, but then its occupants were not pretentious people and found most of their enjoyment in the delights of home and its surroundings. Mrs. Dallas had become quite matronly, while her husband had 'put on flesh," as his friends termed it, to an alarming extent. The babies were round and plump and rosy, quite like country babies in fact, and Mary was an ideal mother, and kept both children and husband in order in her pretty imperious manner.

On this especial day, there was an unusual amount of excitement at the "Cedars," which was the title bestowed upon the villa, for once again the "Infant's Bill" was to be brought before the House, and the fight would be one of the keenest that had as yet taken place. Lady St. Kestor was staying in Town with her sister and the committee of ladies, who had worked so nobly together, were assembled, waiting in suspense to learn the result of their scheme.

When Ashley at length appeared, accompanied by several of his coadjutors, curiosity and excitement rose to the highest pitch and eager questions poured in upon them from every side.

"So," said Mr. Dallas, after relating the events in connection with the proceedings, "we may congratulate ourselves upon a partial success, and though much still remains to be accomplished in the future, still much has been accomplished in the past."

Briefly summarised, the changes made in the law are broadly these:

Extract from the INFANTS ACT, 1886. *The record of a Three Years Effort for Legislative Reform, with its Results.*

1st.—A mother, upon the death of her husband, becomes now, by law, the guardian of her children, and no appointment by the father can set aside her right. She becomes sole guardian, when no other guardian has been appointed by the father, and *joint* guardian should any such appointment have been made, and this applies equally to the case of every mother, *widowed before the passing of the Act*, whose children are yet within the age of legal infancy. She can only be deprived of this, her natural, and now her legal right, by the action of the Court, which may, in pronouncing a decree of judicial separation or divorce, declare the offending party unfit to have the custody of the children. In such a case, the parent, *whether husband or wife*, whose misconduct has led to the separation or divorce, will not be entitled as of right to the custody of the children on the death of the other parent.

2nd.—A mother may, now and henceforth, equally with a father, appoint a guardian or guardians to act as such, after her own death and that of her husband, and where guardians are appointed by both parents they will act jointly.

3rd.—A mother may also *provisionally* appoint a guardian or guardians to act jointly with her husband after her own death; but the Court, after her death, will only confirm such an appointment in case it be clearly shown that the father is, *for any cause whatever*, unfit to be the sole guardian of his children.

4th.—The advantages of the measure are extended to the poor, as well as to those rich enough to have recourse to the superior Courts, since cases under the Act may be heard by the County Courts in England and Ireland and the Sheriffs Courts in Scotland.

5th.—The Act throughout consistently keeps in view the *welfare of the child* or children as the main determining factor in cases of irreconcilable differences between the parents.

" It appears to me," said Mrs. Dallas, " that the most important provision is contained in clause 5, which directs the Court in deciding upon applications as to the mother's right of access, to have ' regard to the welfare of the infant, and to the conduct of the parents, and to the wishes *as well of the mother as of the father.*' "

"You have touched the point exactly, Mrs. Dallas," said an able lawyer who had been one of the most staunch supporters of the measure. "The last sentence is probably the severest criticism that could have been passed upon the proceedings of our Law Courts hitherto. Posterity will observe with amazement that in the year 1886 it was necessary to instruct the Courts that a mother had sometimes 'wishes' regarding her children, and that, if so, some attention is to be paid to them. It remains to be seen whether Judges will do as they have been directed to do, or whether they will still cling to the effete tradition that the mother is sunk in the wife, and that the wife is merely the property of the husband. At all events, they cannot in future plead that they have no power, and are bound by the barbarous precedents of former ages."

A general murmur of assent followed, and a turn was given to the conversation by the announcement that dinner was served.

But it was not until the close of the evening when the two sisters were indulging in a *tête-à-tête*, over the day's events, that Ashley emerged from his sanctum somewhat earlier than usual, for it was his custom always to turn in for a pipe before retiring for the night.

"Well, haven't you two finished your gossip yet, or am I *de trop*?" he asked, in his usual cheery style.

"Gossip, indeed!" said Mary. "Ashley, I am surprised that you dare even insinuate such a thing," said his wife, " we were discussing some most important matters, I can assure you."

Ashley laughed and drew his chair between the two ladies, who were seated on either side of the long French window which opened on to the lawn. The windows were uncurtained, and the light of a full moon was bathing trees and garden with her pale lambent light. And beyond the garden she shone upon the broad bosom of the Thames, glinting and silvering the treacherous waters, as if by shrouding them beneath her sparkling veil, it would render those portals of death, whose gates of temptation stand eternally open, more alluring and fascinating still. Or perhaps she sought to hide the secrets which the river always seems to be telling in its black and sullen moods, when the sun has ceased to blind him and darkness has settled upon the city, unillumined by the silvery lamp of night. It is then that we can look into its face and read the stories of a city's miseries, and with a shudder we realize that it is the treacherous refuge of so many ruined lives and broken hearts. And as it goes gliding along in its course, in imagination, one can picture its deluded victims being borne along also, swiftly and relentlessly as the prisoners chained to a conqueror's chariot wheels. And each victim has his or her life story imprinted on the cold dead face—perhaps it is a woman fair of face and form, whose years have barely reached to womanhood. A false heart and a lying tongue have planted the canker in her soul, and driven her to seek refuge in eternity, with her sin enveloping her in all its hideousness, and unrelieved by an effort of atonement. And if the link could be discovered and followed, we might find in some quiet little village, away from the city's temptations, the broken hearted parents of the unhappy creature, their pride in their beautiful flower crushed, and their lives shattered by the weight of the blow they were so little able to bear. And so the river like a greedy monster swallows the living as well as the dead, and vampire like, absorbs the human interests in its fatal clutch. The murderer, the maniac, the deserted and the bereaved, in all sorts and conditions of life, have from time to time succumbed to its seductions. It seems such an easy way of escaping from the troubles and difficulties of the world, but it is only those who perhaps with the courage born of desperation, have taken the fatal step, from the brink of the river to its bed; who have gulfed the bridge, over which there is no return, who can know what fate is awaiting the suicide when that slender thread of life is snapped and they stand upon the shores of eternity as un-expected and uninvited guests!

"What a glorious night it is!" remarked Ashley. "Why the moon must be at the full I should think!"

"No! not until to morrow!" said Mary, who was quite an authority upon all such matters.

"I feel just in the mood for a spin down the river," said Ashley, rising, and opening one of the windows. "I think moonlight is the best time to enjoy the water!"

"Oh no, not to night Ashley!" Mary interposed somewhat nervously.

"Why not little woman? you are not afraid that I shall come to grief are you?"

"No!" his wife answered, but not with her usual decision of manner, "but it is so late Ashley, and I don't like you to be on the river at night alone!" and Mary looked up appealingly into her husband's face as she spoke.

"Can you imagine Mary growing fanciful?" he asked turning to Lady Laura.

"I think you ought to be very flattered that your wife takes so much interest in your welfare," his sister in-law, answered, as she glanced admiringly at his stalwart form, and graceful nonchalant attitude, as he leant against the frame-work of the window, one foot upon the terrace, on to which it opened.

"Ah, its those precious babies, she's thinking about!" he said, with one of his old ringing laughs, "You know Laura there never were such babies as those in the world before," he added confidentially, with a sly glance across at his wife.

"Ashley, how stupid you are!" Mary exclaimed, but there was a happy light in her eyes, which belied her word. "I am sure if I would only let you, you would spoil them dreadfully! Why, Laura, would you believe it? If ever they cried, or did not want to do anything they were told to, Ashley would appear at the nursery laden with barley sugar or chocolate caramels 'to stop their mouths,' he said."

Lady Laura laughed heartily, "Oh yes, I can quite believe it!" she said—"barley sugar was always Ashley's weakness!"

"Never mind old lady!" and Ashley crossed over to his wife's side and kissed her forehead, "its much better than if I had a weakness for champagne! I'll be a good boy and go to bed, instead of going on to the river, and to-morrow you must let me take you and Laura to make up for my sacrifice of to-night!— What do you say Cousin Laura?"

"Oh I should enjoy it immensely," said Laura, "I think if Mary trusts herself to your oarsmanship I may safely do so."

"Oh, Mary can scull like an Oxford champion! I have taught her something since she has been Mrs. Dallas," and Ashley looked down upon his little wife with love and pride beaming in his blue eyes—their three years of married life had but served to increase their affection for each other, for their mutual esteem had increased as time passed on. There were none of those bickerings and petty arguments, combined with a strife after domestic supremacy, which so frequently forms the groundwork of marital misery. If the fact could only be grasped that the interests of husband and wife are co-equal, and the responsibilities of each co-equal also, the great principle of the dual existence would be at once grappled with, and the secret recognised that a pair can never run smoothly in harness unless both are agreed to travel by the same path. "Don't you think the time has come now, Mary, when you might shew Laura the museum bequeathed to you by Mons. Pierre? I am anxious for her to see the models, and it is quite early yet," consulting his gold repeater, " only just on the stroke of eleven."

Mary glanced enquiringly, and yet somewhat doubtfully, across at her sister. " Would you care to, Laura ? " she asked, " or will it revive old memories too painfully even yet ? "

" No, I think I have almost succeeded in living them down," she answered, and she continued, with a smile, " I am braver than I used to be. Shall we go now ? " and she rose, as if to verify her assertion.

They passed from the small drawing room and down a somewhat long corridor, which led towards the back of the house, then ascended a short staircase which brought them to a sort of square vestibule or lobby.

" Here we are," said Ashley, pausing before a closed door on the far side of the lobby, which was lighted by a swinging lamp, and drawing a key from his pocket, inserted it in the door.

" Have you any matches ? " asked Mary, as the door was flung open.

" Oh yes, any amount." But another halt had to be made on the threshold, while Ashley fumbled in his pockets for his wax vestas, and proceeded to light the gas in the room, before the ladies entered.

The room was small and square. On one of its sides the cupboards containing the models had been fixed in exactly similar positions as they had been when in the perruquier's possession.

Lady Laura examined them with wonder and interest, but started nervously, with an exclamation upon her lips, when Mary unlocked, and threw open the last of the cupboards, which contained the model which had been made up for the original Hester Barnforth.

"He never altered it!" Mary explained, but allowed it to remain as it was, feeling he said that the circumstances connected with it were of unusual interest!"

"It is so like and yet so unlike!" Lady Laura remarked, "Ah, what a fateful time it was Ashley," and she turned away from the contemplation of her sister's uncanny representative with the tears glistening in her eyes. Mary unlocked the cupboard without making any comment—" You'll see little Dick?" she said, apparently not noticing her emotion.

"Oh yes! I have heard so much of him from the children," Laura answered, " really they speak of him quite as if he were one of themselves!"

"And they look upon him as such," said Ashley, "his chair must always be placed at the table and toys found for him and he takes his turn along with them, on the rocking horse—"

"And to think you have never even seen him!" chimed in Mary.

"No, I never felt as if I could bear it before!" and Lady Laura gazed upon the perruquier's little treasure as if fascinated, for Mary had placed him in an upright position upon the little velvet covered couch beside her.

"What different lives and different romances we have!" she said, turning away, "let us leave the morbid side and try to forget it in our living realities."

"Hear, hear!" acquiesced Ashley, and they next journeyed to the two night nurseries which adjoined each other. In the first of them, in two separate beds, were the two boys, Laura's and Mary's. They were both sleeping soundly, with the flush of rosy health upon their faces, and the contented smile of happy childhood upon their lips.

In the next room the two little girl cousins lay together beneath a dainty white curtained bed. They had fallen asleep hugging each other in a good-night embrace, the dark tresses of the one mingling with the golden curl of the other in delightful contrast, while each was tightly clasping within the shelter of a fat dimpled arm a favourite doll, or rather so much as remained of the favourite, for in both instances various parts of the anatomy were at a discount.

The mothers and the father gazed fondly upon their treasures, and as they returned to the drawing room, Ashley said, " Yes, sweet cousin, I trust ere long we may see all reproach of our domestic life swept away; that we may secure family happiness and dignity, to be helpmeets as husband and wife; father and mother sharing equally the privileges of the law!"

"God bless and prosper you in your undertaking, Ashley," Lady Laura replied, "and grant that the day may dawn ere long when marriage will be synonymous with co-operation, and the antiquated standard of despotism will be erased from the Statute Book. I shall be but one of the many wives and mothers who in their hearts, if not with their lips, will bless the zealous reformers who have devoted their energies to the endeavour to sweep away such " Relics of Barbarism!""

CATALOGUE

OF

Messrs. Henry & Co.'s

LATEST PUBLICATIONS.

LONDON:
6, BOUVERIE STREET, E.C.
July, 1890.

By W H. DAVENPORT ADAMS.

A BOOK ABOUT LONDON.
Its Memorable Places, its Men and Women and its History.
Crown 8vo, 6s.

In this volume an attempt has been made to present in a series of striking episodical narratives the principal events in London History, and some of the more striking aspects of London Life. Full particulars are given of plots and conspiracies, forgeries and murders, executions and hair-breadth escapes ; and many favourite old stories not easily accessible now are brought forward in a new dress with all the light of recent research thrown upon them.

THE STREETS OF LONDON.
Their Associations Historical, Literary, Romantic and Social.
Crown 8vo, 3s, 6d.

The work now submitted to the public is the result of very extensive labour, and offers, it is believed, a completer view than has before been attempted of the diverse associations which lend so profound an interest to the Streets of London. It contains more than a thousand succinct references to remarkable persons, incidents and scenes, with illustrative anecdotes and full explanations gathered from a vast number of authentic sources.

By LADY FLORENCE DIXIE.

REDEEMED IN BLOOD.

In Three Vols., crown 8vo, 31s. 6d.   At all Libraries.

OPINIONS OF THE PRESS.

"A novel of stirring adventure, but also one with a purpose."—*Morning Post.*

"In this novel Lady Florence Dixie inculcates her well-known theories about the education and position of women. The way is paved for various thrilling adventures."—*Times.*

"Carries us through at breathless speed."—*Truth.*

"That Lady Florence Dixie can write well is shown not only by her natural sketch Mæva, but by the character of Lady Ettrick, and her charming sketches at the opening of the youthful lovers Rory and Lorna, who certainly do not bend to the customs of conventional society. Whatever else be said for or against the novel, it is indubitably exciting."—*Academy.*

GLORIANA; or, The Revolution of 1900.

With Portrait. Crown 8vo, 6s.

At all Libraries and Booksellers.

"There is abundant play of fancy in the book, as well as some of the ordinary elements of romance."—*Queen.*

"A good many of the characters have a touch of individuality; and in a literary point of view this book is more carefully written and is more interesting than any of our author's previous works."—*Athenæum.*

"A prose Revolt of Islam."—*Saturday Review.*

"It is a book that cannot fail to interest any one who takes it up; and to any one who thinks at all it will, as it has done for us, afford a good deal to think about. It is full of exciting incidents and adventures closely drawn from life."—*St. Stephen's Review.*

"Giving the clever and accomplished novelist all credit for earnestness of purpose, it is scarcely possible to accept wholly the form in which she has urged and illustrated her views; still we must respect and admire the talent with which she pleads the cause she has so much at heart. . . . The tale is well written, vigorous, and interesting."—*Life.*

"The novel is meritorious by reason of its crisp writing and sparkling satire."—*People.*

"A plot which we timidly elect to call unusual, while hastening to add that the book itself is thoroughly sensible where it desists from being clever. . . We admire Lady Florence Dixie's ceaseless vivacity of narration, and her wise and earnest pleading for the truer education of girls."—*Manchester Guardian.*

NEW WORK FOR THE YOUNG.

ANIWEE; or, The Warrior Queen;

A Tale of the Araucanian Indians and the Mythical Trauco People.

In large crown 8vo, 5s. Illustrated. (In preparation.)

By CLIVE HOLLAND.

THE GOLDEN HAWK.

Crown 8vo, 3s. 6d. Illustrated.

"Full of exciting interest. A certain air of picturesque romance is given to the book by dating it back to the middle of the last century, and the author displays a marked aptitude for the conception of the marvellous. . . . The best feature in the story is the weird mystery with which the author surrounds the most sensational marvels that abound in the book."—*Morning Post.*

"A prettily-written story. . . . novel and interesting. . . . Mr. Holland writes clearly and easily, and has evidently studied the period to which his book refers."—*Literary World.*

"*The Golden Hawk* is a tale of the sea which soon enamours the reader's attention, and sustains his interest throughout. It is a capital story, full of incident and bright dialogue. The style is good, and so are the illustrations."—*Star.*

RAYMI; or, The Children of the Sun.

By the Author of " The Golden Hawk."

Crown 8vo, Tastefully Bound, 5s. Illustrated.

" . . . The whole conception here is splendid and novel. The descriptions of the City of the Dead, the embalmed Inca in his Royal Chamber of Death, and other incidents of the Peruvian portion of the narrative, strike us as being thoroughly artistic and finely conceived. In *Raymi* we have a good stirring story of adventure, which is marred neither by improbability nor extravagance. The tone is good, and some of the descriptive portions are really eloquent."—*Public Opinion.*

"Of all the writers who may be described as belonging to the school of Rider Haggard, Mr. Clive Holland is the most original and the most successful. His *Raymi* would do no discredit to Mr. Haggard himself. There is room for improvement in the style, but that will come with use. What is of more importance in a new (and presumably young) writer is that he should have the root of the matter in him ; and in all the essentials for a good story—character, "go," and incidents—Mr. Holland manifests great facility. Hugh Carton, the hero, is put through some sad and dramatic experiences, and not the least enthralling of these is his encounter with Richard Savill, the buccaneer. It is under the most extraordinary circumstances that Hugh makes his acquaintance. Savill is vigorously drawn, so that one is able to realise the man as he was in his habit. Another part of the volume which contains several graphic passages is that devoted to a description of the Children of the Sun, with their rites and customs. Mr. Holland has written a previous romance, with which we are not acquainted, but his present venture certainly warrants the expectation of good work from him in the future."—*Daily Chronicle.*

"This is a good story—a mixture of the real and the romantic. Both elements are well worked out : the real is so like to Nature, that we are ready to think that the marvellous is not so very remote from it."—*Spectator.*

By CECIL HOWARD.

DRAMATIC NOTES —A Year Book of the Stage.
Eleventh Issue. Demy 8vo, 190 p.p., 2s.

"A pretty complete chronicle of the theatrical events of 1890, giving the dates and casts of new plays and important revivals; together with a catalogue of English plays produced in America in 1889. A useful and trustworthy year-book."—*Review of Reviews.*

"*Dramatic Notes for 1890*, written and edited by Mr. Cecil Howard, is a publication of authentic interest, and rich in information exceedingly useful to all who are engaged in theatrical affairs."—*Morning Post.*

"The appearance of *Dramatic Notes* this year has come somewhat 'tardy off'; but the reader has his reward, for this useful record of the past year's dramatic doings is both bigger and better than it ever was before. The lists of productions of the French and American theatres, which Mr. Cecil Howard, the editor, gives in the appendix, are all serviceable features for those who are interested in the contempory stage."—*Daily News.*

"I have received *Dramatic Notes for 1890*, edited by Cecil Howard. I said of the 1889 issue that I had no hesitation in pronouncing it the best and most comprehensive of the series. There are so many improvements in the present volume that I can honestly say the same again—only more so."—*Referee.*

"The long-promised, but only recently published *Dramatic Notes for 1890*, edited by Cecil Howard, once again prove themselves notes even more worthy of extensive circulation among true lovers of the stage than hitherto."—*Fun.*

"The eleventh issue of that useful compilation *Dramatic Notes*, edited by Mr. Cecil Howard, has just been published. As a record of the year's doings in the theatrical world, the volume will be found of the greatest value to all students of the stage. Every piece with the slightest claim to consideration is noticed therein at length, and a carefully arranged appendix gives particulars, not only of all provincial productions, but also of the most important in Paris and America."—*St. James's Gazette.*

"It is as readable and useful as ever, being, indeed, indispensable to the student of the drama. The appendices include a list of the plays produced last year in the provinces, Paris, and America; and the index is admirably elaborate."—*Globe.*

"If anyone should ever take in hand the stupendous task of writing a history of the English drama for the last twenty years, the capable pen of Cecil Howard, the editor of the *Theatre*, must surely be called into requisition. His *Dramatic Notes* ought to be found on the bookshelves of all interested in the contemporaneous story of the British stage, for it is a painstaking record of everything worth knowing in that line, and is practically an annual stage directory. The arrangement of the compilation is equally admirable with the concise methodical style employed by the author, while the accuracy is beyond cavil."
—*St Stephen's Review.*

"To any person having cause to refer to a compendium that gives the happenings and productions on the English stage, this record is invaluable."—*New York Dramatic Mirror.*

By J. T. GREIN and C. W. JARVIS.

No. 1. THE BOUVERIE SERIES.

'TWIXT LIGHT AND DARK.

One Shilling.   At all Bookstalls and Booksellers'.

"These stories are of a high order of merit; they are lifelike sketches, poetically conceived and graphically worked out. There are twelve of them, and if they have a fault, it is that they are too short—which is a tribute to their excellence. They are human and natural, and each is in its way so good that it is difficult to select one from another for special praise. In therefore naming 'Jim,' 'Reduced to the Ranks,' and 'The Swan's Song,' we by no means imply that the others are not in their way as good; but these three may be accepted as special specimens of excellent work. The railway traveller who seeks for a shilling book above the average will do well to invest in '"Twixt Light and Dark.'"—*Life.*

"This volume, the first of the 'Bouverie Series,' contains just a dozen bright, light and entertaining stories and essays, all endowed with literary merit, and with a certain charm of freshness and refinement which commends itself to the critic. The brevity of the tales and sketches makes the little work convenient to take up and lay down, and should make ''Twixt Light and Dark' particularly suitable for railway reading. The book is neatly bound and well printed."—*Era.*

"Taken as a whole the contents of this little volume are very pleasant reading; some of the twelve really short stories are first-rate specimens of their class. 'The Pointsman,' telling how a signalman neglects his duty over a book, and 'Jim,' describing how an elderly bachelor in a railway carriage is saddled with the care of a child, might perhaps disturb the nerves of travellers; but the remaining ten are very suitable for the purposes of a journey. 'My First Murder' is a tragi-comedy, 'The Swan's Song' is melo-drama, 'A Summer Shower' is farce, and 'An Old Man's Home-Coming' is tragedy. 'Found Drowned' is in some respects the best of the lot, but should not be 'taken' immediately before going to bed. If succeeding volumes of the series maintain an equal level it should prove a success."—*Literary World.*

"Under this title Messrs. Henry have brought out a very neatly got up pocket volume of charmingly written sketches of every-day life, in which humor and pathos are continually striving for the mastery. This little work, which is priced at 1s., is just the sort to beguile the tedium of a railway journey, and ought to be found very entertaining by travellers."—*Jewish World.*

By Mrs. A. S. BRADSHAW.

WIFE OR SLAVE?

By the Author of "A Crimson Stain," "A Noble Vengeance," etc., etc
Cloth, 3s. 6d.   In paper boards, 2s.
At all Booksellers' and Bookstalls.   (Just Published.)

www.ingramcontent.com/pod-product-compliance
Lightning Source LLC
Chambersburg PA
CBHW030745250426
43672CB00028B/677